THE
CUL
CLUB

THE CULTURE CLUB

BY CRAIG SCHUFTAN

with illustrations by Brad Cook

ABC
Books

'Eleanor Rigby', words & music by John Lennon & Paul McCartney, reproduced by permission of Northern Songs Ltd (administered by Music Sales Pty Ltd)

Published by ABC Books for the
AUSTRALIAN BROADCASTING CORPORATION
GPO Box 9994 Sydney NSW 2001

First published in March 2007
Reprinted August 2007

National Library of Australia
Cataloguing-in-Publication entry
Schuftan, Craig.
The culture club.
ISBN 978 0 7333 1561 9
1. Popular culture – History – 20th century. 2. Social movements – History – 20th century. 3. Civilization, Modern – 20th century. 4. Art and society – History – 20th century. 5. Music – Social aspects – History – 20th century.
I. Australian Broadcasting Corporation. II. Title.
306

Designed by Christabella designs
Illustrated by Brad Cook
Cover design and illustration by Brad Cook
Set in 10/14pt Sabon by Kirbyjones
Printed in Hong Kong, China by Quality Printing

5 4 3 2

For Kirileigh

INTRODUCTION

In July 2004 I was producing a live broadcast from the Bowling Club in Byron Bay to coincide with the annual Australian Rock festival Splendour in the Grass. At some point during the show there was a call for volunteers from the audience to participate, and those interested were asked to make themselves known to 'Craig Schuftan—over there in the red T-shirt—put your hand up, Schuf!'. At that time, I'd worked as a producer on the show for a couple of years, and listeners would have become used to hearing my name on the radio from time to time, or speaking to me if they called the show with a story. I'd also been presenting a segment called 'Schuf's Mixed Tape', a sort of giant, theoretically never-ending compilation of songs found in the triple j vinyl library.

So, maybe a few people in the audience thought: oh, that guy who plays weird music on a Wednesday or oh, that guy who still hasn't sent me the prize I won three months ago for embarrassing myself on live radio. But for at least one person in the crowd that day, my name was more closely associated with a segment that could be heard on a Monday morning: *The Culture Club*. As I took advantage of the hourly news bulletin to make a mad dash for the crowded bar at the other end of the venue, I heard, in the unmistakable cheery, beery tones of the twenty-something Australian festival-goer: 'Schuf! Existentialism! Whoooooooooo-yeaaaaah!'. I turned around to see a dude in a T-shirt and baseball cap, schooner in one hand, the other arm proudly raised in an air-punching salute to his new favourite philosophical construct.

For the last few weeks, I'd been talking in *The Culture Club* about twentieth-century French Existentialist writers, like Jean-Paul Sartre and Albert Camus, and unearthing fragments of their ideas in various unlikely Pop-cultural places—in Zach Braff's *Garden State*, in The Dust Brothers' soundtrack to *Fight Club*, and in the Bee Gee's 1977 floor-filler *Staying Alive*. As usual, I felt as though I'd just got away with it. When the composer John Cage asked his friend David Tudor how he thought the former should behave when speaking at universities, Tudor replied, 'As a hit-and-run driver', which is more or less the way I approach *The Culture Club* every Monday morning. I happen to find art history interesting and exciting, but have never for a moment assumed that anybody listening could care less about it.

So, it was tremendously exciting to me to find that, here, at the Byron Bay Bowling Club, was evidence that *The Culture Club* actually had a *fan*, and that he—and, potentially, others like him—was prepared to cheer for the history of ideas in the same way that we would all be cheering for Interpol and Mercury Rev the next day at the festival. And why not? If *The Culture Club* had taught me anything over the last four years, it was that most of the great isms of twentieth-century art were connected—usually by far less than the standard six degrees of separation—with the music, movies and magazines that litter our bedroom floors as well as to our memories in the twenty-first century. Not only that, but having made the link, it became clear that one could enrich our understanding of the other, and vice versa. This, to me, is what's most satisfying about *The Culture Club*: It's one thing to realise that listening to The Hives can help us understand Antonin Artaud's Theatre of Cruelty—but what's really amazing is that, having read Artaud, screaming along with The Hives into a hairbrush is even more fun than it used to be. It's these connections—the dimly lit passageways that link oddball composer Erik Satie with The Stooges, the silvery thread that runs from the Marquis de Sade to The Pixies via Salvador Dali and David Lynch, and the wormhole in space-time that begins in Marcel Duchamp's readymade bathroom fixture and comes out of a drainpipe in Abbey Road studios—that I've attempted to map in greater detail in *The Culture Club*.

In setting down the ideas and stories that have appeared in the radio show for this book, I've tried to preserve the curious logic of the segment as it's gone to air, which is to say, it leaps wildly around the last one hundred years of art, music, TV and literature with scant regard for chronology. So, our story starts with media guru and slightly unreliable techno-prophet Marshall McLuhan, jumps forty years back in time to the publication of James Joyce's *Finnegans Wake*, makes a quick detour via the late eighties for a slice of cherry pie in *Twin Peaks*, before dropping us off outside Sigmund Freud's house sixty years before that, where a nervous-looking Andre Breton is working up the courage to knock at his hero's door. This might seem confusing at first, but, being a live-radio segment, *The Culture Club* is driven by conversation, and that's how conversations work. You and your friend start talking about a song, the song reminds you of another song, that song reminds your friend of a book she read once, which gets you thinking about this weird movie you saw one night ... You're not always sure how you got there, but you always seem to end up somewhere interesting. This, to me, is what's fun about art—those manic, two-in-the-morning raves where history seems to come alive, when you're explaining the Futurist manifesto to someone and suddenly Tom Jones and the Art of Noise's 'Kiss' lights up the video jukebox in the pub you're about to get kicked out of. At moments like that, art is a million miles away from the stuffy language of academic writing and exhibition catalogues—it's real, you're listening to it, yelling about it and maybe even *doing* it.

In fact, if there is a common thread running through the ideas and works discussed in this book, it's the notion that art and life can be brought closer together. From Artaud's radical re-thinking of the theatre as a cathartic social ritual to John Cage's realisation that 'everything we do is music'; from the Futurists' brave attempts to bring the sounds of the modern world kicking and screaming (and booming and banging and howling) into the concert hall; to the budding DJs and producers watching Herbie Hancock's 'Rockit' on MTV and realising that that thing on top of Dad's stereo could be used for making music, not just listening to it: all of these tendencies have, at their centre, a wish for art to be more like life, or for life to be more like art.

Well, that's when I'm feeling good about the world. It is possible, of course, that artists, as Freud once observed, are mostly motivated by the prospect of getting laid and/or paid. But leaving aside, for the moment, whatever consolations the former might hold, money—as rich Rock stars never tire of telling us—is no help at all, and may, as my favourite Frankfurt School critic Theodor Adorno would no doubt attest, be the the reason why the gap between art and life persists. If *I* had a lot of money, I'm fairly certain the first thing I'd do is race down the street to the uber-hip bookshop on the corner and buy one of those big, glossy, coffee-table art books I can never afford, or, even better, that boxed set of Fluxus music I saw in the window of the record shop last weekend. I'd have the satisfaction of holding that heavy, shiny, tastefully designed thing in my hand, the feeling that I now owned something significant and important, and that, maybe, just a little of the art-historical fairy-dust that surrounds Fluxus might have brushed off on me. It'd be kind of cool, too, to hear for myself what those crazy nights in New York and Cologne actually sounded like—to hear the sound of Nam June Paik smashing a violin on a table, or George Brecht plucking at the prongs of a comb with his finger ...

But there were two problems with this happy scenario. One is that, having plonked down whatever ridiculous sum was being asked for the Fluxus boxed set, I'd get it home, put the first disc in the CD player and realise, pretty quickly, that I'd paid an awful lot of money for a series of recordings of people playing plastic combs or hitting pianos with shoes—after the first listening, it was most likely destined to be played even less often than my copy of the Sex Pistols' *Never Mind the Bollocks*, that is, never. The second problem is that the whole point of a movement like Fluxus was that you didn't *need* George Brecht to play the comb for you—there was nothing inherently special about any of his performances, the composition requires no real skill to play it. Comb Music could be just as well realised by you, your mum or the guy sitting next to you on the bus as by George Brecht. Scribbled in big capitals on the original Fluxus manifesto was the mandate to PURGE THE WORLD OF EUROPEANISM, to rid the world forever of that litany of Dead White Guys who always seem to be looking down their noses at you whenever you try to do something new and cool.

This book, unfortunately, is full of Dead White Guys. What I've tried to map out here is a scenic route through the history of Modernism in the twentieth century, which is, in many ways, the last gasp of the European classical tradition that preceded it. Modernism can be seen as an attempt, in an increasingly weird world, to keep that tradition alive, even if it meant twisting it into entirely unrecognisable shapes and annoying all the people who claimed to love it and support it in the process. Looking back, it's sometimes hard to see what all the fuss was about, and there's a tendency to think of the various projects of Modernism as over and done with—or at least not worth worrying about too much. Was there really a time when it wasn't OK for cutting-edge American artists to paint pictures of grocery store items? Was Pierre Boulez on crack when he insisted that it was 'historically necessary' to compose according to the laws of Schoenberg's twelve-tone system, despite the fact that nobody was showing up to his concerts? And what was with Andre Breton kicking all those people out of the Surrealists—could the man not take a joke?

Artists certainly seemed to take things much more seriously back then, and it's nice to know that, in these Postmodern times, we can afford to worry a bit less about what's 'historically necessary', since we are now very much aware that the 'history' Boulez was referring to is only one of many—what's historically necessary for a composer in Vienna is of little to no importance for a rapper from New Zealand. Now, you can use Schoenberg's twelve-tone system if you like, but if you want to mix it up with a melody line nicked from an old Bon Jovi song or splice it into a cappella of Missy Elliott's 'Pass that Dutch'—no one's going to ask any questions of you, beyond the obvious one: does it work?

This approach to art-making is the first thing they teach you at Rock and Roll High School. Rock history is, to use Robert Plant's phrase, a long line of 'beggars and thieves', stealing riffs, beats, haircuts and concepts, and adopting them as their own, like thousands of little Mr Potato Heads stealing each other's moustaches and noses. Some of these elements are borrowed from other bands and musicians, but many of them enter the artist's creative orbit from somewhere outside the world of Rock and Roll. In the case of Pete Townshend it was an art-school lecture where the guest speaker unexpectedly destroyed a bass guitar at the lectern, for Jim Morrison, a scuffed copy of Artaud's *The Theatre and Its Double*, and for David Bowie, an early exposure to the cut-up writing of William Burroughs at the Twickenham Arts Lab (OK, OK, the pub). All of these are fairly well-known and documented examples of traffic between the avant-garde and the 'One Hundred Greatest Albums Ever Made', and there are hundreds more examples in this book. But where these connections are often presented as though they merely lend a little art-school cool to a band's mystique—as if it were enough to say, 'Well, they were into some weird shit, weren't they?' and move on—what I've tried to do in *The Culture Club* is show that, through this series of indirect loans and unpaid debts, many of the ideas and aims of Modernism have now become deeply embedded in popular culture. Far from simply functioning as a bit of arty window-dressing for dilettante Rock stars, the isms of the twentieth century have become the founding principles of Pop music in the twenty-first.

1. THE END OF AN EAR-A

Why it doesn't matter what they play on the radio

Q. The other day on the radio I heard NOFX. What's up with that? I thought you didn't want to be played on commercial radio?

A. Our policy of noncooperation toward mainstream press and commercial radio still stands, but I guess if some of those stations want to play a little NOFX instead of a lot of the Red Hot Chili Peppers, thank god. But why does there have to be an instead? Why can't commercial radio play all kinds of shit? Why the same song ten times a day? It's not that radio inherently sucks, it's that all the pay-offs, and ass-sucking, and over-playing of the same songs sucks ... Now there's nothing but crap on the airwaves. My advice to all of you: DON'T LISTEN. Turn off the fuckin' thing.[1]

People have been complaining that the radio sucks ever since radio began—but according to Canadian professor and author Marshall McLuhan, it's nothing to worry about. If he were alive today, he would no doubt tell us that it makes little difference in the long run whether radio stations play NOFX or Nickelback, John Cage or Jon Secada. Same goes for TV and the internet—whether it's porn, politics or poetry, according to McLuhan, makes no significant difference, because the technology by which the signal is delivered is far more important than the contents of the signal itself. The Medium, he said, *is* the Message.

Interviewer: Take 'Peyton Place'. If you put on 'Peyton Place' or if you put on a news documentary, the contents are radically different ... but still from your point of view the medium is transcending the contents ...

McLuhan: It's like changing the temperature of a room. It doesn't matter what's in the room at all or what pictures are on the wall or who's in the room. If the temperature drops forty degrees suddenly, the effect on our outlook, our attitude, is profound.[2]

This, on the face of it, seems like nonsense, and irresponsible nonsense to boot. Surely a country brought up on sitcoms is bound to be stupider as a whole than one that embraces a healthy, balanced media diet of news, current affairs and arty foreign films. Right?

To understand what McLuhan was on about here, we'll need to get to know him, and his ideas, a little better. His early reputation was built on his 1962 book, *The Gutenberg Galaxy*, a study of the effect of print media on society. In it, McLuhan put forward the idea that early civilisation was 'ear-oriented'. A tribal person, he argued, got their information aurally, and from many sources at once: gossip, folklore, tribal drums, smoke signals and the sounds of the natural world, all combined to produce their

sense of the world and how they fit in it. He goes on to say that, since the invention of the printing press, we have changed, as a society, from being *ear*-oriented to *eye*-oriented. By this, McLuhan meant that printed books had taught us to see one thing after another, one at a time. He believed that this helped to create the idea of 'the individual' with a private, fixed point of view, something we took more and more for granted as the eye-era wore on and the ear-era faded into the past.

But thanks to the rise of electronic media in the twentieth century, ear-oriented society was making a comeback. Radio and TV were returning the world to its earlier state of 'allatonceness' by bringing people information instantaneously, and from all directions at once. McLuhan, with his gift for a soundbite, christened this new, re-tribalised world 'The Global Village'.

> Perhaps it is why ... teenagers can listen to the radio full blast, study, and put their hair up in curlers at the same time.
>
> **Howard Luck Gossage, *You Can See Why the Mighty Would be Curious*, 1967**[3]

So when McLuhan said the content of media wasn't important, he probably knew it wasn't exactly true, he was just trying to redirect people's attention and get them to look at the bigger picture. This was a McLuhan specialty: A lot of his pronouncements about the electronic age turned out to be way off the mark—he predicted, for example, that by the twenty-first century cars would be completely obsolete, and would assume the role that the horse had come to occupy in the twentieth—but he wasn't the least bit concerned about being merely right, he just wanted people to start arguing.

This is fantastic when you consider McLuhan's guru status at the time, and the fact that he was being paid a lot of money to fly around the country to appear on chat shows, lecture at universities, and tell large corporations how to run their business. But then, that's part of the reason why he didn't have time to worry about whether or not the things he said were true—he was just too busy. And anyway, wasn't the whole business of having a fixed point of view—and explaining that point of view in a straightforward, one-thing-at-a-time way—more than a little old fashioned, a little ... eye-oriented? This was McLuhan's great all-purpose get-out-of-jail-free card when it came to explaining his ideas—he didn't have to, since the most important thing he had to say was that linear thought was, as he would put it, 'out'. In an interview with Edwin Newman in which he is asked to explain why, exactly, the medium is the message, McLuhan answers Newman's question with a question: 'Where would you look for the message in an electric light?' Having wrong-footed his adversary from the start, McLuhan spends the next hour bamboozling him with totally unprovable assertions such as 'a tribal man has no unconscious' or 'the spin of a satellite has ended nature and turned the earth into an artform'. Instead of dispensing facts, McLuhan believed he was in the business of dispatching *probes*, ideas that would circulate in the culture, without his actually having to be there and argue on their behalf.

McLuhan's next book was a handy collection of soundbites collected from his previous works, a sort of McLuhan Megamix, published under the title *The Medium is the Massage*[4]. No, that's not a typo, it's a pun—McLuhan, subverting the one-thing-at-a-time nature of the outdated medium he was communicating through, was getting his words to work twice as hard for him, using the double meaning to imply that media 'work us over completely' like a massage.

2. THE MEDIUM IS ... THE MASSAGE

How James Joyce can help you understand Marshall McLuhan

Finnegans Wake is one of the books which I've always loved, and never read.

John Cage, 1978[1]

McLuhan's lifelong love affair with the pun was inherited from one of his heroes, the Irish writer James Joyce, whom McLuhan studied at Cambridge. Puns appear in many of Joyce's books, but his last major work, *Finnegans Wake*, is full of them. Almost every single word in it has a double or triple meaning—every sentence explodes as you read it into a kaleidoscope of new ones. Also, the puns are multilingual—*Finnegans Wake* seems to be written in every one of the world's languages simultaneously. Little surprise then that the book, when you first open it, seems almost completely unintelligible, a riot of meaningless babble, which, even as you start to make sense of it, seems to have no plot or consistency, no recognisable characters, no reason to keep reading other than to impress people who are impressed by that sort of thing.

But for McLuhan, Joyce's book seemed to anticipate the return of an ear-oriented world. The fact that *The Wake* refused to be read as a series of 'rite words in rote order' suggested the simultaneousness of the new electronic age, and the title ('fin' meaning 'end' in French plus 'again') meant that Joyce saw history as circular, that it would return to an earlier state[2]. Was McLuhan just reading too much into it? Could Joyce possibly have put all those obscure multilingual meanings in there on purpose? All those, and more. It took Joyce seventeen years to complete *Finnegans Wake*, and as fragments of his work in progress started to appear, many of Joyce's contemporaries thought he'd lost his mind, or worse, that he was being deliberately obscure or 'modern' for the sake of it, trying to out-Stein Gertrude Stein (whose 1913 poem *Bee Time Vine* was one of the few precedents for *Finnegans Wake*). Ezra Pound said that unless the book actually contained a cure for the clap, then he saw no point persevering with it. More recently Seamus Deane, who wrote the introduction to the new Penguin edition, had to admit that it is 'basically unreadable'[3], while at the same time making a case for it as one of the most important books of the twentieth century. The composer John Cage, who spent many years 'working through' *Finnegans Wake*, using it as a text for his music and happenings, claimed to love it, while cheerfully admitting that he'd never made it all the way through. 'I've dipped into it', he said.[4] How is this possible?

3. THE FINNEGANS WAKE

How Sigmund Freud can help you enjoy James Joyce

According to Freud, a dream is a code waiting to be cracked. In 1913's *The Occurrence in Dreams of Material From Fairy Tales*, Freud examines a recurring nightmare described to him by a patient, in which seven white wolves appear sitting in a tree at the dreamer's window[1]. Freud interviews the patient further and concludes that the image of the wolf derives from a picture his sister used to frighten him with when he was a child, the tree from a story his grandfather once told him, the number seven from a fairy tale called 'The Wolf and The Seven Little Goats', and the colour white from the flocks of sheep his father used to take him to visit on the estate he grew up on as a child. Drawing all these strands together, Freud decided that this was an anxiety dream relating to repressed feelings about the patient's father.

Freud believed that the dream expresses a wish, a wish that the sleeper's conscious mind will not allow. That's why the dream's real subject always appears disguised in some way, to protect the dreamer from the horrible truth. Sometimes this 'disguising' is done with imagery (as in the dream of the seven wolves) and sometimes it's done with language. This happened in one of Freud's own dreams, where the mysterious made-up word 'autodidasker' was later revealed to be a punning combination of several names and ideas that were the source of anxiety in his waking life.[2]

Finnegans Wake is a book about a dream—the whole story takes place while the main character is asleep and comes to an end in the morning when he wakes up. But it wasn't enough for Joyce to write a book describing a dream—he wanted the book to be *like* a dream, so that you, the reader, have to do a bit of Freudian detective work to decode the dream and find out the characters' secrets[3]. Once you start doing this, you begin to realise just how much work Joyce put into his puns. For example, the book's main character is known as Mr Porter, but in his dream he becomes Humphrey Chimpden Earwicker—Humphrey, because he's a porter and he humps things, not just heavy bags, but heavy secrets. What's the secret? He's an Earwicker, or an earwig, a type of insect that in the book's dream-code translates as incest, his unconscious mind expressing a forbidden sexual desire for his own daughter. His guilt is exposed in a satirical song called 'The Ballad of Persse O'Reilly'. In his *A Shorter Finnegans Wake,* Anthony Burgess explains how 'Persse O'Reilly' is derived from the French *perce-oreille*, meaning earwig.

So Mr Porter has repressed longings, but of course he's not the only one. His dream-name is represented by the initials HCE, which, elsewhere in the book, are shown to stand for Here Comes Everybody or Haveth Childers Everywhere. *Finnegans Wake* is not just about Mr Porter's problems, it's about everybody's problems, and while Ezra Pound may not have found his cure for the clap in there, if you take the time you'll find a cure for something much more serious.

The fall (bababadalgharaghtakamminarronnkonn bronntonnerrontuonnthunn-trovarrhounawnskawntoohoohoordenethenthurnuk!) of a once wallstrait oldparr is retaled early in bed and later on life down through all Christian minstrelsy

***Finnegans Wake*, James Joyce**[4]

As it turns out, Joyce's Humphrey is also Humpty, the self-satisfied egg that Alice meets, perched precariously on a wall, in Lewis Carroll's *Alice's Adventures Through the Looking Glass*. The 100-letter thunderclap reprinted above is, as Martin Gardner points out in his *Annotated Alice*, just one of thousands of examples in *Finnegans Wake* of what Humpty would call *portmanteau* words. Humpty reads Alice a poem called 'Jabberwocky', which contains many words not included in Alice's English textbooks, such as 'brillig' and 'slithy'. 'Well', Humpty explains, '"slithy" means "lithe" and "slimy" ... You see it's like a portmanteau—[a type of suitcase]—there are two meanings packed up into one word.' Humpty refuses to be bound by the conventions of standard English—either in his poetry readings or his conversation:

'When I use a word,' Humpty said in a rather scornful tone, 'It means exactly what I choose it to mean—neither more nor less.'

'The question is,' said Alice, 'whether you can make a word mean so many different things.'

'The question is,' said Humpty Dumpty, 'which is to be master—that's all.'[5]

Joyce would no doubt have had the same answer for those who wondered whether or not it was possible to cram so many layers of meaning into the text of *Finnegans Wake*, and, he would have maintained, like Humpty, that the speaker, not the word, should be the master. But Humpty inevitably falls off the wall and can't be put back together again, and in *The Wake* Joyce makes Humpty's fall the fall of the whole human race, the point at which things stopped being themselves, and experience became broken up by language. After the fall, the free, playful babble of the unconscious was bound tightly in the straitjacket of sense, squeezed into a sequence of 'rite words in rote order', and this, in the book, becomes the source of humanity's neurosis, the repressed wish for a life lived directly, without the mediating effect of words.

It's quite appropriate that, in making this point, Joyce should make reference to a children's book, since in a sense, the 'fall' in his story is replayed in all our lives from the moment we are first taught to read and write. As film director David Lynch explained to Chris Rodley (speaking about his early short film, *The Alphabet*), in learning to shoehorn our thoughts into language as children, we may be losing much more than we gain:

> See, I never had to articulate anything ... Every idea was in another language down, deep inside. I never had to bring it to the surface. So things were pure and, you know, better that way ... It just struck me that learning, instead of being something that's a happy process, is turned around to being almost a nightmarish process, so it gives people dreams—bad dreams.[6]

4. BREAK THE CODE, SOLVE THE CRIME

Dream Interpretation in 'Twin Peaks'

In Lynch's 'Twin Peaks' the detective work of dream-analysis becomes the *actual* detective work of crime solving. After a day of questioning the locals about the mysterious death of homecoming queen Laura Palmer, FBI agent Dale Cooper literally solves the case in his sleep. He immediately calls Sherif Truman, saying that he knows who killed Laura Palmer, but the next morning when they meet, Cooper admits that he's forgotten—or rather, he knows that he knows, but the knowledge is being kept from him by the confusing form of his dream. 'Harry', Cooper says, 'my dream is a code waiting to be cracked—break the code, solve the crime.'[1] Cooper's dream involves several of the aspects of dream-work identified by Freud including 'condensation'. In *The Interpretation of Dreams*, Freud explains that while a description of the actual events of a dream generally fill about half a page, the analysis of the dream, the recording of the thoughts and wishes expressed within it, can run to six pages or more[2]. This 'condensation' can be done with images or (as is the case with Mr Porter's dream in *Finnegans Wake*, as well as Freud's own 'autodidasker') with language—and Cooper's dream includes a combination of both. For example, in the dream, Cooper meets a woman who looks like Laura Palmer, but a dwarf in a red suit tells him that she is 'his cousin'. When the dream-Cooper asks her, 'Are you Laura Palmer', she replies with the mysterious sentence 'I feel like I know her, but sometimes my arms bend back'. All of these exchanges as well as visual aspects of the dream—including the red curtains in the room and the music that plays in the background—refer to facts relating to the night she was murdered and the identity of the killer, and even point to future events such as the killer's next victim. Freud would scoff at the idea that a dream could be used to predict future events, but if we accept the idea that Cooper has psychic abilities, then it still holds that some of the knowledge he has gained from these powers is being suppressed by his conscious mind.

What's even more interesting is that Lynch himself did not know the meaning of the dream when he created it. The scene itself was virtually an afterthought, the day's shooting had finished and Lynch was leaning against a car that was hot to the touch from being in the sun all day. Lynch remembers putting his hand on the hot metal of the roof, and at that moment a vision entered his mind of the actor Mike Anderson, whom he had met two years previously and would be cast as the dwarf in Cooper's dream, speaking backwards in a red room. So Lynch was, in a sense, decoding this 'waking dream' himself, looking for meaning in its images over the course of the series. It's not surprising, then, to discover that he wrote most of the first series of 'Twin Peaks' lying on a psychiatrist's chaise-longue, while his partner Mark Frost dutifully recorded his free-associations.[3]

5. LIE DOWN ON THE COUCH ...

Why poets make terrible psychiatrists, and how Salvador Dali embarrassed the Surrealists

> ... The magnificent discoveries of Freud offer ... a startling revelation of the depths of the abyss opened up by this abandonment of logical thought ...
>
> **Andre Breton, *Limits not Frontiers of Surrealism*, 1936**[1]

The French poet and later leader of the Surrealist movement, Andre Breton, first came across Freud's writings on the unconscious while working as an orderly treating victims of shellshock in 1915[2]. Breton was fascinated by the semiconscious ravings of his patients and even considered becoming a psychiatrist, although it's doubtful that he would have been a particularly good one, since his main interest in psychiatry, and Freud, had to do with the strange and mysterious terrain of the unconscious for it's own sake—he just liked the weird things people said when they were semiconscious, and hoped to be able to create the same kind of unexpected beauty in the poems he was writing. This led him to the discovery four years later, of what he called 'Automatic Writing':

> I resolved to obtain from myself what we were trying to obtain from my patients, namely, a monologue spoken as rapidly as possible without any intervention on the part of the critical faculties, a monologue consequently unencumbered by the slightest inhibition ...[3]

Using this method, Breton and his friend Philippe Soupault began churning out Automatic Writing at a frightening rate. After six straight days spent sitting at a desk, writing down, uncensored, the first thoughts that came into their heads, they had produced the world's first fully automatic novel—*Les Champs Magnetiques*.

> Sun of the astral seas, torpedoing of the black beams of great long-boats, uneasiness corridor and glares of capers, of muscatels, of maraschinos! Darling, where is that acrobat, where the little nest in which I was born?[4]

Breton and Soupault were pleased. They had cunningly tricked their unconscious minds into revealing something very special and rare, a quality that the Comte de Lautreamont had identified years earlier as the result of 'a chance meeting between an umbrella and a sewing machine on a dissecting table', a thing which would later be referred to by the Surrealists as, 'The Marvellous'.

Freud, on the other hand, couldn't have cared less about marvellousness. He was interested in exploring the unconscious only to the extent that it would lead to a cure for his patients' neuroses. Unsurprisingly, when Breton sent him a copy of *Les Champs Magnetiques*, Freud wasn't all that impressed.[5] By 1922, having exhausted the possibilities of automatic writing, Breton and his associates would move on to an interest in dreams. The Surrealists organised 'sleeping-fits' where one member of the group would fall asleep with a pencil in his hand and, prompted by questions from the others, produce a stream of mysterious dream-imagery on cue. Robert Desnos, in particular, possessed singular gifts as a sleeper. 'He "dozes"', Breton wrote in 1928, 'but he writes, he talks.'[6] But, here again, where Breton would have agreed with Freud that the interpretation of dreams could form a road map of the unconscious, Breton, once he got there, was quite happy to just drive around enjoying the scenery.

This difference in approach didn't stop Breton from idolising the good doctor. While in Vienna in 1921, Breton spent days hanging around outside Freud's house clutching a photograph of him, finally working up the courage to knock. Unfortunately, when they did eventually meet, Breton found that his admiration

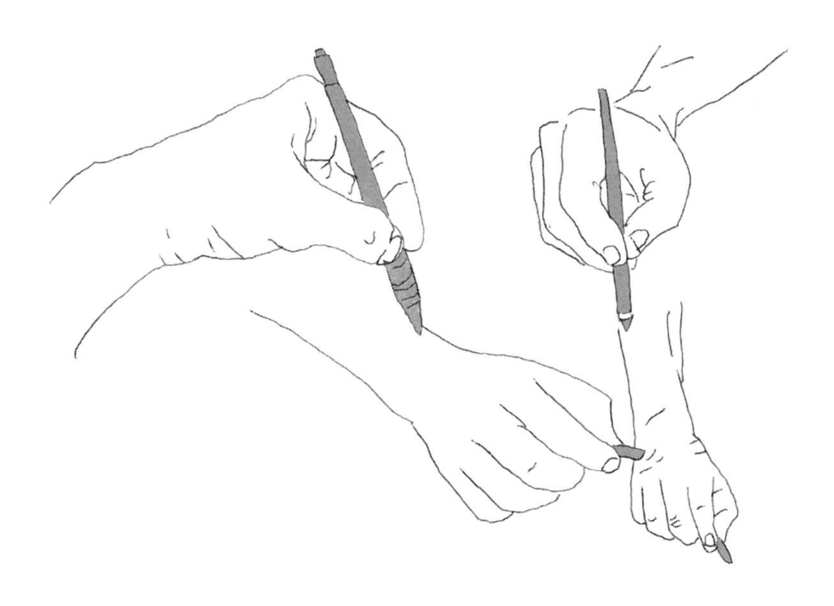

was not reciprocated. The meeting was more than a little awkward and later, Freud would tell his friend Stefan Zweig that he regarded the Surrealists as 'one hundred per cent fools'.

Freud did, however, make an exception for the Spanish-born Surrealist painter Salvador Dali, whose paintings he found interesting, and perhaps even worthy of analysis. This would have annoyed Breton a lot, since he and Dali had recently had a blazing row over the future direction of Surrealism, ending in a kind of bizarre avant-garde court-martial. Their disagreement had to do, appropriately enough, with dreams.

Dali often said, 'The only difference between a madman and myself is that I am not mad.' It's actually a very useful and accurate description of his working methods, a system he defined in a 1930 essay as 'paranoiac-critical'. According to this method, Dali would look at an image as though he were a paranoid—he would allow himself to see things in the image that were not actually there and, by doing this, he would come to see its deeper meaning. In other words, Dali was being 'mad' on purpose, because he believed that the things seen by the mentally ill were not delusions, but truths.[7]

So, Dali's paintings became recordings of his obsessions as he deliberately set out to psychoanalyse himself on canvas. His works from the 1930s are populated by images of rotting and putrefaction, soft, flabby forms propped up by stilts and crawling ants, set in desolate landscapes hung with long, late-afternoon shadows. Some of these horrors have specific meaning for Dali—lobsters in his paintings tend to stand in for female sexuality, while grasshoppers (which as a child filled him with an unholy terror) are associated with thoughts of his father.

At first, Breton found Dali's paranoiac-critical method tremendously exciting. He had come to realise, after the initial burst of excitement, that automatic writing and the recording of dreams had their limitations—they were just that: recordings. But he was still committed to an art that would plumb the depths of the unconscious, and Dali's new technique seemed to offer a new avenue for exploration while remaining true to Surrealism's mission statement.

But when Dali began to speak openly of his desire to have sex with Adolf Hitler, of his fantasies of being ravaged by Hitler's white skin, of seeing his black leather holster pressing into his pudgy back, and, most disturbing of all, of becoming aroused by seeing a photo of the Fuhrer torn up into a bowl of eggs, Breton found himself facing a dilemma. By this point Surrealism had become politicised, and Breton was trying to forge links with the Communist party. So, by loudly proclaiming that he had a crush on the leader of a political movement whose aims and philosophy were in every way opposite to those of the Communists, Dali had chosen as a subject the one thing that the movement could not be seen to associate with. Dali had hit Breton where it hurt—Surrealism was supposed to be all about keeping the imagination free, but Dali knew the Surrealist leader had his limits and threw his own theories back in his face. At his trial, Dali loudly proclaimed his loyalty to the movement's principles, assuring Breton that if he were to dream the following night of buggering his fearless leader, he would not hesitate to record his unconscious desires, uncensored, on canvas the very next day. Breton had no choice but to kick Dali out, but by then it was too late. Dali's bizarre personal appearance, as well as his handy way with a soundbite—he made sure to repeat the bit about the difference between himself and a madman at every opportunity—had made him a hit in the United States from the moment he got off the boat brandishing an 8-foot long baguette and explaining excitedly to the press why he had painted a picture of his wife with a cutlet on her shoulder. To Breton's annoyance it was Dali, more than anyone else, who would come to be associated in the public imagination with Surrealism in the years after the Second World War.[8]

6. SURREALISM IN SPACE

Dali, H.R. Giger and Alien

For his graduation show at Switzerland's School of Arts and Crafts in 1965, the Swiss painter Hans Ruedi Giger put together a portfolio of Surrealist-influenced India-ink drawings collected under the title, 'A Feast for the Psychiatrist'[1]. Looking at the pictures, though, you'd have to wonder whether there was really anything left for the psychiatrist to do. Giger had done such a thorough job of illustrating his hang-ups and anxieties that, even if you'd only skimmed through *The Interpretation of Dreams*, you'd have little trouble deducing that the man suffered from a castration complex. By 1969, Giger was aware that he'd superseded the need for psychoanalysis—or at least found a way of doing it himself. His 'Passages' series was painted after a recurring dream in which Giger found himself stuck in a dark metal opening, unable to move forward or back. Having given form to what he referred to as his 'birth trauma', Giger found that the nightmares stopped. The 'Passages' are unusually subtle for Giger, whose work throughout the seventies was a riot of psycho-sexual imagery: deathly looking femme fatales grafted onto towering industrial machines or skewered by an endless mass of sinister plumbing; babies' faces rotting away in mechanical tombs; and embryonic monstrosities hatching in the walls of dark, grimy factories—all rendered with meticulous precision by Giger's airbrush. In all of this, Dali's influence loomed large. Giger updated Dali's horror of 'soft' forms to an atomic-age obsession with boiling, bubbling flesh and mutated humanoid monsters, while his Biomechanoids, with their oddly distended, veiny skulls, recalled the phallic growth of William Tell's right buttock in Dali's *The Enigma of William Tell*. Like Dali, Giger did not believe in censoring his thoughts: 'The drawing arose spontaneously', he said of his first airbrush works from 1972. 'I tried to switch off my thoughts as far as possible, so as to bring the debris in my mind uncensored into the daylight', and like Dali, he was sure to render his nightmares with crystal clarity and an obsessive attention to detail. The critics might have written off Giger's work as 'kitsch', but if kitsch was good enough for Dali by this point, why should Giger care?

It was Dali himself who provided Giger with a Hollywood connection, initially by getting him involved in a slated adaptation of Frank Herbert's *Dune* in 1975. After this project fell through, Giger was invited to design the monster for Dan O'Bannon's *Alien* and, by 1979, audiences around the world were being scared witless by the uncensored imaginings of Giger's id. The 'penis with teeth' that had first appeared in his Biomechanoids of the early seventies could now be seen exploding out of John Hurt's chest in a geyser of blood, while the 'face hugger' that had implanted the little sucker in him in the first place looked so much like a vagina that it had the cast and crew erupting into Freudian giggles during filming. Maybe Giger hadn't entirely dealt with his 'birth trauma' after all.

7. THIS IS NOT AN APPLE

René Magritte's poetic shock

... I create, using things known, the unknown ...

René Magritte, 1967[1]

Like Dali, the Belgian painter René Magritte was a realistic Surrealist—he painted very strange things in a very normal way—but where Dali gave his precisely rendered nightmares a kind of slippery, liquid texture, extending and distorting his forms, Magritte allowed himself no such crazy flights of fancy—at least not when it came to style. In fact, Magritte has *no* style or if he has one, it's the purposefully bland, factual style of a 'how-to-paint' book bought from a craft shop. When he paints an apple, it's the kind of apple that might have been used for the label of a bottle of apple juice in 1955—maybe even that's too exciting and dynamic. There's certainly no trace of modern painting in it: an Impressionist like Pissarro might break down the same apple into an atomic pattern of coloured dots; Van Gogh might imbue it with the brilliant twitch of life he gave his *Sunflowers*; and Picasso would slice up the apple and redistribute it across the surface of the painting. Magritte, on the other hand (apart from some mild Cubist flattening of the picture plane), just painted an apple that looked like an apple—as though the previous thirty years of art hadn't happened.

This is one reason why Magritte's work is so easy to like, even if you don't really like modern painting. Looking at a Cezanne or a Picasso, let alone a Pollock, can be a very disorientating experience—and, for the viewer who's used to the conventions of pre-Impressionist art (which is to say, painting that looks like stuff, you know, with shading, perspective and everything in its right place), abstract art offers very little by way of a secure foothold. Even if you can decipher the technique to the point where you can see what it is, it's still sometimes very hard to work out whether it's any good or not.

In stark contrast, Magritte offers you art as you've always known it—nicely rendered pictures of things. But Magritte is still enough of a Modernist to want to upset your expectations, and if he paints an apple on the canvas, he's only doing it in order to put the apple (or whatever he happens to be painting) somewhere it shouldn't be. So, in *The Son Of Man* (1964), the apple appears floating incongruously in front of a businessman's head, in *Time*

Transfixed (1938), a small steam train (rendered with all the pedantic workmanship that a model enthusiast would bring to painting the train itself) appears instead of a fireplace in the family living room, and in *The Rape* (1934), a woman's torso straight out of Walter T. Foster's *How To Paint the Female Nude* is shown in place of her face.[2] Magritte's is an ordinary world painted in an old-fashioned way, but reorganised with a sense of Modernist uncertainty and more than a hint of dread. Not the full-blown psychic horrorshow of Dali's nightmares, but something closer to a vaguely disturbing dream.

8. DAYDREAM BELIEVERS

Magritte and David Lynch's daylight hallucinations

Magritte's *The Lovers*, painted in 1928, is one of the artist's most unsettling images. The idea of two people posing for a snapshot with their faces covered by white sheets is disturbing enough, with all the connotations that face-covering carries (body in the morgue, prisoner about to be executed). But what makes the picture really weird is the sheer, boring, normalness of everything else. The pretty but unremarkable landscape, the casual intimacy of the pose, where the woman nestles her head on the man's shoulder, even the time of day—it's not a moody sunset or a mysterious night, Magritte's hallucination takes place in broad daylight.

> **Interviewer:** There's something very unnerving about it. Uncanny. As if the apparition hasn't learned its proper place.
>
> **David Lynch:** I think it's because at night time you're prepared for something like that to happen. It would still be a terrifying thing, but in the daytime you figure—in the brightness of the sun—they're not going to appear. It's like in *The Shining*, when the kid's on his bike and he rolls round the corner and there they are! You know it's not right for them to be there at that time.[1]

Little Danny Torrance in *The Shining* is scared out of his mind by the sudden, inexplicable appearance of two little girls standing in the corridor of the Overlook Hotel, and so are we—but why? There's no logical reason, other than that the girls are somehow not where they should be—they belong to another world.[2] David Lynch used this trick a number of times in 'Twin Peaks'. The first time Sarah Palmer sees the face of her daughter's killer, it's in a brief, daylight hallucination, where the murderer can be seen crouching at the foot of Laura's bed. It's not dark or even dimly lit in the room, and Bob is no H.R. Giger monster or decaying ghoul—he looks like a call-centre worker who listens to Crosby, Stills, Nash and Young. And yet the brief scene is every bit as scary as anything from *Alien*, simply because Bob is out of place—a normal man in a normal room, but who is nevertheless *wrong* in every way. It's true that the scene is accompanied by an extraordinary bit of incidental music (somewhere between an atonal big band tuning up and a ship's foghorn) and that Sarah Palmer's screaming makes the shot retrospectively scary, but the moment is just as terrifying with the sound off.[3] Bob's unexpected appearance in the Palmer's house is an example of what Magritte's friend Camille Goemans once described as 'poetic shock'.

> I woke up in a room in which someone had put a cage containing a sleeping bird. A magnificent error caused me to see in the cage not a bird but an egg in its place. I thus came upon a new, astonishing poetic secret.
>
> **René Magritte, 1930s[4]**

Magritte, like Lynch, was less interested in dreams as such than in *waking* dreams—the intrusion of the irrational or the unconscious into waking life, the marvellous in broad daylight.[5] In 1953's *Golconde*, hundreds, possibly thousands, of bowler-hatted businessmen (identical to the one obscured by a wayward apple in *The Son of Man*) descend from a clear blue sky as though it were nothing out of the ordinary. Six years later in *The Month of the Vintage*, they crowd at the window of an empty house with a similar nonchalance. The viewer's line of sight is directly level with the top of the hats, meaning it's impossible to tell how many of them there are ... they could go on forever. The businessmen seem to be able to multiply themselves in space and time—flip back to 1926 and there they are, hovering impossibly at the window of a sparsely furnished house in the Swiss Alps in *The Threatened Murderer*. Inside, the similarly besuited killer listens to his favourite records while the body of his most recent victim cools on the couch.

9. WALK AWAY RENÉ

Magritte in the music industry, from Pink Floyd to The Mars Volta

Jump forward to 1975 and one of Magritte's conformist commuters is working A&R for a major record company, his hand is extended towards you holding a test pressing of a new album, but something isn't right—underneath his bowler hat his face is blank, like an unfinished shopfront mannequin, and between his gloved hand and the cuffs of his shirt is nothing but clear blue sky. This confusion of figure with background is another favourite technique of Magritte's (1953's *The Seducer* shows a ship which seems to be nothing more than a continuation of the ocean), but the phantom record company representative is not actually a Magritte at all. It's an image from a record cover by British graphic design company Hipgnosis. The photomontage is one of several created for the 1975 album of longstanding clients Pink Floyd, *Wish You Were Here*—and any one of them could have been painted by Magritte. On the front of the album cover, two businessmen (updated from Magritte's prototype to a 1970s moustache and sunglasses version) shake hands outside a Hollywood studio—that one of them is on fire (another recurring image in Magritte's work) seems not to bother them in the slightest. On the accompanying poster, a man dives head-first into a lake—but there's no splash. In an impossible flouting of the laws of physics, the diver seems to have inserted himself smoothly into the glassy surface of the water without displacing a molecule.

Hipgnosis's work in the seventies—as a quick flick through its retrospective book *Walk Away René* will show—is a near-perfect grafting of Magritte's techniques onto Rock album cover designs.[1] Unlike the light-shows and tie-dyes of Hapshash and The Coloured Coat, or the Dali meets Tolkien dreamscapes of Roger Dean's sleeves for Yes, Hipgnosis found the extraordinary in the everyday. And yet, for all its restraint and sobriety, the company's best work is perfectly suited to post-psychedelic Rock music. Thanks to the popularity of LSD in the sixties, it wasn't just Belgian Surrealists who now got to enjoy the poetic shock of seeing a bird turn into an egg. In *The People's Music*, Ian MacDonald relates one story out of many thousands in which the singer Nick Drake is shown a blackberry at a party and told that it is, in fact, a bunch of grapes. 'The amazing thing', Drake laughed, 'was that there was no question: it was a bunch of grapes.'[2]

Unlike Magritte, however, Hipgnosis—being graphic designers and therefore guns for hire—had always to explain the *meaning* of its pictures, whereas Magritte consistently refused to do so. For Magritte, the painting always had to stand by itself, without words to back it up—which is nice, but cuts no ice in the business of graphic design, which, at least since the 1960s, has been all about the *idea*. And you'd better be able to explain the *idea* to the *client*—otherwise, well, there's always Roger Dean ...

Hipgnosis was very big on the *idea*. A couple of early exceptions aside, its designs are usually based on some fairly easy-to-read Freudian visual puns, a sort of dream-condensation for dummies—if these are repressed desires that the unconscious is trying to disguise in the form of a dream, then the unconscious is doing a lousy job. For example, the flaming man on the cover of *Wish You Were Here* is literally 'getting burned' in a bad deal, and the invisible businessman is literally 'transparent'—you can 'see right through him' and his promises, and see that the dreams he's peddling, like the record in his hand and his own body, are liable to melt into air. Elsewhere, the title of 10cc's 1977 *Deceptive Bends* spins off a series of word-associations that find visual form in Hipgnosis's famous cover. 'The bends' conjures up images of deep-sea diving, but the undersea explorer in the old-fashioned diving suit on the cover is holding the near-drowned body of a femme fatale in a red dress in his arms. Her curves (bends) are attractive—as is the ever-popular scenario of the damsel in distress—but has our helmeted hero somehow been duped by the lady in red?

Interestingly, Hipgnosis's most famous image was too obvious a pitch even for the designers themselves—which is a bit rich when you consider that these guys thought nothing of illustrating The Winkies' album with a crotch-shot of three men in swimming trunks, and that partner Storm Thorgersen tried for years to get his 'ducks up the wall' (three real, dead ducks brutally stapled to a living room wall) accepted as a cover design. For the *Animals* album, Pink Floyd rejected Hipgnosis's suggestions in favour of an image of a pig levitating over Battersea Powerstation—nothing more than an illustration of the old cliché about unlikely events, 'pigs might fly'. After much shenanigans with the inflatable pig (including a near disaster on the second day of shooting when it broke from its moorings and sailed off into the heavens, achieving an altitude of thirty thousand feet, only to come down later that evening on a farm in Kent), they got the shot, and the incongruous porker can be seen sailing over the smokestacks of the powerstation, as the sun sinks in a gloomy sky.[3] The pig casually defies gravity and sense with the same insouciance as Magritte's bowler-hatted gents in *Golconde* or the giant apple suspended over the ocean in 1964's *Fine Realities*.

Despite supposedly having waved goodbye to Surrealism in the late seventies (the title of its coffee-table book alludes to this), Hipgnosis's Storm Thorgersen is still in the business of using the known to create the unknown and in many ways his approach is closer to Magritte's now than it ever has been. For the cover of Muse's 2003 album *Absolution*, he's made an arresting update of *Golconde*, this time seen from the point of view of the swarming clones, as the bright midday sun casts their shadows onto the concrete below. For The Mars Volta's *Frances the Mute* cover (2005), he's transposed Magritte's *Lovers* into the driver's seats of vintage cars, passing each other slowly in the street. This time, the figures have red cloth bags instead of white sheets on their heads, creating a chilling portrait of alienation in city life. The two passing motorists, despite their physical proximity, simply do not exist for one another.[4]

Well, maybe that's what it's about—neither the band nor the designer is talking too much about what the image means, so we're on our own—'I'm not afraid to admit that we like to make the listener work a little', said Cedric Bixler in an MTV interview. Likewise Magritte, while he frequently spoke and wrote about art, was not about to give you any easy answers when it came to his work. *The Lovers* is seen by many as a painting about loneliness and alienation—the idea of being so close to another human being, but so far from understanding them—but if it is, Magritte certainly wasn't telling, and he wouldn't have been all that interested in your ideas on the subject either. As far as Magritte was concerned, a painting was not something in need of 'translation', as though it was another form of speech or writing. 'The image', he said, 'must suffice.'

Much to the irritation of critics and movie-goers, Lynch has adopted a similar 'not telling' stance in interviews about his films.[5] He'll tell you how he came up with something, but he's not about to explain the 'hidden meaning' of his images, and refuses to validate others' interpretations of them. For Lynch, as with Magritte, what usually passes for 'interpretation' or 'analysis' is an essentially destructive process, in which a beautiful, mysterious image is reduced to a set of clichés based on a superficial understanding of the artist's biographical data. You know, 'he made a movie about a monster baby (*Eraserhead*), because he was a young bohemian who wasn't ready for fatherhood'. Well, maybe, but maybe he just dreamed up the idea of a monster baby and thought it would be a cool thing to make a movie about. As Lynch himself said to Chris Rodley, 'Everybody has a kid, and they [all] make *Eraserhead*? It's ridiculous! It's not just that. It's a million other things.' In the case of Magritte, much has been made of the fact that his mother committed suicide by drowning, and that when her body was retrieved from the water, her head was covered by her dress. Certainly, this fact could be used to explain the many examples of wrapping and covering that appear in Magritte's work, as well as the recurring motif of a woman's face or upper body being obscured by some unlikely object, the bunch of flowers in *The Great War*, or her own naked body in *The Rape*. But maybe it's a mistake to reduce paintings as complex and mysterious as Magritte's to a simple regurgitation of an early trauma, as though that's all they amounted to. Maybe we should just take him at his word when he says that the image of the wrapped couple in *The Lovers* simply floated into his mind one day, much as the image of Laura Palmer's body, wrapped in plastic, washed up in Lynch's mind on that day in 1987, setting in motion the thought process that would bring Surrealism to soap opera the following year. Here, Lynch's suspicious attitude towards language and words, a trend in his work that dates back to *The Alphabet*, comes to the fore again. Laura Palmer's autopsy reveals that the killer has inserted cut-out *letters* under her fingernails.

10. HAPPENING THINGS

How Allan Kaprow took painting off the wall

Magritte might not seem to paint like a Modernist, but his work fits into the Modernist timeline in at least one important respect: he refuses to take for granted the idea that a painting is a window onto a world, a scene that you can 'walk into'. Magritte repeatedly sets up the conventions of Renaissance-style perspective and three-dimensional modelling, and invites you into his neatly furnished room of painterly illusions, only to pull the rug out from under you, just as you're getting comfy. In 1933's *The Key To The Fields*, a window looking out onto a pastoral scene shatters, and as it does, we see that it wasn't a window at all, but a painting. 'Don't be fooled', Magritte seems to be saying, 'paintings are flat.'

In his essay, 'Modernist Painting' art critic Clement Greenberg argued that the whole point of painting since Manet was to emphasise the painting-ness of painting, to move towards what he called 'purity'. Up until the end of the nineteenth century, he says, painters had used art to hide the art, blending their colours so as to conceal the brushstrokes, applying varnish to smooth out the surface texture, and using perspective and shading to give the illusion of three-dimensional space. For a lot of people this had been (and for many still is) the whole point of painting, to create convincing pictures of things on a flat surface. But, as Greenberg observed, the Modernist painters had been slowly but surely dismantling this assumption by emphasising exactly those qualities of painting that the Old Masters had gone to so much trouble to hide.[1] For Greenberg, Jackson Pollock and the Abstract Expressionists represented the culmination of this process. Pollock's most famous paintings, from the period after 1947, contain no figure, no landscape and very little illusion. There's no narrative, why should there be—that's literature, not painting, and no three-dimensional modelling, because modelling is for sculptors. What they do have is paint, and lots of it. Pollock was particularly interested in the Surrealists' idea of the unconscious being the source of art and in Breton's concept of 'automatic drawing', a visual equivalent of automatic writing in which the artist simply draws without thinking, his hand thus becoming a conduit for psychic energy. These ideas were first introduced to Pollock by Robert Motherwell, a keen student of Surrealist thought and an important builder of bridges between the new American painters and the older generation of Europeans, many of whom had moved to New York over the previous decade. Pollock synthesised these influences along with ideas from Native American art, and came up with an up-sized version of automatic drawing, criss-crossing his canvases with long lines of paint which he flung and dripped onto the surface. He worked on a large scale, so as to involve his whole body in the making of the painting, and laid his canvases on the floor of his studio, circling and dancing around them with his sticks and old dried brushes.

Having announced that modern painting had reached its ultimate state of painterly flatness, Greenberg and the Abstract Expressionists would have been quite happy for it to stay like that for a while; unfortunately, this was not to be the case. In fact, Greenberg had helped to create a monster with his reductivist theory of art, and now that narrative, space, shading, varnish and all those other non-art elements had been done away with, it was only a matter of time before someone decided to get rid of the canvas.

That's exactly what Allan Kaprow did. Pollock, with his flinging, dripping and dancing, had already been described as an 'action painter', now Kaprow was taking away the painting and becoming an action man. In 1959 he decided he wanted to make 'spatial representations of a multi-levelled attitude to painting'. That's artist-talk for throwing paint around the *whole* room—not just the flat surface on the floor—and not just paint either. Kaprow's interest in Pollock had led him from action painting to action collage, including tin foil, straw, newspaper and 'occasional food'. Soon he was filling up the entire gallery with these accumulations of stuff, incorporating flashing lights and tapes of electronic sound to create 'environments', a painting you could walk around in. Since this process produced no saleable result (a painting to take home and hang on the wall), the *work* became the *process* of making the thing (something Pollock had already anticipated with his ritual dance around the canvas), Kaprow quickly realised that the audience could become part of this process, too.[2]

In 1959 Kaprow made a new work called *18 Happenings in 6 parts*. The blurb on the invitation implied that the artist planned to 'increase the responsibility of the observer'—more artist-talk for 'audience participation may be required'. When they arrived at the Reuben Gallery in New York, the guests were given little cards featuring instructions for moving around the space, while all around them people did spontaneous paintings and spoke spontaneous poetry; 'We have known time ... spiritually!'.

11. SPACE INVADERS

Why Yves Klein jumped out the window, why Piero Manzoni's shit is worth its weight in gold, and how Kazuo Shiraga challenged mud to a mud wrestle and won

As the fifties turned into the sixties, the quest for 'direct' expression that had guided Pollock to get his whole body in on the act had some surprising consequences. Dali had hinted at the direction this might take when he suggested to the gallery owner Julian Levy the possibility of creating 'superior sculpture of the interior' by squeezing his blackheads, but it was an Italian artist named Piero Manzoni who really took the idea to its logical conclusion. Manzoni's notorious *Merde d'Artiste* is exactly what it says on the tin, an edition of ninety cans each containing thirty grams of the artist's own shit, which Manzoni sold at the current market price of gold. He also sold *Artist's Breath* in the form of balloons full of his own air, and, for a price, you yourself could be signed by Manzoni and become one of his living sculptures.

In these works, Manzoni followed closely in the steps of the French artist Yves Klein, who designated the artist's breath 'a precious material' in 1960, and created the prototypes for Manzoni's 'Living Sculptures' with his *Anthropometries* that same year. In front of a slightly bemused crowd of onlookers, Klein created the most 'direct' form of figure painting in history. Instead of making paintings of girls, he put the paint on the girls and then put the girls on the canvas—the resulting imprint became the work of art. Like Manzoni, Klein was not above using his own body to realise his projects, and in 1962 he created one of the most famous images in modern art when a camera caught him doing a spectacular bellyflop out of a first-floor window onto a Paris street, in a work he called *Leap into the Void.*[1]

Klein's very brief space mission could have been the end of him, but we know that he lived long enough to set up the Spanish Judo Federation in 1964, so he must have come out of it OK. In fact, Klein's parallel career as a martial arts expert—he was a black

belt and wrote a textbook on the subject—gives us some clue as to what he was doing hanging in mid-air like that. When Klein talked about the void, which he did, frequently, he was referring to something close to the Japanese concept of 'Ma', where the 'empty' space around events or shapes in music and art is considered as important as the sounds or forms themselves. In the fifties, Klein became aware of the Japanese artists of the Gutai group, and works like Saburo Murakami's *At One Moment Opening Six Holes*, where Murakami flung himself violently through a paper screen, or Kazuo Shiraga's *Challenging Mud*, in which the artist challenges mud to a mud wrestle, with a dried mud sculpture being the result.[2] Klein was one of the few Western artists to make a meaningful connection with this kind of art—the direct, physical nature of the Gutai group's works seemed to him to be closing the gap between art and life. Looking back in 1959's 'Overcoming the Problematic of Art', he wrote:

> *I am against the line and all its consequences: contours, forms, composition. All paintings of whatever sort, figuratives or abstract, seem to me like prison windows in which the lines, precisely are the bars.*[3]

Klein subsequently began exhibiting monochrome paintings done in pure, unmixed blue pigment, but soon realised that even these were merely remnants of his 'pictorial sensibility in the raw, material state', in other words—his real art was invisible and could only be displayed in an exhibition of the void. Having filled the Iris Clert gallery with the stuff in 1958, and invited 3500 people to the opening, he encouraged the crowd of people at the opening 'not to stay too long in the gallery so that other visitors who are waiting outside can enter in their turn'. Later in the evening, he ordered security guards to forcibly remove a young man who was drawing on the perfectly blank walls, and thereby compromising the void.[4]

Klein, with his keen eye for spectacle and thirst for publicity, considered the night a huge success, and was particularly pleased to notice an entry in the gallery guestbook from the French writer and philosopher Albert Camus that read: 'with the void, a free hand'. Camus had been part of a group of Paris intellectuals and writers, including Jean-Paul Sartre and Simone de Beauvoir, who were the leading lights of a philosophical movement called Existentialism. Actually an update of the ideas of nineteenth-century thinkers like Nietzche and Kierkegaard, Existentialism was a philosophy tailor-made for the twentieth century, a strategy to help you cope with the meaninglessness of existence (or at the very least, a stylish way to be grumpy about it). No wonder Camus liked Klein's exhibition of the void—he'd been spending a lot of time staring at it.

12. ROCK AND ROLL

Soundtracks for the void—four songs to help you cope with the death of God in the modern world

The story goes that Sisyphus was condemned by the ancient Greek gods to push a big rock up a hill for all eternity. Day in, day out, Sisyphus humps his boulder up the slope, only to have it roll straight back down the hill again.

Thousands of years later, in 1940, Albert Camus used the myth of Sisyphus as a handy way of explaining Europe's hottest new philosophical concept—*Existentialism*. Camus asks us to imagine Sisyphus, having pushed the rock to the top of the hill for the ____th time, watching numbly as the boulder slowly begins to move again, throwing his hands in the air and saying, 'Oh, what's the freakin' point?'. In that moment, Camus says, we need to imagine Sisyphus happy.

We are all, he argues, a bit like Sisyphus. Human life is basically meaningless and without purpose, as we push our boulder (or equivalent) up the side of a mountain until we're dead. But it's not all bad news. If nothing you do means anything, and if God does not exist, then the human individual is free to invent his own life. This new life, rather than being based on roles established for us by society, would be based on lived experience, on existence *as it is*—hence: Existentialism. Scary, but fun.[1]

THE CURE, *KILLING AN ARAB*, 1979

'Mother died today. Or maybe yesterday. I can't be sure.' So begins Camus's Punk classic of 1946, *The Outsider*. His protagonist, Meursault, feels nothing much for the death of his mother—or anything else for that matter—but he's not a robot or a psychopath, he's just suffering from the twentieth-century disease and, boy, does he suffer for it.

At first, everything is fine. Shortly after the funeral, our anti-hero is out on the town, going to the movies, having a quick dip at the local baths and pashing strange girls. Later, he's down at the beach with his new girlfriend, Marie, and his friend, Raymond. It's here that Meursault's troubles really begin, as Raymond is stalked by a group of Arab men in boiler suits, one of whom is the brother of Raymond's girlfriend. A fight on the beach ensues, Raymond is attacked with a knife, but in the end the Arabs retreat, and Meursault, Raymond and their mutual friend Masson head back up to Masson's house to treat Raymond's wounds.

But then Meursalt does a strange thing. Wanting to clear his head, he walks back down to the beach by himself, where he finds one of the Arabs lying near a rock in the sun. The Arab pulls out a knife, and Meursault shoots him, seemingly for no better reason than because he can't decide whether to continue walking towards the man or to turn back and get out of the sun. He's arrested, and we're given the impression he'd probably be acquitted, or at least given a light sentence, if he weren't so damn casual about the whole affair. But as Camus puts it in the book's afterword:

> *[Meursalt] refuses to lie. Lying is not only saying what isn't true. It is also, in fact especially, saying more than is true and, in the case of the human heart, saying more than one feels. We all do it, every day, to make life simpler.*[2]

This, when you think about it, is true. Most people, when asked how they are, reply 'fine'. They're probably not, there's probably a million things on their mind, they could be mildly irritated by a persistent rash, or suffering from crippling depression, but the transaction is much simpler if they just stick with 'fine'. Likewise, if they really did tell you how they're feeling ('Well, not so good—I have this rash, you see ...'), unless it's someone you really like and care about, chances are, you're not all that concerned or interested. But it's a brave soul who is prepared to say 'so what' or 'who cares', when it's so much simpler to lie.

But Meursault, as Camus points out, is not interested in making his life simpler, and in the end, he's sentenced to death for the crime of living his life authentically. His trial hinges not so much on the actual events at the beach that day, but on his reaction (or lack thereof) to the death of his mother. As they prepare for Meursault's day in court, his well-meaning defence lawyer asks his client if he'd felt 'any grief' upon hearing the news:

> *I found it difficult to answer his question. I probably loved mother quite a lot, but that didn't mean anything. To a certain extent all normal people sometimes wished their loved ones were dead. Here the lawyer interrupted me, looking very flustered. He made me promise not to say that at the hearing.*[3]

Needless to say, things go badly at the trial. The lawyer, convinced that Meursault is doomed—'That's all for today Mr Antichrist', he says, slapping our anti-hero on the back as he leaves his office—more or less gives up on his defence. Not that Meursault cares much. 'Whatever I choose it amounts to the same', he wails at the judge and jury, grabbing some kind of makeshift guitar, his hair standing dramatically on end from the shock of modern life, 'ABSOLUTELY NOTHING!'.

This last quotation is not from *The Outsider*, but from a mini-musical version of Camus' novel, the first single by UK goth-rockers The Cure. 'Killing an Arab' focuses on the story's pivotal moment, that sweltering day on the beach when Meursault made his choice and sealed his fate:

Standing on the beach with a gun in my hand,
Staring at the sky, staring at the sand ...[4]

THE BEATLES, *ELEANOR RIGBY*, 1966

As the prosecutor in *The Outsider* is asking the jury to demand Meursault's head in return for his crime, he tells the court that he has looked into the accused's soul and found 'nothing'. But just to make sure, the state sends in a chaplain to visit Meursault during his last days. Meursault tells him to get lost, in no uncertain terms. 'I was aware that I didn't have much time left', he says, 'I didn't want to waste it on God.'[5]

Father McKenzie,
Wiping the dirt from his hands
as he walks from the grave.
No-one was saved.[6]

The absurd, as Frederick Karl and Leo Hamalian define it in *The Existential Imagination*, is 'a condition that results when man, seeking happiness and reason confronts a meaningless universe'.[7] In the Beatles' 'Eleanor Rigby', both Eleanor and Father McKenzie are living in this universe, but neither is prepared to admit it. The priest goes on writing sermons that 'no-one will hear', and Eleanor lives in her dream, wearing 'the face that she keeps in a jar by the door' (this is no more than the face Meursault refuses to wear, the lie that makes life simpler). Even Eleanor's sudden, meaningless death won't stop them from pretending: Father McKenzie keeps up his absurd rituals for the sake of his congregation—and himself, because the idea that we are alone is, as Meursault's chaplain more or less admits, 'too much to bear'.

For the Existentialist, God is a fairytale, a shabby display erected to hide the meaninglessness of existence. Meursault, staring death in the face in complete solitude, and knowing that all of his choices were made by him and for him alone, feels truly alive, while the chaplain, convinced that he will live forever in the afterlife, is 'living like a dead man'.

THE DUST BROTHERS, *FIGHT CLUB*, 1999

> *You have to realise that someday you will die. Until you know that, you are useless.*
>
> **The Dust Brothers, 'This is Your Life', 1999**[8]

In post-war Paris, Sartre and his entourage of hangers-on spent a lot of time in cafés—so much, in fact, that the replacement of Sartre's favourite table at the Café de Flore with a fridge caused a national uproar. It was this lifestyle of conspicuous bohemianism that made Sartre, and Existentialism, such a popular craze in the fifties and early sixties. Among the tourists and students who made the pilgrimage to Paris, hoping to catch a glimpse of 'The Sartre' in his natural habitat, were the Beatles, who derived much of their early style (lots of black), as well as the philosophical ideas at the heart of songs like 'Eleanor Rigby' and 'Nowhere Man', from this experience.[9]

It was in the café, too, that Sartre situated a demonstration of 'Bad Faith', an important idea in Existentialist thought. In 1943's *Being and Nothingness*, Sartre observes a waiter, carrying trays and taking orders:

> *His movement is quick and forward, a little too precise, a little too rapid ... all his behaviour seems to us a game ... he is playing, he is amusing himself. But what is he playing at? We need not watch long before we can explain it: he is playing at being a waiter in a café.*[10]

This 'playing' is what Eleanor Rigby was doing with her stick-on smile, masking her loneliness and alienation, but preventing her from living her life authentically. Her Bad Faith means that she's always living for something outside of, or beyond, herself—a promotion, a party, a new pair of shoes, the afterlife, and never for the moment.

Years later, noted philosopher Brad Pitt delivers a neat précis of Sartre's idea on The Dust Brothers' *Fight Club* soundtrack:

You are not the car you drive ... You are not your fucking khakis!

In the film, Pitt, in the role of Tyler Durden, chastises the film's protagonist, 'Jack', for putting his faith in *things* ('Ikea-boy', he calls him), and for living his life as though he were playing a role. Durden invites him to join his Fight Club, where young men confront the meaninglessness of existence by punching the crap out of each other for no reason. In *Fight Club*, the vague promises of the Church, or its more recent replacements, consumerism ('you are not your grande latte') and new-age spirituality ('you are not a beautiful and unique snowflake'), are replaced by Durden's brutal insistence on the here and now. 'This is your life', he tells the new Fight Club recruits. 'It doesn't get any better than this.' Here, 'Jack' comes to the same conclusions reached by Sartre in his 1938 novel, *Nausea*. 'I am free', says Roquentin, 'I haven't a single reason for living left.' This is freedom, Fight Club style. After all, as Tyler Durden reminds his assembled faithful, 'It's only after you've lost everything, that you're free to do anything'.[11]

THE BEE GEES, *STAYING ALIVE*, 1977

I saw something which disgusted me—I no longer know whether it was the stone or the sea.[12]

Standing on a beach with a rock in his hand, Roquentin, the hero of *Nausea*, suffers an Existential crisis. Everything he looks at, from the rock to the braces worn by the café owner downstairs, makes him want to hurl. Relief from this philosophical tummy-trouble comes in an unexpected form, as the voice of a Blues singer floats into the room:

I felt my body harden and the nausea vanish ... I am in the music. Globes of fire turn in the mirrors, encircled by rings of smoke.[13]

Most art, by trying to describe or make sense of a pointless world, gives Roquentin gastro, but the Blues song is more than a depiction of life; it seems to *be* life, cutting through the Existentialist quandary and giving Roquentin his first actual happy feeling. This is why the Existentialists had a lot of time for Jazz. The improvising black musician, inventing his music (and his life) before an audience night after night, seemed to be the perfect Existentialist hero. You can find this heroic figure reincarnated as a freestyling rapper in the Eminem vehicle *8 Mile*. Step back another thirty years and he morphs into Vincent, the disco-dancing protagonist of Nik Cohn's 1975 magazine story *Tribal Rites of the New Saturday Night*, later filmed as *Saturday Night Fever.*

By day, Vincent works in a hardware store, a living, grinning reincarnation of Sartre's café waiter—Bad Faith in tight pants. Vincent plays his role to perfection, and this, as Sartre writes in *Being and Nothingness*, is nothing less than what is required of the tradesman:

> Their condition is wholly one of ceremony ... there is the dance of the grocer, of the tailor, of the auctioneer, by which they endeavour to persuade their clientele that they are nothing more than a grocer, an auctioneer, a tailor. A grocer who dreams is offensive to the buyer, because such a grocer is not wholly a grocer.[14]

But Vincent does have dreams—he's disguised it well, but he's not wholly a hardware store employee—in his dreams, he's a star. Come the weekend, Vincent is transformed: 'Promptly at five, the manager reversed the "open" sign', Cohn writes, 'and Vincent would turn away, take off his grin.' Leaving behind the face that he keeps in a jar by the door, Vincent steps out into the night. On the dance floor of the 2001 Odyssey, he swaps his twentieth-century angst, the nausea he feels for the people and things outside of himself, for pure action, light and speed.[15] In the film, as Vincent (now Tony Manero) struts down the street, the Bee Gees provide us with a commentary. 'We're goin' nowhere', they sing, like a falsetto Greek chorus. But if there's nowhere to go, you can do anything, and disco dancing is Tony's way of celebrating this sublime pointlessness. Unlike his family, Vincent is not living for the promises of the next world, or the 'rainy day' his boss at the hardware store tells him he should be saving for. 'Save a little; build a future', says his well-meaning boss, admonishing his employee for blowing his wages every week at the 2001 Odyssey. 'Fuck the future', replies Tony.[16]

13. STAYIN' ALIVE

Why modern life is rubbish, and Rock music and pinball are better than art

Sartre and Disco are, in a sense, both products of Nazi repression. Sartre's later philosophy was formed during the German occupation of France, where, as a member of the resistance, he found himself daily having to make decisions that put his own life and the lives of his colleagues at risk. Meanwhile, what later became known as Disco, the practice of playing records for people to dance to, was also in trouble. In his history of Disco, *Turn the Beat Around*, Peter Shapiro shows how the discotheque evolved from small clandestine gatherings of Jazz and Swing fans in Nazi Germany and occupied France, who wanted to dance to music that Hitler had explicitly condemned as 'degenerate', and would risk their life and liberty to do so.[1]

Not that Nik Cohn needed this kind of history lesson to make the connection in *Tribal Rites of the New Saturday Night*. Cohn, a teenage prodigy and one of the first real Pop writers, lived and breathed Existentialism. He shared Roquentin's disgust at the idea of 'art' (not to mention Tyler Durden's; 'deliver me from clever art', he demands in 'This is Your Life'), and valued danger, gesture and style above all else. Writing about Rock and Roll in his book *Awopbopaloobopalopbamboom: Pop from the Beginning*, he reserves a special place in Pop hell for those who invoke the A-word.

> ... while it lives off flash and outrage, impulse, excess and sweet teen romance, it's perfect. But dabble in Art and it immediately gets overloaded ... the words of Little Richard sum it up now and always: AWOPBOPALOOBOP ALOPBAMBOOM.[2]

When Cohn sensed that the flash and outrage were running out, and that Pop was becoming too serious, he moved from Britain to the United States, hoping to rekindle the flame. In 1975 he pitched a story to his editor at *New York Magazine* about Disco dancing, and set out to get the story—although this turned out to be easier said than done. At first, Cohn was too petrified even to walk through the door of the 2001 Odyssey nightclub. On his second try he made it inside, but found that he, as an already slightly over-the-hill British journalist, had no frame of reference, no way of talking to the club's ultra-hip clientele.

Cohn, under the gun—and with no interviews to build his story around—simply made it up. Or rather, he made up a story about a figure he'd glimpsed in the doorway of 2001 Odyssey—giving him the attributes of the violent, mysterious Teddy Boys he'd seen growing up in Derry and the style-obsessed Mod 'Faces' he'd come to know in the sixties, and peppering the story with enough local colour to make it convincing as a portrait of New York nightlife.[3] As a result, Vincent is in many ways just another version of a character Cohn never tired of describing; the violent, narcissistic anti-hero Pop star of his second novel, *I Am Still the Greatest Says Johnny Angelo*. In a press conference at the Excelsior Hotel, Johnny tells the crowd of reporters that he hates women and human garbage, causes riots because he is 'fond of fun', and when asked what his hobbies are he replies, 'pinball'.[4]

> For hours each day I learned my trade, and when the ball dropped down toward my flippers, I hit it back up again.
>
> **Nik Cohn, *Arfur: Teenage Pinball Queen*, 1971**[5]

Pinball is the ultimate Existential pastime. Cohn's Arfur, like Camus's Sisyphus, always finds her burden again as the ball rolls

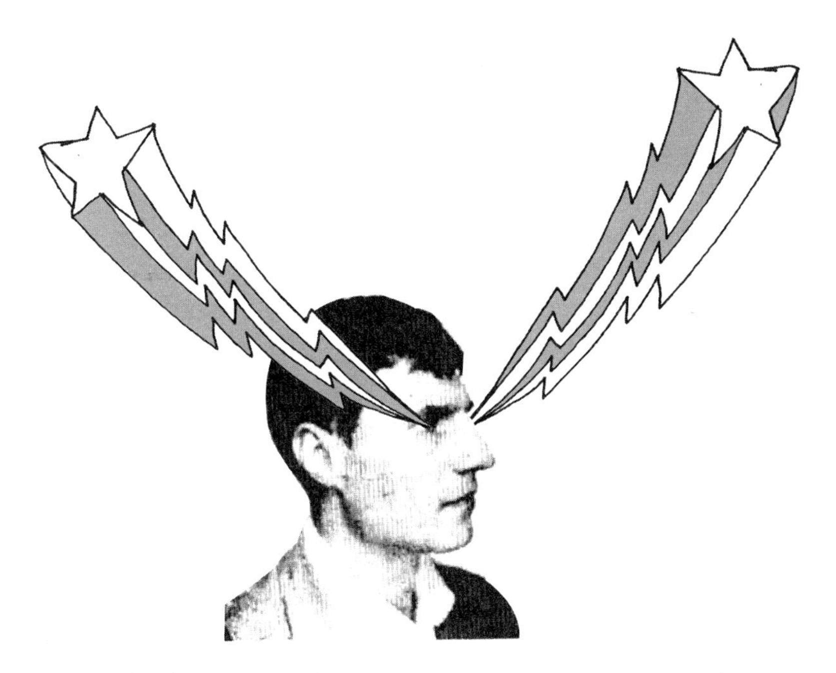

down the slope and, in that moment, we have to imagine her happy. Likewise the Scottish-born writer Alex Trocchi, soaking up the café life of Sartre's Paris, found in the pointless beauty of the pinball machine America's 'greatest contribution to culture'—although by this point he might also have mentioned the atomic bomb. Harry Truman's decision to drop uranium and plutonium bombs on the Japanese cities of Hiroshima and Nagasaki in 1945 did more than just end the war—it changed the world, and artists, writers and intellectuals had to run to catch up. In Don Delillo's novel *Underworld*, the painter Klara Sax is speaking to a reporter about the difficulties of trying to find an appropriate artistic response to the bomb in the Cold War era. 'They had brought something into the world', she explains, 'that out-imagined the mind.'[6]

14. VIOLENT PORNOGRAPHY

Austryn Wainhouse and the Marquis de Sade

By the 1950s, the daily possibility of the end of the world, combined with the still-fresh memory of the war in Europe, had created a new mood in the avant-garde, a deep sense of crisis and disillusionment. These were hothouse conditions for Existentialist thought—with a nuclear sword of Damocles hanging over everyone's heads, what else was there left but 'freedom in terror'. For many writers and artists, the bomb virtually defined absurdity—there was no appropriate response to it other than hysterical laughter, or even, as the American poet Gregory Corso believed, loving embrace:

> O Bomb I love you
> I want to kiss your clank eat your boom
> You are a paen an acme of scream
> a lyric hat of Mr Thunder
> O resound thy tanky knees
> BOOM BOOM BOOM BOOM BOOM[1]

But not everyone could learn to love the bomb—certainly not the students at London's New College who, horrified at Corso's blasé acceptance of nuclear holocaust, chucked shoes at the poet during a reading of *Bomb* in 1957[2]. For the students, as for many others in the Cold War era, the existence of the H-Bomb raised questions too big to be ignored, questions that probed at the heart of modern society. It had taken billions of dollars and 50,000 people to perfect the atomic bomb at Los Alamos—50,000 people working overtime in order to bring into the world something which had the power to destroy the world itself. What was wrong with all those people?

Sitting at a café table not too far away from Trocchi's pinball machine, scribbling frantically in a notebook, Austryn Wainhouse thought he might have the answer. Western society was sick, it was sick because people were repressed, and neither the victory over fascism in Europe nor the defeat of the Japanese in the Pacific was going to change that in the slightest. As far as he was concerned, the freedom won by the Allies had nothing to do with real freedom, by which he meant, freedom of the imagination. Wainhouse's thinking was indebted to Freud in that he believed that the roots of society's neuroses lay in the repression of its citizens' desires. But anyone peering over his shoulder as he wrote would have seen that he was not working on a treatise on psychiatry or drafting a manifesto for a new political movement. Instead, Wainhouse was busy translating, from the French, some of the most violent and explicit pornography known to man—the novels of the Marquis de Sade.[3]

Sade was, as Simone de Beauvoir has observed, neither a great writer, nor a particularly original thinker. His philosophy was born of a monumental selfishness, a desire to please himself and indulge his own fantasies. But the further Sade went in search of kicks, the harder he came up against the limits imposed on the pleasure-seeker by the church and the state. It was his refusal to accept those limits that made him a darkly attractive hero, not only for Wainhouse and the Paris Existentialists, but for an earlier bunch of café-dwellers, the Surrealists.[4]

Sade was related to French royalty, and so belonged to a class of people who were used to doing whatever they liked and getting away with it. But the Marquis's proclivities ran to the extreme—and the extremely violent—and his increasingly extravagant sex crimes eventually became too much for his fellow libertines, and saw him repeatedly locked up in jail. Here, Sade developed his personal philosophy, believing that if it's in your nature, then it's natural, and should therefore be tolerated by the state. He believed, for example, in a man's right to kill, but not in the state's right to execute.[5] More importantly for the Surrealists, Sade believed that the imagination must be kept free, and that only God could punish him for his thoughts (which was another way of saying that there was no God, since Sade thought about whatever he liked, and God never seemed to do anything about it). It was also in prison that Sade began to write the violent, blasphemous pornographic novels that he would later become famous for, including *Justine*, the first to be published during his lifetime. Here, his anti-clerical streak is well to the fore—the man who some years earlier claimed to have disproved the existence of God by placing a communion wafer in a prostitute's vagina, then fucking her while screaming 'If thou art truly god, avenge thyself!', wastes no opportunity to punish his hapless heroine for her misguided belief in a merciful God.[6]

Roland in a still crueller manner intensifies, upon the hindquarters I expose to him, his vexations and his torments ... each blow draws a gush of blood, which springs to the walls.

'Why,' he continues with a curse, 'he doesn't much aid you, your God, does he ... What a bloody fine God you've got there, Therese, what a superb God he is!'

The Marquis de Sade, *Justine*, 1791[7]

Encouraged by the example of the 'Divine Marquis', the Surrealists embarked on a relentless program of god-baiting, from Benjamin Peret's proto-performance art photograph, *Benjamin Peret Insulting a Priest*, to the eye-opening spectacle of *Conroy Maddox Entertaining a Nun*[8] (it's hard to say who's corrupting whom here, but it looks like a fun night). Paul Eluard rams the point home in the Surrealist treatise, 'Poetic Evidence'. 'Christian morality', he asserts, 'is no more than a mockery. All the apetites of the imaginative body revolt against it.'[9]

15. YOU LITTLE LIBERTINE

Dali, Bunuel, The Pixies and The Breeders come to grips with the Marquis de Sade

'The imagination is free', said film-maker and sometime Dali collaborator Luis Bunuel, 'man is not.' Dali and Bunuel made cinema history in 1929, with the premiere of their film *Un Chien Andalou* (An Andalucian Dog). The movie began one day when the two were swapping dream stories—Dali had dreamed about a hand crawling with ants, Bunuel about the moon being traversed by a cloud, like a razor blade cutting an eye. Both of these images appeared in the film, but it's the second, where a shot of the moon as it appeared in Bunuel's dream is immediately preceded by a woman's eye being sliced with a straight razor, that made the film's reputation.[1]

Got me a movie/oh ho ho ho ho!
Slicin'up eyeballs, oh ho ho ho!

The Pixies, 'Debaser', 1989[2]

Un Chien Andalou is Dali and Bunuel's love letter to Sade. Anything they imagined—as long as it was approved by the other—would be included in the film, and what they imagined, as Bunuel later admitted, was largely concerned with sex and death, with a healthy dose of anti-clericalism thrown in. Their next film together, *L'Age d'Or*, was even more heavily indebted to Sade—Bunuel had just read *The 120 Days of Sodom* for the first time. So where *Un Chien Andalou* had Marist brothers dragging rotting donkeys on top of pianos, *L'Age d'Or* ends with a character from Sade's *The 120 Days of Sodom* dressed as Jesus Christ, followed by a shot of women's scalps nailed to a crucifix.

Sade, had he been in the audience, would no doubt have cheered—but for contemporary audiences there are some troubling questions raised by the Surrealist's enlistment of The Divine Marquis in the service of the sexual revolution. Why is it a woman's eye being cut in half? Why women's scalps nailed to a crucifix? Dali and Bunuel's films are just one example of the myriad images of violence against women in Surrealist art—from Hans Bellmer's mutilated doll sculptures and Alberto Giacometti's *Woman with her Throat Cut*, to Max Ernst's collage-novel *One Week Of Goodness*, in which women are variously raped, tortured, knifed and flogged. Why, in the course of the Surrealist's 'research into sexuality', did women always get the sharp end of the poker?[3]

These questions may have been running through the mind of The Pixies' Kim Deal as she played bass on the band's tribute to *Un Chien Andalou*, 'Debaser'.[4] While Black Francis was hollering about slicin' up eyeballs, Deal might have been starting to formulate her own thoughts about the Marquis de Sade, thoughts that would eventually surface in her work with The Breeders. In 1993's 'Cannonball', Deal addresses Sade directly: 'I know you, little libertine', she sings, mockingly, 'I know you're a real koo koo.'[5] Deal's sister, Kelly, was reading a biography of Sade at the time of the song's writing, and, as she said in an interview the same year, the lyrics began with Deal 'making fun of the Marquis de Sade'. As well as implying that Sade may not be so much a revolutionary thinker as a spoiled, infantile brat who was used to getting his own way, Deal may be wondering, as many commentators have, whether or not Sade's elaborate fantasies had more to do with his difficulty achieving an orgasm than with any real desire to 'keep the imagination free'. And who says his imagination was the freest anyway? Deal was pretty sure she could think of worse stuff than the litany of horrors described at the end of *The 120 Days of Sodom*. 'But then I read that he used to suck the snot out of other people's noses', said Deal, 'and I thought OK, you win, big guy!'[6]

16. DE LA SADE

Keeping the imagination free with Pos, Trugoy and Mase

Less than two weeks before the storming of the Bastille, a key moment in the French revolution, Sade was still locked up in one of the fortresses' towers. As crowds of Parisians agitated for democracy in the streets below, the Marquis, with his own axe to grind against the monarchy, urged the demonstrators on from the window of his cell, using a metal funnel (which had been given to him so he could piss out of the window into the moat) as a loudspeaker. Democracy left Sade with mixed feelings—the fact that the revolution virtually outlawed Christianity in France must have pleased him—and the old regime made him 'too miserable to lament it', but you could be sure that the 'liberty' in 'liberty, equality and fraternity' was not quite so liberal as he might have hoped.[1]

> If I want to, I can jump off this building—it's delacratic
> I can hold two pieces of doo doo in my hand—it's
> delacratic ...
> I can do anything that I want
>
> **De La Soul, 'I Can Do Anything (Delacratic)', 1989**[2]

De La Soul's Delacratic society, with the suggestion that it will tolerate everything from suicide to copraphilia—as well as more esoteric practices such as 'wav(ing) my hand in my air'—might have suited Sade better. While Pos and Trugoy's rhymes never approach the extremes of *The 120 Days of Sodom* or *The Bedroom Philosophers*, as the sleevenote explains, 'this album does not contain explicit lyrics—but the thought is erotic!'[3]

Erotic thought, the uncensored enjoyment of one's innermost desires, is what made De La Soul's debut stand out as much as it did when it first appeared in 1989. When the dominating trend in Hip-hop was towards gritty urban realism or brutal bragadoccio, the Long Island trio turned their gaze inward. The world as it is is still present on tracks like 'Ghetto Thang' and 'Say No Go', but mostly *3 Feet High and Rising* describes a mental landscape of dreams, jokes and slips of the tongue. Pos, Trugoy and Mase chat with a squirrel, host an orgy and play you learn-to-speak French records for no reason, before laying down their manifesto toward the end of the album. 'This is a DAISY age.'

Daisies appear on the album's cover, too, floating improbably above the group's heads. But they're not real daisies—DAISY, like Joyce's HCE, is a dream-anagram, standing for Da Inner Sound Y'all. The DAISY age would be a revolution of the mind. Unfortanutely, it seemed that most of the 2 million or so people who bought the album missed the point slightly, seeing only a rap group sporting daisies and peace signs, and lazily pigeonholing them as 'hippies', (a label the group had already disowned on 'Me Myself and I'). In 1991 it released *De La Soul is Dead*, an album which set out to explode the image of the group as positivist flower children, and hinted that violence and crime formed a part of its philosophy as much as flowers and squirrels.

17. DESTROY PASSERS-BY

The Sex Pistols, Vivienne Westwood, and the simplest Surrealist act

We've already seen how important the idea of freedom of the imagination was to the Surrealists in the tussle between Breton and Dali. Dali's insistence on including Adolf Hitler in the pantheon of Surrealist heroes, and his refusal to renounce his obsession with the Fascist leader ('In my view', he said, 'Hitler has four balls and six foreskins'), hit Breton where it hurt. But this showdown was only one in a long line of expulsions and excommunications from Breton's circle. On the one hand, Breton was a control freak, and the twin imperatives of maintaining a firm grip on the movement's direction while at the same time trying to bring about the liberation of the imagination often caused him to blow a fuse.[1] But there was also something more personal at stake. In elevating figures like Dali (and previous to that, the Dada mastermind Tristan Tzara) to such lofty heights of esteem, Breton was in many ways searching for a substitute for the one great intellectual love of his life, Jacques Vache. Vache, unlike Tzara, Dali, Picabia, Valery or any of Breton's other infatuations, had the good sense to die young and leave a good-looking corpse, but not before providing Surrealism with its founding moment. In 1917, at the premiere of Guillame Apollinaire's play *La Mamelles de Tiresias*, Vache pulled out a pistol and waved it at the crowd, saying that he wanted to shoot the audience because he didn't like the stage décor. Breton looked on, mesmerised, the experience left him feeling 'charged'. Later, in the second manifesto of Surrealism, Breton described the simplest Surrealist act as, '... going down into the street, revolvers in one's hands, and firing at random, wilfully, into the crowd'.[2]

> It was in the middle of 'Pretty Vacant'. All of a sudden, Vivienne is slapping this girl's face ... Vivienne said afterwards that she was bored, that the Sex Pistols were boring, she decided to liven things up. So she slapped this girl for no reason, just did it. It was extremely electrifying.
>
> **John Ingham, quoted in Jon Savage's *England's Dreaming*, 1991**[3]

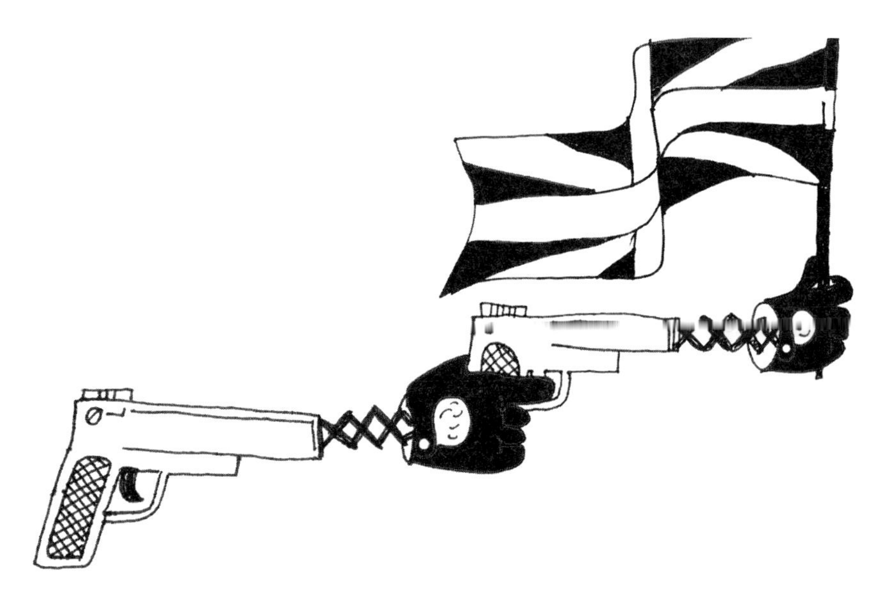

In the photos from this early appearance by the Sex Pistols in April 1976, John Lydon looks down and smiles mischievously at the chaos erupting in front of the stage. To his right, guitarist Steve Jones plays on, wearing a T-shirt printed with a photographic image of a pair of breasts, part of a new range of clothes designed by Westwood and her partner Malcom McLaren, and available from their shop at 430 Kings Road—Sex. Prior to opening under its new moniker, Sex had gone through a number of image-makeovers since McLaren and Westwood had started renting the space in 1971. At first, attracted by the flash and casual violence of the Ted subculture, the pair had sold early rock 'n' roll 45s, powder blue suits and winkle-picker boots under the name Let It Rock. In the Teds' absurd rituals and dress codes, McLaren saw something of what Trocchi had glimpsed in the pinball machine, a sublimely modern pointlessness, a way of living that was purely 'of the moment'.

But when the Teds got to be a bore, McLaren decided to shift the emphasis towards biker culture—leather jackets, silver studs and hand-painted glitter slogans, one of which became the shop's new name, Too Fast to Live, Too Young to Die. This was quickly followed by Modernity Killed Every Night (from a quote attributed to Jacques Vache) and, finally, in 1974, Sex. By now, the retro rock n' roll clothes were nowhere to be seen, and the biker look had mutated into S&M—Sex sold the kind of clothes and accessories you used to have to order from the back of specialist fetish magazines, off the rack. Wearing these clothes in public, especially in Britain in the late seventies, involved an Existential choice. Sex associate Alan Jones was actually arrested for wearing one of McLaren's designs (a T-shirt featuring two cowboys standing facing one another, naked from the waist down), and there was every chance that the very same Teds McLaren had been outfitting only a couple of years previously would beat you to a pulp for wearing a pair of bondage trousers in public.[4]

More recently, in her essay 'The Philosophy of the Catwalk', Juliet Ash (who elsewhere writes of the delicious thrill of going to a board meeting wearing, under her skirt, a pair of knickers with a penis graffiti'd on the front from Westwood's 1990 collection) quotes Westwood herself on the importance of fashion as an artform: 'It's still vital and valid', she says, 'it has to be because it's defined by the fact it's got to be worn.'[5] But even in early stages of Sex, McLaren and Westwood were already concerned with fashion as a kind of lived philosophy, and the designers wore their influences on their sleeveless T-shirts. The shop's assortment of rubber and leather-wear was augmented by hand-made tees printed with slogans taken from Alex Trocchi's revolutionary pornography, and from the SCUM manifesto by radical feminist Valerie Solanas, who, in 1968, had walked into Andy Warhol's Factory, revolver in hand, firing wilfully into the crowd.

It was around this time that McLaren's long-held ambition to put together a teenage pop group in order to model his Sex-wear began to bear some fruit. Having assembled a band of working-class street urchins in Steve Jones, Paul Cook and Glen Matlock, the search for a charismatic lead singer finally came to an end late in 1975. John Lydon, a kid who had been hanging around Sex with his friends, gawping at the tit-clamps and rubber skirts, passed his audition by singing into a shower attachment while Alice Cooper's 'Eighteen' played on the shop's jukebox. By the following year, Lydon (re-christened Johnny Rotten) was writing his own songs, including what would become the band's first single, 'Anarchy in The UK'.[6]

> Don't know what I want but I know how to get it,
> I wanna destroy passers-by![7]

'Anarchy' was written with McLaren sitting over Lydon's shoulder, feeding him ideas from McLaren's own background in underground art and late-sixties revolutionary politics. Most prominent among these are the cryptic pronouncements of the Situationist International, whose spray-painted slogans appeared in Paris around the time of the student strikes and sit-ins of May 1968, and would subsequently appear on McLaren and Westwood's hand-printed Sex T-shirts. The Situationists' leader,

Guy Debord, was committed to re-activating the Surrealist's program to revolutionise everyday life, but his heroes were not painters and poets. Debord identified more closely with characters like Vache, who instead of just *making* art, lived their life *as* a work of art, as he'd done that night at the theatre, waving his gun at the audience for no reason other than because he didn't like the show.[8]

18. THE DIVINE MARQUIS

Doing what comes naturally with the Marquis de Sade

At the heart of Breton's (and Debord's) appreciation for Vache's dangerous stunt is the idea that human beings have a right to realise their desires. If the Surrealist desired, at any given moment, to start firing on strangers for no reason, then she should be allowed to do so. Why? Because it's in her nature, and it's good to be natural. This might sound crazy, but the idea that it's better for people to be 'closer to nature' has been popular at least since the writings of Jean Jacques Rousseau in the eighteenth century, and as John Weightman has pointed out in his article 'Rousseau and the Concept of Nature', many people today are Rousseauistic, without ever having heard of him. But what's natural? It's natural for people to want to love each other and eat fruit and spend time in the outdoors, but it's also natural for some people to want to kill other human beings or sodomise the wildlife or whip prostitutes with a thong. This was the leap of logic made by the Marquis de Sade[1]. In her essay 'Must We Burn Sade?', Simone de Beauvoir shows how Sade took the generally accepted eighteenth-century credo, 'nature is good; let us follow her', and reversed the first part while keeping the second. For Sade, nature is cruel and violent, and if he is sometimes too—well, that's only natural.[2]

> O mankind, is it up to you to pronounce what is good—or what is evil; is it up to a puny individual of your species to assign limits to nature, to decide what she tolerates ...?[3]

Sade's *Justine* went through six printings in the ten years following its publication in 1791, but, by the time the Surrealists got to him, it had been out of print for almost one hundred years. After the Second World War a new French edition finally appeared, and shortly after that Austryn Wainhouse began his translation of the 'monster author' into English, for the first time in history. Trocchi had agreed to publish Wainhouse's translations of *The Bedroom Philosophers* and *Juliette* under the auspices of his literary magazine *Merlin*, but changed his mind when he realised he could get deported for it. Luckily, however, Wainhouse had just met another publisher, a man who liked nothing better than testing the limits of the state when it came to obscenity, especially if there was a chance of making a quick buck along the way.[4]

19. DIRTY BOOKS

How Maurice Girodias launched the sexual revolution with a truckload of canned celery

> Moral censorship was an inheritance from the past, deriving from centuries of domination by the Christian clergy. Now that it is practically over, we may expect literature to be transformed by the advent of freedom ... as the means of exploring all the positive aspects of the human mind, which are all more or less related to, or generated by, sex.
>
> **Maurice Girodias, 1965[1]**

Girodias ought to know a thing or two about moral censorship. His father, Jack Kahane, having moved from England to France, founded the Obelisk Press and was the first to publish the novels of Henry Miller[2], a thing he would never have got away with in Britain's prudish Victorian climate. Kahane, who was also brave enough to publish a fragment of *Finnegans Wake* (then still a work in progress published as *Haveth Childers Everywhere*) instilled in his son a deep regard for intellectual freedom. Girodias writes with horror about the way English society could 'cover with abuse a man like DH Lawrence, and let him be tormented and quartered by the hounds of decency'. Unfortunately, apart from a sizeable collection of bar debts, this was about all the young Girodias stood to inherit from his father, and when he decided to start up his own publishing company, he did so with assets amounting to no more than 'one ton of canned celery ... which proved to be entirely worthless'.

Soon Girodias found himself in court for publishing obscene books (after he started reprinting some of the Henry Miller titles from his father's press), but this experience did not deter him in the slightest. In fact, when he launched his new imprint, the Olympia Press, in 1953, it was with a catalogue of titles virtually guaranteed to get him into trouble, including Austryn Wainhouse's brand new translation of *The Bedroom Philosophers*.

Girodias devised an ingenious scheme for his new publishing enterprise. He knew from the beginning that his main clientele would be made up of American tourists and servicemen stationed in Paris, so he created a catalogue of exotic-sounding soft-porn titles and started taking orders. At this point, none of these books actually existed, but the only thing surer than the fact that sailors get lonely at night was that Paris was full of skint writers who weren't above adopting a pseudonym and churning out a bit of made-to-order smut. Girodias's going rate of five hundred dollars per db (dirty book) could buy you a lot of espressos.

So when the orders for *With Open Mouth* and *Roman Orgy* started appearing in the mail, Alexander Trocchi became Carmencita de las Lunas, Christopher Logue became Count Palmiro Vicarion, and within no time the db's were flying off the shelves. As 'Marcus Van Heller' (the nom-de-plume of John Stephenson, *Merlin*'s business manager) later said, it was 'a devil-sent way of keeping the wolf from the door'. Of course, these titles were automatically seized and banned by the French authorities, but since it always took six months for the ban to come into effect, Girodias had a small grace period in which to turn a profit. But for Girodias, this wasn't about money. Well, not *all* about money. His conception of the Olympia Press as a stick with which to beat the 'Hounds of Decency' meant that he also published books that are now considered great works of art, but which no one else would touch because of their controversial subject matter. *The Bedroom Philosophers* certainly fell into this category, as did Vladimir Nabokov's *Lolita*, and the novels of Samuel Beckett and Jean Genet. Which is why, in November 1957, when a young American poet named Allen Ginsberg was looking for a publisher for his friend William Burroughs's new book *Naked Lunch*, it was Girodias he went to see first.[3]

20. THE MAN WHO TAUGHT HIS ASSHOLE TO TALK

William Burroughs and *Naked Lunch*

> One of the foulest collections of printed filth I've seen publicly circulated ...
>
> **Jack Mabley on an excerpt of *Naked Lunch* published in *Chicago Review*, 1958**[1]

Burroughs's manuscript was such a mess that Girodias passed on it, but after the US Post Office seized copies of the magazine *Big Table*, containing excerpts of the new novel, people began talking about *Naked Lunch*, and Girodias, with his keen ear for scandal, started to get interested. 'Dear Mr Burroughs', he wrote in June 1959, 'what about letting me have another look at *Naked Lunch*?'.[2]

Burroughs's book certainly was filthy, but maybe not in exactly the way that fans of *Roman Orgy* or *White Thighs* were expecting. Instead of Hsi Men's 'thrusting charger' or the 'glossy swellings' of Lady Clodia's breasts, readers of *Naked Lunch* were treated to the story of the man who taught his asshole to talk.

What started out as a harmless carnival act—'Oh I say, are you still down there old thing?'—soon turns into a nightmare as the ass grows teeth, eats its way through his pants, and eventually takes over the subject's entire body, sealing over his mouth with globs of jelly-like ectoplasm. Even the actual sex scenes have a disturbing Sade-meets-the-atomic-age flavour about them, as in this routine from the Johnny and Mary section. Mary is soliloquising while preparing to sodomise Johnny with a dildo nicknamed 'Steely Dan III':

> When I was a transvestite Liz in Chi used to work as an exterminator. Make advances to pretty boys for the thrill of being beaten as a man. Later I catch this one kid, overpower him with supersonic judo I learned from an old lesbian monk. I tie him up, strip off his clothes with a razor and fuck him with Steely Dan I. He is so relieved I don't castrate him literal he come all over my bedbug spray.[3]

Naked Lunch was shocking—especially to Burroughs's mother, who was so embarrassed she threatened to cut off his allowance if he ever set foot in the United States again—but Burroughs really felt as though he had no choice but to write it: he couldn't write anything else. In a letter to Ginsberg in 1955, he describes the process in terms of Breton's Automatic Writing gone horribly wrong. Where Breton had, in 1919, felt moved to transcribe a phrase, an image from his subconscious that was 'knocking at the window',[4] Burroughs, subjected to the same knocking, would just as soon have left some of those undesirable phrases out in the cold. But he felt himself, and his typewriter, to be controlled by a hostile entity from which he was forced to take dictation. To prove the point, in the same letter, he includes a draft version of the 'talking asshole' section of *Naked Lunch*, explaining that *this* is the kind of stuff that comes out when he tries to write something popular and commercial.[5]

In many ways, Burroughs *was* the man who taught his asshole to talk. His second novel, *Queer*, had been based on the time Burroughs had spent living in Mexico, and his attempts to seduce a young man called Eugene Allerton. In the novel, Burroughs's alter ego Lee—a pseudonym he often used in his letters—chats up Allerton with a disgusting but slightly titillating story about a wise old queen called Bobo who taught him to be proud of his homosexuality:

> Poor Bobo came to a sticky end ... his falling piles blew out of the car and wrapped around the rear wheel. He was completely gutted, leaving an empty shell sitting there on the giraffe-skin upholstery. Even the eyes and the brain went, with a horrible shlupping sound.[6]

Burroughs called these stories 'routines'. As long as there was a receiver for the routine, it was relatively harmless, but in the international zone of Tangier, where Burroughs lived at the time of writing what would become *Naked Lunch*, stimulating company was scarce. In another letter to Ginsberg he complains that he has no one to talk to but his young Arab boyfriend Kiki—'Some artist and writer colony!' It was contact with Ginsberg that Burroughs craved above all else, but when his friend failed to reply to his increasingly desperate letters for months at a time, Burroughs's routines turned in on themselves and grew a life of their own. Where previously he was a writer, now he felt himself being written, but by what or whom?[7]

21. LESBIAN SARDINES

How Burroughs took on the ugly spirits with a pair of scissors borrowed from a Zurich nightclub

Having finished *Naked Lunch*, Burroughs moved to Paris, where he ran into the painter Brion Gysin whom he had met (but not liked very much) in Tangier. Gysin had the dubious honour of having been kicked out of the Surrealists by Andre Breton in 1935, but not before he'd picked up from them a technique that would prove very valuable to both himself and Burroughs over the next ten years—cut-ups.

The cut-up technique had been invented in 1916 by the Romanian-born poet Tristan Tzara. Tzara got his start in show business in Zurich, Switzerland, when he answered an ad in the local press soliciting 'young artists' to contribute to a new variety nightclub called Cabaret Voltaire. Forty years before Allan Kaprow's first happenings, the Cabaret hosted wild nights of avant-garde craziness—sound poems, cardboard masks and costumes (the performers disguised themselves as 'languorous foetuses' and 'lesbian sardines'), 'negro' music, and Tzara 'wiggling his behind like the belly of an oriental dancer'. The Cabaret's contributors were constantly experimenting. Soon the painter Jean Arp (who never performed, but decorated the walls and stage of the club) had invented a new form of picture-making by tearing pieces of painted paper, dropping them onto a sheet and gluing them where they fell. Applying this method to the written word, Tzara came up with the following set of instructions for aspiring poets:

> Take a newspaper
> Take some scissors
> Choose from this paper an article of the length you want to make your poem.
> Cut out the article.
> Next carefully cut out the words that make up this article and put them all in a bag.
> Shake gently.
> Now take out each cutting one after the other ...
> The poem will resemble you.[1]

This was the technique Gysin had rediscovered in his room in Paris in 1959. When Burroughs, who was staying at the same hotel, came back from a long lunch—with a couple of reporters from *Life* magazine who were interviewing him about *Naked Lunch*[2]—he found Gysin in a state of great excitement. While cutting a mount for a drawing, Gysin's Stanley blade had inadvertently sliced through a few pages of newspaper underneath. Rearranging the fragments of the text, he found that he had accidentally made poetry from the random assortment of newspapers and magazines on the table (which coincidentally included a copy of *Life*). Gysin and Burroughs then proceeded to cut up everything in sight. On the one hand, it was just the kind of game people played when they were stoned on hashish. In his book *The Beat Hotel*, Barry Miles transcribes a tape recording of Burroughs cutting up a letter and reading the results out loud, accompanied by a lot of stoned laughter from Gysin and Gregory Corso. But Burroughs wasn't just amusing himself, even at this early stage he realised that the cut-ups contained *secret messages*, or rather, that the writer's real intentions could be revealed by the cut. So when Burroughs cuts up the letter in the tape recording, his amusement comes from the idea that he has decoded the letter's hidden meaning—'Wanna hear what he's really saying?'[3]

The next step for Burroughs was obvious. *Naked Lunch* had been, in many ways, a novel about control—who controls you? The question was never far from Burroughs's mind, especially since the events of 6 September 1951. That night, his friend Kells Elvins had a dream about Burroughs stirring a pot over a stove. When Kells asked him what he was cooking, Burroughs replied, 'Brains!', and showed him a pot full of what looked like squirming white worms.[4] Meanwhile, the real Burroughs had accidentally shot and killed his common-law wife, Joan Vollmer. 'I guess it's about time for our William Tell act', he'd said, in front of a group of bemused onlookers. Joan, despite never having played the game before, balanced a glass on her head, and Burroughs, usually a very good shot, missed the glass completely and hit Joan in the forehead, killing her instantly.

Burroughs has described this as the event that, more than any other, made him a writer, and although Joan's death is never mentioned in *Naked Lunch*, the novel can be seen, on one level, as a kind of detective story, as Burroughs attempts to crack the case of himself, to unmask the evil spirit that had guided his hand on that day in 1951.

But Burroughs had spent enough time in analysis by this point to realise that the unconscious keeps its secrets well hidden, and even as early as 1956, he knew that mere automatic writing 'would never get past the censors'[5]—you had to sneak up on those ugly spirits with a sharp pair of scissors. If what Tzara said was true, that a cut-up would resemble the author, then Burroughs couldn't wait to get a look.

Burroughs's next book, *The Soft Machine*, also published by Girodias, was mostly comprised of cut-ups. Just as Joyce's abandonment of 'rite words in rote order' for *Finnegans Wake* had many of his contemporaries scratching their heads, feeling that he'd abandoned his God-given gifts as a storyteller to pursue obscure literary parlour games, so the reaction to the cut-ups from Burroughs's peers ranged from slight disappointment (Ginsberg) to indignant outrage (Corso).

Ginsberg actually wrote the jacket blurb for *The Soft Machine*, but later complained in a letter to a friend that Burroughs's new writing was 'toneless'. But Burroughs paid no attention to this, rightly pointing out that he and Gysin were simply bringing writing up to date with painting, where the use of collage and found objects and the incorporation of chance procedures had been a commonplace since the days of the Cabaret Voltaire. And besides, as Gysin observed, even when none of his own material was used in the process, Burroughs's cut-ups *always* read like Burroughs. The man inside, you might say.[6]

22. RETURN ME BACK TO THE CIGARETTE

Interrogating the mass media with Burroughs, Bob Dylan and Marshall McLuhan

> One afternoon, he was trying to explain his novel, the as yet unpublished *Tarantula*, to a journalist. He'd written it, he told her, using William Burroughs and Brion Gysin's cut-up technique. The woman was initially intrigued: 'Oh what's that', she asked, 'is it a literary theory?'. Dylan proceeded to explain it to her, using a copy of the *Daily Telegraph* and a pair of scissors. But as soon as he started trying to assemble the scraps of newspaper, you could tell he'd never actually done it.
>
> **Marianne Faithfull, quoted in Clinton Heylin's *Behind The Shades* 2000**[1]

Despite Marianne Faithfull's scepticism, Bob Dylan can be seen making a real-time demonstration of Tzara's Dada poetry method in the documentary film *No Direction Home*. Here, the original text is not a newspaper, but an advertisement painted on a wall. Not having a chisel or bandsaw handy, Dylan performs a mental cut-up, rearranging the elements of the sign's text in his mind and spitting them out at random. So:

We will collect clip bathe and return your dog
Cigarettes and tobacco
Animals and birds bought or sold on commission

becomes, after Dylan's cut-up:

I wanna dog that's gonna collect and clean my bath, return my cigarette and give tobacco to my animals!

And later, after several more permutations:

I wanna place that's gonna collect my commission, sell my dog, burn my bird and sell me to the cigarette! I'm looking for a place that's gonna animal my sold, commit my return, bathe my foot and collect my dog! Commission me to sell my animal to the bird to clip, buy my bath and return me back to the cigarette!

The result is hilarious, but also faintly disturbing. Dylan has, on the one hand, proved the effectiveness of Tzara's poetry recipe—despite using almost no words of his own (apart from 'foot' and 'burn' which seems to have been extrapolated from 'cigarette'), the seven variations he produces all somehow sound like Bob Dylan poems. But Dylan's live cut-up also seems to reveal something about the sign, something that had been there all along, but only became evident after his intervention. The weird, crazy monologue of desire Dylan has spun off from the original text ('I want ... I want ... I want ...') makes the sign itself now seem very strange.[2] Is it possible that the person who wrote it may have harboured a secret desire to burn Bob's bird or get his pets hooked on tobacco, which was then repressed and hidden beneath the more obvious, intentional message of the sign, to be subsequently unearthed by Dr Dylan's Surrealist psychoanalysis?

For Burroughs, the answer was, emphatically, yes. He believed that it was possible to unmask and destroy the control mechanisms of the mass media by scrambling (which is to say, unscrambling) its code, a practice taken up by many of Burroughs's acolytes in the seventies and eighties. One day in

1979, sculptor and performance artist Mark Pauline was driving down a San Fransisco freeway when he saw an enormous hand-painted billboard advertising imported scotch. The billboard showed the actor Telly Savalas reclining in an elegant suit, underneath the legend 'Feel the Velvet, baby'.

> I looked at it and I said, NO! Not feel the Velvet, Feel the PAIN. I knew that Feel the Pain was the hidden meaning—you had to drink the scotch so that you wouldn't feel pain anymore.

Pauline and his associates scaled a building and abseiled down the billboard in the dead of night in order to cut-in the word 'pain' to the advertising catchphrase, as well as modifying Savalas's teeth and adding a small leaping dog in the corner of the picture. Soon after, the *San Fransisco Chronicle* reproduced a photo of Pauline's handiwork, with its hidden message uncovered for all to see.[3]

Burroughs's method is very similar to Marshall McLuhan's Freudian reading of the media. If a dream is an acting-out of repressed desires from the dreamer's unconscious, he argues in *The Mechanical Bride*, then the repressed desires of society as a whole could be manifested in the advertising and entertainment that surround us every day.[4] But, just as the dream must appear in code, so as to maintain the conscious mind's belief that everything is OK, so the coded forms of the mass media maintain control over society. But, Burroughs reasoned, if their hidden messages could be revealed somehow, the spell might be broken—no more control. By cutting in new words, sounds and pictures to the existing media landscape (as Pauline did with his billboard vandalism), the story could be changed—control was now in the hands of individuals, and anyone with a camera, a tape recorder or a simple pair of scissors could take over at any time. Burroughs eagerly embraced this serendipitous side-effect of the cut-up, as he began to realise, as Joyce had earlier in the century, the extent to which human behaviour is controlled by language. Indeed, Burroughs began to wonder if our whole perception of time was limited by the sequential nature of language. 'Cut word lines', he proposed, 'and the future leaks out.'

This line of thinking, expounded upon at length in *The Job*, a book of interviews with Daniel Odier released in 1974, leads Burroughs into some decidedly crazy territory, as he insists (on fairly flimsy evidence) that the cut-up can be used to predict future events, as well as to force the proprietors of a café that had served him a dodgy cheesecake to close down.[5] By this time, he had expanded the cut-up idea to include film—which, as he rightly points out, has always been a cut-up—and sound—making recordings of himself, Ian Somerville and Brion Gysin and then 'dropping in' at random new recordings during playback, hammering away at the pause button as though he were the Little Richard of the tape recorder.

Burroughs admitted to Odier that he had some competition in this area. 'John Cage', he said, 'has taken this idea much further in music than I have in writing.'[6]

23. THE SOUND OF SILENCE

Dead air or live music? John Cage's 4'33"

From the early 1950s until his death in 1992, most of Cage's music was created using random, or 'indeterminate', processes. On the surface, Cage's methods have some similarities to Burroughs's cut-up techniques, but, in reality, they couldn't be more different. Where Burroughs used chance as a tool to help him discover his own true intentions (or the intentions of others), Cage wanted to have no intentions at all. 'I have nothing to say', he would say, 'and I'm saying it.'[1]

This is so completely at odds with the way we usually think about art and music that, fifty years later, it's still hard to get your head around it. What's the point of art if not to express yourself? And furthermore, how can you possibly hope to make good art if you, the artist, make no decisions at all about what it's going to look or sound like?

Cage is best known, notorious even, for composing a piece of music with no music in it at all. Its real name is *4'33"*, but a lot of the time people refer to it as 'Silence' or 'The Silent Piece'. The score (yes, it actually has a score), calls for the performer to sit at the piano without playing a single note, over three separate movements totalling four minutes and thirty-three seconds. But the piece is never really silent, because the world never stops producing sound.

Cage himself knew very well the impossibility of creating a genuine silence. He'd been kicking the idea around since 1947, when he first referred to a planned piece of music called *A Silent Prayer*. Around this time Cage, like many composers in the age of recording, began to feel that the world already contained far too much music, and that the most useful thing he could do as a composer, rather than adding to the overall racket, was to make a subtraction, an absence of sound. In a lecture at Vassar College that year, Cage put forward the idea of making a silence that he could sell to the Muzak Corporation to include in its playlists of background music for offices and hotels. Here, Cage is still thinking of silence as non-sound, a reprieve from the problem of a noisy world.[2] But over the next few years, his thinking began to change. He started to entertain the idea of silence *as* music, and an exhibition of paintings by his friend Robert Rauschenberg gave him a push in the right direction.

Rauschenberg's 1949 exhibition consisted of all-white and all-black paintings, and in many ways, the show seemed to be a joke at the expense of modern art, a grim view of the future of painting if Greenberg's insistence on 'flatness' and 'purity' continued to hold sway. But a few people, Cage included, saw something beautiful in the blankness. If you paid attention, you could see that, far from being empty, Rauschenberg's canvasses played host to a constantly changing series of visual effects. Cage saw complex interplays of shadows cast by people and objects in the room, migratory patterns of dust across the surface, tiny imperfections in the canvas and the paint itself—all those accidental things that people usually tried to ignore at an art show had now become the whole work of art.

Of course, Rauschenberg hadn't planned any of these effects, he'd merely created what Cage called 'airports', fields on which they could land. This was in stark contrast to the popular trend in American painting at the time—the late forties and fifties were the time of the Abstract Expressionists. For a painter like Mark Rothko, art was largely a matter of the artist expressing his tragic self through the medium, a highly *subjective* style of painting. But Rauschenberg said he wasn't interested in using painting to express his personality, and it was this 'disinterestedness' that Cage found so attractive. 'The highest purpose is to have no purpose at all', he was fond of saying. 'This puts one in accord with nature in her manner of operation.' Cage, under the influence of Eastern philosophy and Zen Buddhism in particular, wanted his art to be less ego-driven, to have less of him in it. So Rauschenberg's paintings made his next move seem obvious. In fact, Cage remembers thinking that he *had* to compose a silent piece of music after seeing the show. 'Otherwise', he thought, 'music will be lagging behind.' He consulted the *I Ching*, or Chinese *Book of Changes*, to determine the lengths of the three movements.[3]

4'33" had its first public performance in August 1952. In his book on Cage, *The Roaring Silence*, David Revill describes the sounds heard by the audience as, '... wind in the trees, rain blown onto the roof and, in due course, the baffled murmurs of other audience members'. Was Cage upset by these environmental interruptions? Should the room have been better soundproofed so as to make the silence more silent?

As it happens, Cage had already been to the most silent room he could find, the Anechoic Chamber at Harvard University. Excited by the prospect of experiencing, for the first time, a near total absence of sound, Cage stepped into the chamber, but was disappointed to find that he could still hear two distinct sounds. Asking to be let out, he explained to the engineer that something must be wrong with the chamber, since he could quite clearly hear a low pulse and a high singing tone. The engineer explained that the first sound was Cage's own blood circulating around his body, and that the second was produced by his nervous system—so much for silence. At that moment, Cage realised there was no need to worry about the future of music—as long as there was someone around to hear it, there would always be sound.[4]

> **Interviewer:** But then, as there's sound all around us, why bother to make music?
>
> **Cage:** Well, why not?[5]

Far from being emptied of sound, *4'33"* admits that all sound, from the nervous coughing of the person sitting next to you, to the singing of the performer's own nervous system, can be considered as music. Just as Rauschenberg's white paintings became a field for unplanned events, so Cage's piece becomes a kind of frame for the sounds contained within it. Not only that, but the choice of where the piece is going to be performed, what time of day, who will be in the audience and all the other things people normally think of as being 'outside' the work become integral to it. The fact that the composer and performer do almost nothing to realise it means that the responsibility for the work shifts from the artist to the audience. In other words, *4'33"* is about listening.

24. THE SOUND MEASURER

How Cage rolled Beethoven with an eighteen-hour piano marathon

While in Paris in 1949, Cage found a score by the French composer Erik Satie entitled *Vexations*. The piece itself was very short, or seemed to be, until you read the note Satie had scribbled in the margin—'to be played eight hundred and forty times'.[1]

Before Cage, most people who had heard of *Vexations* took it to be a joke, and there was every reason to think that it was. Satie, who wrote the piece in 1893, was known to have a sense of the ridiculous—he wore seven identical grey felt suits for seven years and gave his compositions names like *Four Veritable Flabby Pieces for a Dog* or *Three Pieces in the Shape of a Pear*. He was just as likely to write 'white and motionless' or 'pale and hieratic' in the margin of a score as 'to be played eight hundred and forty times'. Satie's self-deprecating streak was such that he eventually downgraded himself from a composer to a simple 'sound measurer'. In his book *Noise Water Meat*, Douglas Kahn quotes an excerpt from Satie's *Memoirs of an Amnesiac*, which gives us a unique insight into the life and times of a 'phonometrographer':

> The first time I used a phonoscope, I examined a B flat of medium size. I can assure you that I have never seen anything so revolting. I called in my man to show it to him.[2]

But in spite of these shenanigans, Cage took Satie very, very seriously. As he saw it, Western music was still overly concerned with harmony, which Cage thought was a dead end. Satie's work, on the other hand, seemed to point to the future, having more to do with structure and time. In 1948, in a lecture at Black Mountain College, where he first met Rauschenberg, Cage caused an uproar when he pitted Satie against Beethoven and picked Satie as the favourite.

So, having made a copy of the score for *Vexations*, Cage turned his attention to organising a performance of the work. This was easier said than done, and when the piece was finally realised in September 1963, it took a relay team of pianists playing for eighteen hours and forty minutes—one person would perform, while another waited to perform and another kept count. It was five dollars to get in, but if you managed to stay awake till the end you got a twenty-cent refund. As with *4'33"*, what seemed like a ridiculously simple idea on the surface revealed itself, in performance, to be very complex, but in a way that had nothing to do with traditional European ideas of the composer-as-genius, or the idea that art is a means of projecting the individual's ego. Those who looked at the score and saw only a proto-Surrealist gag assumed that there would be nothing new to hear after the eighteen notes were performed for the first time. But *Vexations*, as Cage's study of Zen would have told him, was full of changes; it's just that most of those took place at the level of perception rather than performance.

> In Zen they say, 'If something is boring after two minutes, try it after four. If still boring, try it for eight, sixteen, thirty-two and so on. Eventually one discovers that it is not boring at all, but very interesting.'[3]

Hearing the same thing eight hundred and forty times allows the mind to focus on tiny variations in timing and timbre that, in most Western music, with its focus on narrative and resolution, fly by without the listener even noticing them. Cage left the Pocket Theatre in New York feeling as though something very important had been set in motion, and he was right.

25. HARDER, BETTER, SLOWER, STRONGER

Getting in tune with the Theatre of Eternal Music

Among the piano tag-team that night in 1963 was a young Welsh music student named John Cale, who, when he wasn't studying or working at the local bookshop, was selling drugs for a composer who had moved from California to New York (to be closer to

Cage) called La Monte Young. In 1960, Young had performed his #6, which calls for the performers to stare at the audience as though they were the performers—a neat reversal which recalls *4'33"*, in the sense that the audience becomes responsible for the form of the piece. In the same year, he out-Satied Satie with his *X for Henry Flynt*, an unspecified sound played over and over for an unspecified period of time. Young, perhaps recognising their shared interest in repetition, invited Cale to join his new group, The Theatre of Eternal Music, along with his wife Marian Zazeela and violinist Tony Conrad. Originally, Young played saxophone in the group, but he soon changed to singing when he found that he couldn't get in tune. This doesn't sound like such a big deal until you realise that The Theatre of Eternal Music did nothing *but* get in tune.[1]

It was Conrad who brought the importance of correct tuning to the group's attention. He had learned from his violin teacher the importance of slowness—if you play too fast you can't tell if you're in tune.[2] But Young's music at this point was slower than anything else in the history of Western composition—his #7 of 1960 calls for two notes to be held for as long as possible, and the Theatre of Eternal Music was known to hold notes for up to six hours. As Cage had shown with *Vexations*, reducing the number of events in a piece of music while extending the duration had the effect of focusing the performer's attention in a way that had never happened before. Now, for the first time, the players could get inside the sound and walk around, and they were not entirely satisfied with what they heard there.

The problem lay in the Western system of tuning itself. The intervals between the notes on a piano keyboard are not mathematically correct, but represent a compromise, a fudge designed to help keyboard musicians jump from one key to another without having to re-tune their instruments. So technically, all Western classical music since Bach (who consolidated the new tuning system with his *The Well Tempered Klavier*) has been out of tune. Of course, we've got so used to it now that we don't even notice it, but for Young's group with its endless dronefests there was no getting around it. As Terry Riley, a later member of the group, explained it years afterwards in an interview: 'If you threw up a bunch of slides on a wall that were out of focus, you'd tend to go through them quickly.'[3] Which, he argued, is exactly what Western musicians have been doing with their ever-so-slightly out of tune instruments for centuries. The Theatre of Eternal Music scrapped Bach's keyboard-centric compromise, and tuned to pure, mathematical intervals.

Only one problem remained: finding a constant drone for the group to tune to so that their notes didn't 'drift' too much over the course of the performance. Young eventually found the solution by amplifying the small electric motor in his turtle aquarium and, after that, there was literally no stopping him. Some of Young's performances from the 1960s are *still going*.[4]

26. THE WELL-FED PIANO

The Fluxus variety hour—George Brecht plays a comb and produces an egg, while La Monte Young feeds a piano and hits the wall

Composition 1960 #10;
Draw a straight line
And follow it.

La Monte Young

Young first performed the piece above at one of a series of concerts that he had organised at Yoko Ono's loft in the winter of 1961, and it's an important step in the development of his ideas. On the one hand, it looks ahead to the endlessness of the Theatre of Eternal Music and later works like *The Well-Tuned Piano*. But there's also a certain amount of quasi-mystical silliness in its brief form, not to mention its slightly absurd realisation, where Young measured the floor of the performance space until he hit the wall. This is by no means the most ridiculous work that Young performed in the early sixties. His *Piano Piece for David Tudor #1* calls for the performer to bring a bale of hay and a bucket of water onto the stage for the piano—the performance is over when the piano has had enough to eat and drink or when the piano has decided not to. These exercises, with their mixture of Cage-like conceptual thought and stand-up comedy sight gags, were typical of Fluxus, an international art-amusement collective that Young had a brief but important association with in the early sixties.[1]

Fluxus began, appropriately enough, in John Cage's classroom at the New School for Social Research in New York in 1958. It was a course in 'composition', but nobody was learning harmony and counterpoint. Instead, Cage's students came to understand what he himself had learned in the process of composing and performing his *4'33"* eight years earlier—that *everything we do is music*.

Of course, if that's true then music is easy—and it really was. One of Cage's students, George Brecht, wrote his *Comb Music* the following year, in which the performer is asked to 'slowly and uniformly' move her finger along the prongs of an ordinary plastic comb—the piece is over when all the prongs have been used. Another of Brecht's scores *Egg* simply reads 'at least one egg'. At first Brecht thought of these works as private, 'little enlightenments' that he could share with his friends in New York's artistic community—but this cosy state of affairs would not continue for long.

Solo For Balloons
blow balloon up
let air from balloon slowly / fast
rub fully blown balloon with hands
strike balloon with hand
pierce balloon with pin

George Maciunas, January 1962

Every art movement needs a tyrannical leader, someone to organise the shows, write the manifestos and, most important of all, draw up lists of who's 'in' and 'out' of the group. The Dadas had Tristan Tzara, the Surrealists had Andre Breton, and Fluxus had George Maciunas, who, according to Flux artist Emmett Williams, was still planning exhibitions and writing lists of potential collaborators as he lapsed into a coma in 1978. Maciunas paid the bills for Fluxus with his job as a graphic designer for the American Air Force in Weisbaden, and he used his knowledge of design and printing processes, as well as his international connections, to promote the movement all over the world.[2] Pretty soon, Brecht found himself performing his events in concert halls in Europe, where audiences who'd been enticed by Maciunas's snappy Modernist posters promising 'the newest music' looked on, baffled. Meanwhile in the United States, Fluxus concerts were getting an equally chilly critical reception.

Part of the problem was the concurrent happening of the Happening. In fact, Fluxus and Happenings were often confused with each other in the mind of the art audience and critics, and with good reason. Kaprow, the inventor of the Happening, was also enrolled in Cage's experimental composition class in 1959, and there were a lot of personal connections between the perpetrators of the two movements, who often appeared in each other's performances. But Fluxus, from the audience's point of view, often suffered by comparison. If Maciunas, Brecht, Vautier and co. took *4'33"* as their starting point, then Kaprow and other early Happeners like Jim Dine and Claes Oldenburg were more inspired by Cage's Black Mountain event of 1952. This performance, which involved poetry, piano, dancing, DJing (Robert Rauschenberg on the wind-up gramophone) and Cage himself standing on top of a ladder and delivering a lecture, gave Kaprow the idea of the Happening as a kind of simultaneous spectacle, with many different art forms combined in a total 'environment'.[3]

Of the two developments to have evolved from his classroom, Cage seems to have preferred Fluxus, whose events he often contributed to, whereas Happenings seemed to him to have too much intention, too much of the artist's ego. But for the paying public, the choice was a no-brainer. Are you going to see *Eighteen Happenings in Six Parts*, with its simultaneous onslaught of lights, sounds, paint and poetry, or go across the street and watch some guy holding an egg? The Happeners had clearly put a bit of thought and effort into their events—but playing a comb? 'Boo', shouted the audience, 'So what? I could do that!'

But for the Fluxus artist, 'I could do that' is the best possible response to a work of art. Maciunas believed that it was in the interests of the art-business to keep up the appearance that art was difficult, profound and complex—this simply pushed art out of reach of the people, and kept the value of masterpieces up. By making art that was more like life (as Brecht did with his everyday Events) and by living life in a way that was more like art (La Monte Young's endless music), Fluxus was trying to move art and life closer together, and ultimately, do away with art entirely.

> Promote living art, anti-art, promote NON ART REALITY to be fully grasped by all peoples, not only critics, dilettantes and professionals.
>
> **George Maciunas, 'Fluxus Manifesto', 1963**[4]

Fluxus artists were a motley bunch, with such diverse practices that it was hard for them to agree on anything, which is why Ben Vautier would later describe the movement as 'a pain in art's ass'[5]—it was, then as now, very difficult to sum up what the movement was 'about'. Nevertheless, this goal of de-specialising art, of taking art out of the hands of experts, and finally realising the Surrealist's dream of 'poetry made by all' rings true for most of their work, at least at this early stage. It also reflects the movement's beginnings—earlier in the same manifesto, Maciunas calls on Fluxus to 'purge the world of Europeanism', by which he means the cult of the individual and artist-as-genius that Cage had been trying to undermine through his interest in Zen and chance operations.

27. THE YEAR OF THE SCAVENGER

A trip to the tip with Al and Beck Hansen, Bob Dylan and David Bowie

> The incredibull egghead software chick-a-deli simple
> sams camera
> no she sushi merchant of tennis.
> Experience: weightless macho combo burrito del taco
> over 1 pound.
>
> **Al Hansen, *Venus Rap*, 1992**[1]

Al Hansen, another of Cage's students, seemed to slip easily between worlds in the sixties art scene. He was the social glue that held the disparate Fluxus group together, he lent a hand at some of the most famous early Happenings (including Claes Oldenburg's *Ray Gun* events), helped name the Velvet Underground, and had many fans at Andy Warhol's Factory, where the amphetamine-heads enjoyed the shiny, trashy surfaces of his Hershey Bar collages. Not having a newspaper handy, Hansen had applied Tristan Tzara's famous recipe for Dada poetry to a pile of chocolate bar wrappers collected from the pavement, and as the cut-up fragments came out of a hat, he pasted them onto a sheet of paper in the shape of a curvy Playboy pin-up. *Miss Stuff* (1967) is a self-advertising Pop princess, her body is covered in brash slogans extrapolated from the words 'Hershey's Chocolate':

HEY EYES
COOL IT
HEY HEY HEY HEY
HER COOL SMILE
HER YES
OH OH OH YES
HER SWEET COOL
IN OH HER
ATE WITH AL
OH HER[2]

In the late seventies, Hansen was still picking up trash from the streets—but by this time he was taking the grandkids along with him for the trip. For little Beck Hansen, picking up cigarette butts and chocolate bar wrappers from the side of the road with Grandpa Al would be a formative experience. Al had already achieved 'legendary status' in his imagination before they even met, and the deal was sealed when, as Beck tells it, at the age of seven, his semi-mythical Grandpa finally showed up at his house and gave the boy 'a kiss on the head and an African machete ... I immediately found several large boxes to destroy'—his first cut-up.[3]

> My man Al revolving door spitting out holy debris/
> Dismantler of cankerous machinery
>
> **Beck, 'Masai Ticket for Al', 1995**

What Beck learned from Al Hansen was that anything could be used to make a work of art. Al had already demonstrated that the cigarette butt, possibly the most despised, useless item in the modern world, could be transformed by the imagination and resourcefulness of the artist into a sculpture of the goddess Venus. Hansen approached the garbage bin or ashtray as though he were a primitive man from pre-historic northern Spain, driven by a basic human desire to realise his visions despite the poverty of his materials—in other words, turning shit into gold. His grandson inherited the idea that beauty could be found in the everyday, and by the 1990s, Beck was making his own art from the stuff shoppers throw away. The lyrics of a Beck song often sound like they were torn from the pages of a pile of month-old celebrity gossip mags and retail catalogues, stuffed with what Al would call 'objectionable, shitty, funky material':

> Evaporated meats
> On high tech streets
> We go solo
> Dance floors and talk shows
> Hot dogs, no doz
> Hot sex in back rows
>
> **Beck, 'Hollywood Freaks', 1999**[4]

Beck's very first single, 'Loser', which he performed on British TV as a performance art event, hiring a group of eighty-five-year-old men as his backing band, already revealed a sensitive ear for audio junk sculpture. 'Don't believe everything that you breathe', he wheezed over a creaky readymade loop from an old Dr John song, 'you get a parking violation and a maggot on your sleeve'.[5]

Shortly before his death in 1997, Allen Ginsberg praised these lyrics as 'the best since Dylan's'.[6] Ginsberg, who was an important influence on Dylan and knew him personally (that's him in the background in DA Pennebaker's film clip for 'Subterranean Homesick Blues'), was well placed to see how Beck's odd assemblages of personal reflections, overheard talk, neon signs and shopper dockets not only connected him to Dylan, but to a Surrealist tradition which includes Ginsberg's own work and extends as far back as Guillame Apollinaire's 1916 poem, 'Zone'.

> You read handbills catalogues posters singing aloud
>
> That's what poetry is this morning and for prose there are the papers[7]

Two years later, Apollinaire's friend Andre Breton had incorporated this magpie approach into his own poetry. 'Andre Breton', he wrote in 1918's *For Lafcadio*, 'collector of indirect loans/is dabbling in collage/while waiting to retire', implying that the world contains more than enough readymade phrases and sentences to keep any number of young poets in verse, without having to invent new ones all the time. Breton's 'indirect loans' included borrowings from his friends' letters, other writers' work, and slogans glimpsed in the arcades and shopfronts of Paris:

> Out
> Tender capsule etc. derby
> Madame de Saint Gobain finds time goes by slowly
> when alone
> A cutlet wilts
> Outline of fate
> Where shutterless this white gable
> Waterfalls
> Log-haulers are favoured
>
> **Andre Breton, *Black Forest*, 1918**[8]

Just because your poetic material came readymade didn't necessarily save you time. Breton insists that the poem above took him six months to write. 'You may take my word for it', he later wrote, 'that I did not rest a single day.'[9] But as the century progressed, the one-thing-at-a-time print culture that Breton grew up with disintegrated into the 'allatonceness' of the electronic age, and Surrealist poetry got faster as a result. Ginsberg's verse roared past Breton's at 'one thousand four hundred em pee haich', and Dylan made automatic poems out of shop signage before your very eyes. In Dylan's 1966 book of poetry, *Tarantula*, Crow Jane delivers a manifesto of collage-poetry, 'don't do your ideas—everybody's got those—let the ideas do you ...'[10]. Meanwhile, as we've seen, Burroughs was splicing his own literary DNA with newsprint, Kafka, Ezra Pound and Shakespeare to create new, super-powered mutant writings in the collage novels *The Soft Machine* and *Nova Express*. Writing with scissors might have seemed like a radical break with the past, but Burroughs insisted that it wasn't:

> All writing is in fact cut-ups. A collage of words read heard overheard. What else? Use of scissors renders the process explicit and subject to extension and variation.[11]

Burroughs's cut-up novels might not have been flying off the shelves like Len Deighton or Barbara Cartland, but they went down a storm at the Twickenham Arts Lab in the late 1960s, where a young folk-singing Dylan fan calling himself David Bowie was organising a series of Sunday night Happenings featuring mime, Free Jazz and tie-dyeing classes. In this milieu, Burroughs had achieved the status of a god. Later, when Bowie found himself at creative impasse, burned out on drugs and fame after the monstrous Ziggy Stardust tour, he cut his way out of the stalemate with Burroughs's scissors. Burroughs had, in the early sixties, compared cut-ups to the use of chance in games and military tactics—if your strategy was arrived at by random process, how could your opponent possibly predict your next move? Bowie wrongfooted his audience's (and his own) expectations by allowing chance to guide his hand in writing the lyrics for *Diamond Dogs*: 'I use Burroughs's cut-up technique', he explained in the 1974 documentary, *Cracked Actor*.[12] *Diamond Dogs* is a fake science-fiction musical that attempts to predict the future by cutting Orwell's *1984* and Burroughs's *The Soft Machine* with Dylan's urban Surrealism, 'in the year of the scavenger, the season of the bitch'. Twenty-five years later, the title song would turn up in a real musical, Baz Luhrman's Postmodern evocation of Parisian bohemia, *Moulin Rouge*, where Beck sings it as though the year of the scavenger was 1894, not 1984. The following year, Beck turned up in a future vision far worse than anything imagined by Orwell or Bowie, as he found himself revived in the thirtieth century as a head in a glass tank attached to an android body in 'Futurama'. Beck consoles the irascible robot Bender by explaining the transformative power of art. 'When I'm feeling bad, I write a song about it. Like, when I wrote "Devil's Haircut" I was feeling really ... What's that song about?'[13]

Love machines on sympathy crutches
discount orgies on the dropout buses
Hitching a ride with the bleeding noses
Coming to town with the briefcase blues.[14]

It might not be *about* anything, but as Bowie said, speaking of his use of cut-ups on *Diamond Dogs*, it created an atmosphere—the meaning was out of the artist's control, and it was just old-fashioned to imagine otherwise. When Burroughs's friend and fellow Beat hotel resident Gregory Corso objected that the cut ups were ruining poetry, Burroughs replied, 'Oh Gregory, these days nobody cares about poetry. Too much colic in your ego like that', echoing Breton's reminiscences of Jacques Vache, 'If not for him, I might have become a *poet*'.[15] Poetry, if it was to continue in the modern world, could no longer be left to the 'muse' (as Corso would have it); it had to be found, as Apollinaire had predicted, in the streets.

28. SATORI

How Yoko Ono snuck Expressionism in the back door at the Festival of Fluxus

One of the qualities that characterised Fluxus was its truly international membership. Other art movements had looked to the East before, but no actual Polynesians got to be post-Impressionists, and African sculptors never got invited to Cubist exhibitions. By contrast, twenty-three Japanese artists made contributions to Fluxus during its lifetime, a mutual admiration society that began in 1961 when Maciunas invited a young Japanese artist named Yoko Ono to exhibit her works at his gallery in New York.

Since the late 1950s, Ono had been experimenting with 'instruction pieces', which superficially resembled Brecht's 'little illuminations', short texts describing an action to be performed by the artist. For the Japanese, this type of thinking had deep historical roots, most clearly in Zen *koan* such as, 'to turn a somersault on a needle's point'. Like Young's plan to feed a piano, this phrase appears at first to make no sense, but in contemplating its meaning, the reader will eventually experience what the Japanese call *satori*, a moment of profound understanding.[1]

But while Ono's work had enough stylistic similarities with Fluxus for Maciunas to want to include her in his big list, a great deal of her work explores darker, more personal terrain. It's interesting to compare Ono's *Cut Piece* of 1964 with Robert Watt's *Two inches* from the previous year. *Two inches* is a typical bit of Fluxus low-budget art-amusement, where a ribbon two inches in width is 'stretched across the stage or street, then cut'. It's brief, it's elegant, it doesn't mean anything outside itself, and thereby follows Cage's dictum; 'to let sounds be themselves'. *Cut Piece*, while employing the same technology (fabric and scissors) and the same brief, 'instructional' style, is a totally different beast. Ono sits motionless on the stage with a pair of scissors by her side, and audience members are invited to come up to the stage and cut parts of her dress off until she is naked. It's hard to imagine a more personally expressive work, or one more loaded with meaning, conjuring as it does images of voyeurism, rape and violence. And yet, as Hannah Higgins points out, *Cut Piece* is regularly performed to this day in Fluxus anthologies and concerts.[2] How did she get away with sneaking Expressionism into a movement that aimed to 'purge the world of Europeanism'?

While Maciunas would have been loath to admit it, Fluxus was actually closely related to Expressionism in many ways. In order to see why, we'll need to revisit the era of the Tenth Street School, the glory days of Abstract Expressionism, when men were real men, paint was plentiful and The Big Canvas stretched out in front of American artists like a field ... a field in which to *act*.

This idea of painting as an event was first identified by the art critic Harold Rosenberg in 1952. For Rosenberg, Pollock's paintings were not so much an expression of his feelings as a residue of his actual physical presence on the canvas, the evidence of action. As we've already seen, Kaprow picked up on the 'action' in this equation, and soon started throwing paint, straw and occasional food around the gallery. But for George Brecht, Pollock's dripping and flinging led him in quite a different direction. Brecht liked the accidents in Pollock's method, the way he incorporated chance into his paintings by abandoning his forms to the effects of gravity as the paint sailed off the stick and splatted onto the surface. For him, this was actually closer to Cage's 'nature in her manner of operation' than the usual interpretation of Pollock as an expressive genius; Pollock himself would probably have both agreed and disagreed—in an interview he once described himself as 'working from the inside out, like nature'. B. H. Friedman recounts how Pollock once tried to settle an argument about what is and isn't art in a decidedly Fluxus way—by driving a large nail into the floor with a hammer. 'Dammit', he said, 'that's art!' Far from putting art up on a pedestal, Pollock seemed to Brecht to be bringing art and life closer together by doing something very ordinary—dripping.[3]

Drip Music (Drip Event)
A source of dripping water and an empty vessel are arranged so that the water falls into the vessel.

George Brecht, 1959–62[4]

In this confusion over Fluxus's position in relation to 'expressive' painting, it's easy to see how Ono could have slipped through the cracks. Her *Blood Piece* (1960) is drip music of a different kind—the artist is instructed to paint with her own blood 'until you die'. It's almost more Pollock than Pollock—talk about 'painting from the inside out!'.

29. THE ART PILL

How Joseph Beuys enlarged our understanding of art by hitting a piano with a shoe

The German artist, Joseph Beuys made his debut as a Fluxus performer at the Gallerie Parnass in Wuppertal in 1963. Dressed like a concert pianist, he sat down at the keyboard and proceeded to beat hell out of the piano with a pair of old shoes until the instrument disintegrated. Later, by way of explanation, Beuys said that the purpose of his concert had been to bring about a 'new beginning ... an enlarged understanding of art'. The point, as is often the case with a FLUXUS was to re-integrate the art object into everyday life – just with a little more force in this instance. But Beuys later criticised Fluxus for not going far enough, saying that the movement 'held a mirror up to people without indicating how to change things'.[1] This would never be good enough for Beuys who, in his own eccentric way, wanted to change everything.

Beuys: Two years ago I created a political party for animals.

Interviewer: Do you have a lot of animals in the party?

Beuys: It's the largest party in the world.

Interviewer: And you are the leader?

Beuys: I am the leader.

Interviewer: You're crazy.

Beuys: And therefore I am a very mighty man. Mightier than Nixon.

Joseph Beuys, Interview with Willoughby Sharp, 1969[2]

For Beuys, the above interview was an example of what he called 'social sculpture'. Like McLuhan with his 'probes', Beuys wanted to get people thinking, talking and arguing by saying and doing thought-provoking things, as he did in 1964 when he suggested to

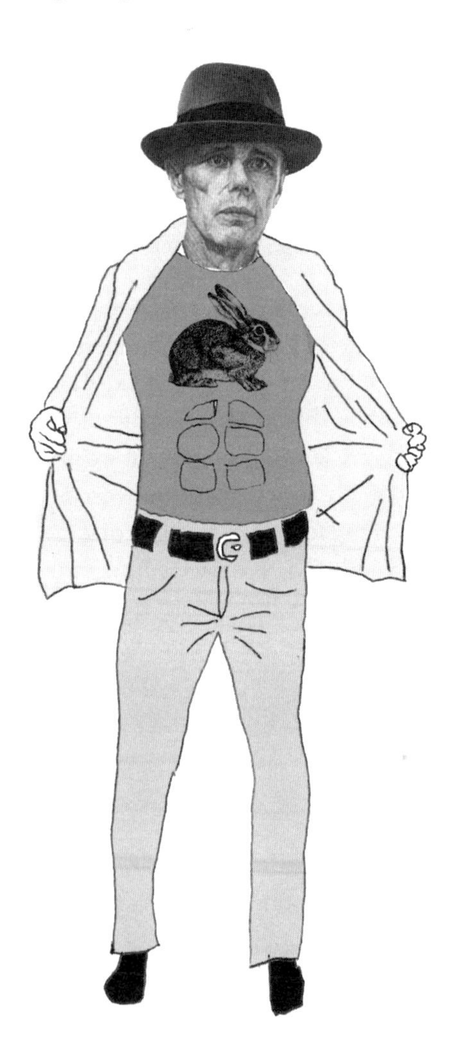

the German government that the Berlin wall be heightened by five centimetres in order to improve its proportions. Beuys later explained that his idea had been to ridicule the 'physical wall', and thereby re-focus people's attention on the 'social wall' that had led to its construction in the first place.

So when he talked about making social sculpture, he wasn't talking about making monuments out of plaster and bronze, he was talking about changing life through art, and everything Beuys did was part of his art. Whether he was clobbering a piano with a shoe, making a drawing with hare's blood or beeswax, or saying loony things in an interview about starting a political party for animals, it was all part of Beuys's big project, which was to unlock the creative potential of human beings everywhere.

What Beuys took from Fluxus was that the boundaries between art and life had to be removed (which is why his objects never sit on plinths or bases), but he knew that this was not going to be brought about with just one egg. In turn, the other Flux artists criticised him for making his art too 'complicated'—Beuys's actions and sculptures were a good deal more spectacular than Brecht's barely perceptible 'events'. In 1963's *The Chief*, the chief of the stags (Beuys, in his official role as the leader of the animals) appeared rolled up in a rug made of felt, with a dead hare placed at each end of the roll and fat sculptures in the corners of the room. Inside the rug, a microphone picked up the chief's vocalisations and amplified them through speakers placed in the street outside the art gallery. Not only is this a lot more ambitious technically than Fluxus, it flies in the face of the movement's manifesto by being symbolic—it's *about* something, but what?

Beuys's early interest in natural science had been interrupted by Hitler's rise to power and the outbreak of the Second World War. Drafted as a pilot in the Luftwaffe, he experienced death on an unimaginable scale, 'dead people ... everywhere',[3] and while Sartre was fighting the Nazis in the French Resistance, Beuys was going through his own Existential crisis. By the time the war had ended, he had decided he wanted to be an artist. Beuys studied sculpture in Dusseldorf, but the war had taken its toll on his mental and physical health, and he spent the next decade in a state of self-imposed exile. He made no sculpture during this time, but he drew constantly—when he ran out of sketchbooks he drew on notepads, graph paper, calenders and paper bags. *Swan* from 1954 is a drawing in blue ink on a page torn out of a diary. It's recognisably a waterbird, but Beuys seems somehow to have drawn the energy produced by the bird, the heat given off by its body and the molecular disturbances caused by its movements, as well as its physical form. 1952's *Stag in the Rock* is harder to decode—the shape of the stag's head can be seen poking out from underneath a larger form, which could be the animal's own skull, as lines of kinetic energy shoot off toward the cluster of organic shapes to its left.[4] Again, you get the feeling that Beuys sees the animal and the landscape as a continuum—the relationship between the two is what concerns him. According to Beuys, the pictures he produced during this time—more swans, bees and stags as well as obscure machines and instruments involving wax, fat and felt—would guide him in the rest of his life's work.

In works like 1965's *How To Explain Paintings to a Dead Hare*, where the artist appears speaking to said hare for three hours with his face covered in gold foil and a heavy weight attached to his shoe, Beuys took the animal forms he had used to reconnect himself with his own creative energy and staged them as public spectacles in the hope of awakening the potential for creativity in all people everywhere. Not that he expected everyone to start going to painting classes on Sunday or rolling themselves up in a rug in the loungeroom and talking to the pets—you could keep doing what you were doing, just do it more *creatively*:

> At the moment art is taught as a special field which demands the production
> ... of artworks. Whereas I advocate an aesthetic involvement in every sphere
> of human activity. Even the act of peeling a potato can be a work of art if it is
> a conscious act.[5]

30. ART AND THE PEOPLE

How Marcel Duchamp made art without making anything at all

> Perhaps it will be the task of an artist as detached from aesthetic preoccupations ... as Marcel Duchamp, to reconcile art and the people.
>
> **Guillame Apollinaire, *The Cubist Painters,* 1913**[1]

According to Beuys, Marcel Duchamp had hinted at the direction he hoped that art would take as early as 1917, with a work he submitted for (but which was not exhibited in) the Society of Independent Artists annual exhibition that same year. The work that Duchamp had produced was chastely referred to in newspaper reports at the time as a 'bathroom fixture'—it was, in fact, a urinal. Not a painting of a urinal, or a sculpture of a urinal or a replica cast in bronze of a urinal, just the thing itself; ordinary, factory made, purchased from the JL Mott Iron Works on 118th street in New York. Duchamp had done nothing to it besides turning it upside down, crudely lettering the words 'R Mutt 1917'on the bottom left-hand side, and giving it the title *Fountain*.[2]

Of course, Duchamp had done *one* other thing to it—he had tried to hang it in an art exhibition, thereby creating, as was said at the time, 'a new thought for the object'. For Beuys, the significance of *Fountain* was clear—by putting an everyday item in the art gallery, Duchamp had shown that all people, not just artists, are creative and make beautiful objects.

Leaving aside for the moment the question of what, if anything, Duchamp had intended by his now legendary art-prank, for Beuys, it was a start, but not enough. As with Fluxus, Beuys parted company with Duchamp for not being committed enough to solving the problem of how to change life through art—this is what Beuys meant by his statement 'the silence of Marcel Duchamp is overrated'.[3]

Beuys was by no means the first to be disappointed by Duchamp. He disappointed his brothers by abandoning a promising career as a Cubist painter in order to spend more time writing obscure Surrealist puns, he disappointed the New York art world by giving up a promising career as a Surrealist in order to play chess, and in a final outrage, he disappointed all the people who considered him a hero for giving up art by making another artwork just before he died in 1968.[4]

But Duchamp wasn't lazy, he was just more honest than most artists are prepared to be. Usually, in order to be recognised, you need to have a style, and in order to have a style, you need to produce things in a series of some sort, so that your audience can see a progression. But Duchamp never saw any point in repeating himself (unless he really *wanted* to repeat himself, in which case he was careful to make an exact copy). He only made art when he had an idea, and because he often kept a day job (he took up a position as a librarian after deciding to quit painting in 1912), he never relied on his own art as a source of income. Keeping art and work separate meant he was less susceptible to the demands of collectors who may have wanted him to churn out 'more Duchamps'. He was becoming aware, as he would later write, that art was 'a habit forming drug', and that sometimes it was better to just say no. This is why he was careful never to get too involved in movements. During the heyday of Dada in Paris, Tristan Tzara invited Duchamp to contribute a work for a group exhibition, to which Duchamp replied with a brief telegram reading, 'BALLS TO YOU'. Later, Duchamp would contribute to Surrealist exhibitions and publications, but always keeping a safe distance. In fact, his most prolific and successful collaboration with Breton's group was done without his being involved at all—at least not in a physical sense. At the height of the sleeping-fits craze, the Surrealists' most talented sleeper, Robert Desnos, claimed to be channelling Duchamp's female alter ego, Rrose Sélavy. Breton, having struck out repeatedly in trying to permanently recruit Duchamp to the cause, happily settled for Rrose's paranormal manifestations as the next best thing.[5]

Fountain is actually just one of a series of no-art artworks that Duchamp had been 'making'—which is to say 'choosing'—since 1913, when he attached an ordinary bicycle wheel to an ordinary stool so as to have something pretty to look at in his studio. This was soon followed by a bottle-drying rack, which unlike the wheel, was not altered in any way.

Duchamp himself did not grasp the significance of these objects until a couple of years later. In 1915 he was walking down a New York street with his brother-in-law Jean Crotti when he saw a snow shovel in a hardware store window and bought it, on a whim. Like the bottle-drying rack, Duchamp claims to have chosen the object in a spirit of complete 'visual indifference'—there was nothing special about it. But only one year later, Crotti was describing the shovel (now hanging from the ceiling in Duchamp's studio) as 'the most beautiful object I've ever seen'. Duchamp quickly realised that this could form the basis for a whole new way of making art. The 'Readymade', as Duchamp called it, existed in a state completely outside of good or bad taste—and yet by signing it and designating it a work of art, he had, nevertheless, made an artistic decision, and within no time at all, the thing had become 'beautiful'. He immediately wrote to his sister with instructions as to how to transform the bottle rack into a Readymade, only to find that she had thrown it out, being slightly more indifferent towards it than he was.[6]

31. A RIDDLE TO FREE THE MIND

Biz Markie, the Dust Brothers, your mum, and the assisted readymade

Rubbish piles, fresh and plain
Empty boxes in a pawnshop brain
License plates, stowaway
Standing in line like a readymade

Beck, 'Readymade', 1996[1]

In his excellent book on the aesthetics of Hip-hop production, *Making Beats*, Joseph G. Schloss recounts a conversation with producer Mr Supreme. Supreme is telling the story of an argument he had with his mother about sampling—his mother says that what he does is not art, because he's taken the sounds from someone else. Supreme makes the very good point that as a producer, he is in the business of putting sounds together—whether he had someone walk into a room and hit a drum with a stick, or whether he takes that sound off a record makes no difference; he's still composing. 'And she paints, so I told her, "You don't actually make the paint", you know what I'm saying?'[2] Duchamp would have called what Mr Supreme's mum does 'an assisted readymade', as he explained in 1961:

> Since the tubes of paint used by the artist are manufactured and ready made products, we must conclude that all the paintings in the world are 'Assisted Readymades'.[3]

It's a shame, considering how persuasive his argument is, that Duchamp wasn't around to deliver his lecture on 'The Creative Act' in 1991 when Gilbert O'Sullivan took rapper Biz Markie to court for sampling the piano intro from the English Pop star's hit, 'Alone Again, Naturally'. US District Court Judge Kevin Thomas Duffy effectively ruled against the assisted readymade as a valid musical form when he ordered Biz's record company to pay damages to O'Sullivan for breach of copyright, creating a precedent that had enormous repercussions for Hip-hop in the nineties. After this, it became impossible to release albums like De La Soul's *3 Feet High and Rising* or the Beastie Boys' Dust Brothers'-produced *Paul's Boutique*.[4] Paying for all those samples from Bob Dylan, The Beatles, The Commodores and the soundtrack to *Psycho* would cost a fortune. By the time they came to work on Beck's *Odelay* in 1996, the Dust Brothers were being very careful to dot their i's and cross their t's when it came to using other people's stuff. The sizeable chunk of Antonio Carlos Jobim's 'Desafinado' that pops up in the last few bars of 'Readymade' is duly credited.

Legalities aside, for many, the revolution in thought implied by the assisted readymade is still a leap too far from the idea of the artist as craftsman. Perhaps this is why Allen Ginsberg once described Duchamp's assisted readymade, *Why Not Sneeze Rrose Sélavy?*, as 'a riddle to free the mind'. Comprising a wire birdcage which Duchamp half-filled with small cubes of white marble along with a cuttlefish bone and a thermometer, *Why Not Sneeze* was commissioned by Dorothea Dreir in 1921, but although she paid Duchamp for the work, she never liked it very much and eventually gave it to her sister, who also hated it[5]. You can bet that Judge Kevin Thomas Duffy and Mr Supreme's mum wouldn't have thought too much of it either; 'That's not art!', they'd protest, pointing to the bit in the Bible that says 'thou shalt not steal'.

While in Paris, Ginsberg actually met Duchamp and Man Ray (who had been one of the first to jump on the readymade bandwagon with his *Gift* of 1921, a clothes iron modified with thumbtacks, conceived 'after a couple of grogs' with composer Erik Satie) at a party in 1958. According to Ted Morgan, Ginsberg, who had brought Burroughs with him, got very drunk and tried to feel Duchamp up—he later managed to convince the artist to give Burroughs a kiss[6].

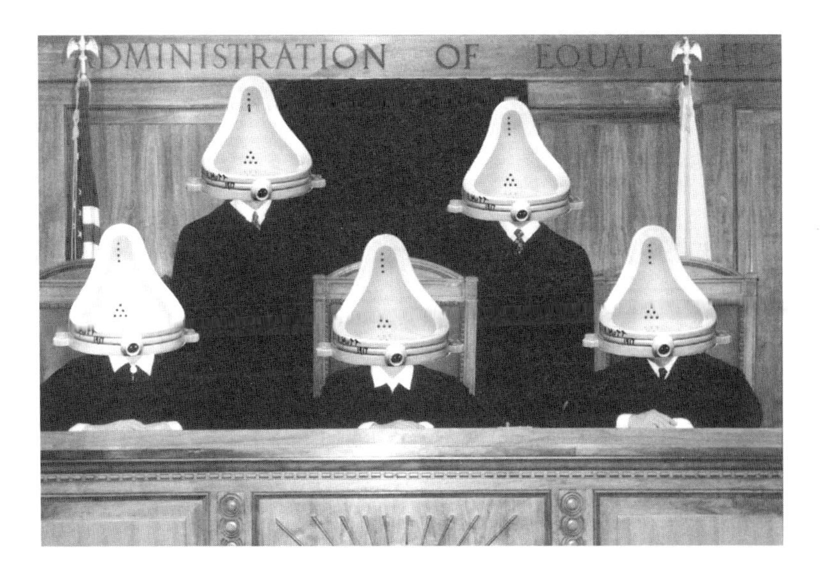

32. RE-COMMODE-IFICATION

Duchamp, John Cage, Brian Eno and David Bowie

Duchamp's readymades are strongly related to his interest in chance. In 1913, (the year John Cage was born), he and his sisters composed a piece of music by drawing notes out of a hat and transcribing the results. That same year, as part of the preparations for his *The Large Glass or The Bride Stripped Bare by Her Bachelors, Even*, he created *3 Standard Stoppages*. These were threads exactly one metre in length, which Duchamp dropped from a height of one metre onto a canvas and glued down in the shape they had fallen. The point of this, as with the readymade, was to subvert his own tastes, which, even at this early stage, were already beginning to bore him. He already knew where he would *choose* to place the thread—how much more interesting, more surprising, to let the thread decide? This was the principle Duchamp observed some years later when, having left *The Bride Stripped Bare* unfinished, the glass panel on which it was painted was shattered in transit. Duchamp decided to accept the accident as part of the work, gluing the glass fragments back into their original shape.[1] If good taste, as Duchamp once said, was the enemy of art, then accidents could prove to be an artist's best friend.

> Honour thy error as a hidden intention
> Make a sudden, destructive unpredictable action; incorporate[2]

These are just a couple of the helpful aphorisms included in a deck of cards called 'Oblique Strategies', produced by Brian Eno in collaboration with the painter Peter Schmidt in 1975. Eno came up with the idea while still at art school in the sixties—having read about John Cage's use of the Chinese *I Ching* as a compositional tool, he decided to create an 'oracle' of his own, more suited to his own creative needs. Eno continued to consult the Oblique Strategies throughout the seventies and eighties, not only while recording his own albums, but also in his collaborations with

David Bowie. Eno had noticed that the creative blocks that musicians sometimes experienced in the highly pressurised environment of the recording studio could be easily broken by the introduction of a random element into their thinking. So, 'don't be afraid of things because they're easy to do' could be the perfect piece of advice for a musician who's struggling with a needlessly complicated guitar solo, when two well-chosen notes would suit the song better. 'Which frame would make this look right?' Maybe the music the band has been working on is useless as a Pop song, but perfect as a film soundtrack.

Bowie was particularly taken with the Strategies—the track 'Sense of Doubt' from his album *Heroes* was composed by Eno and Bowie taking turns at overdubbing parts, each following an Oblique Strategy card as faithfully as they could.[3]

Eno has spoken at length about his indebtedness to Cage, and thanks to his highly influential role as a producer and musician, many of Cage's, and by extension, Duchamp's, ideas have become part of the mainstream of Rock music. Perhaps this is why Eno decided to repay the debt by making his own, very personal contribution to Duchamp's *Fountain*. In 1994, Eno, dismayed at the way Duchamp's conceptual joke about the role of the artist had become misunderstood to the point that a replica (not the original) of R Mutt's bathroom fixture was being insured for something in the order of thirty thousand pounds, decided to restore the *Fountain* to it's original non-art status by pissing in it—a process he cheekily referred to as 're-commode-ification'.[4]

33. INDETERMINACY—THAT'S WHAT I WANT!

Sheet music, tinfoil, pie plates and other ways to prepare a piano

During the recording of The Flying Lizards' 1979 cover of 'Money (That's What I Want)', pianist Julian Marshall recorded his part of the song while Lizards producer and mastermind

David Cunningham threw sheet music, a glass ashtray and a cassette recorder into the piano[1]. This form of piano abuse can be traced back to the music Cage wrote for dancer Syvilla Fort in 1940, and his subsequent discovery of the Prepared Piano. Cage had agreed to write a percussion score for Fort's performance, but the space she'd booked was too small—if they set up a percussion ensemble there'd be no room for the dance. So Cage turned the theatre's piano into a percussion instrument by preparing it—inserting ashtrays, pie plates and other foreign objects between the strings in order to turn them from pitched sounds into percussion sounds, thumps, clicks and rattles. Cage continued to experiment with the prepared piano over the next decade, and he got it down to such a fine art that soon his scores included very precise instructions for how to prepare the instrument—including exact measurements for where the screws should be inserted, how far they should be turned, even what gauge of screws to use.[2]

'Preparing' is not just for pianos—Sonic Youth have been known to insert things between and beneath the strings of their guitars or to play them by dropping objects onto the strings in a decidedly 'indeterminate'[3] way. But as with Eno's use of chance operations in the making of a David Bowie album, the differences from Cage's approach are as important as the similarities. If Cage, like Duchamp, had been trying to remove himself from the process, then for him *that* was the goal—as he put it 'to have no purpose at all'. Rock musicians, however, while happy to use indeterminacy as a way of subverting their own thinking, will always reserve the right to 'chuck the system', as composer Earle Brown puts it, and turn the results of their experiments into something pretty. Where Cage sought to free himself from likes and dislikes entirely, Eno, Bowie and The Flying Lizards (not to mention The Flaming Lips, Wilco, Frank Zappa and other musicians who have used indeterminacy in their work) are in the business of making likeable music. Sonic Youth are a good example of this. The band's catalogue includes some 'pure' avant-garde music, including the SYR release 'Goodbye 20th Century' where it interprets scores by various luminaries of modern music including Cage[4] and the 1983 live recording 'Audience', a remixed version of *4'33"*, in which the band electronically manipulates and amplifies the sound of the crowd while remaining completely silent.[5] The group until recently had a fifth member in multi-instrumentalist Jim O'Rourke, who Thurston Moore has described as 'kind of like our Brian Eno'. O'Rourke has actually played accompanying music for dancer Merce Cunningham, a frequent collaborator of Cage's, and his position as a 'fly in the ointment' within the group was specifically intended to upset the band members' tastes and habits[6]. But Sonic Youth is also unashamedly interested in emotional Rock music—Neil Young, Black Sabbath and Boston albums share space on the band's shelves with Tudor and Cage.

34. AGAINST AESTHETICS

What's the difference between an artist and a dry-cleaner?

Duchamp's abandonment of his art-making to chance and indifference raises important questions about what art is, and what it is that we like about it. If the shattered glass of *The Bride Stripped Bare* looks good, can we say that Duchamp is a good artist for putting it there? No, it was an accident. But he chose to accept the accident as part of his work, and if you think it looks good, then *The Bride* is still good art. This was the argument set in motion by the non-exhibition of R Mutt's *Fountain* in 1917.

Beuys's understanding of the work, that Duchamp had demonstrated that art exists outside of art galleries by putting a factory-made object in a fine-art context, was partly true. Duchamp had often expressed admiration for machine-made forms and 'mechanical' drawing. 'Painting is finished', he said to the sculptor Constantin Brancusi in 1914. 'Who can do anything better than this propellor? Can you?'[1] But he had also said that he wanted to 'discourage aesthetics', so it's not quite right to see him as arguing for beauty in the everyday. Duchamp, like his friend

Picabia, knew that the business of 'aesthetics' was so subjective as to be virtually meaningless. That's why he'd given up being a modern painter—why would he go looking for the same thing at the flea market? As Picabia wrote in 1920, in an open letter to the art-going public:

> You are always looking for an emotion that has already been felt, just as you like to get an old pair of trousers back from the cleaners, which seem new, as long as you don't look too close. Artists are cleaners, don't be taken in by them.[2]

Is it possible Duchamp was just using a urinal to take the piss—having a go at the seriousness and pretentiousness of modern art by seeing how far his audience could be pushed? He certainly had a wicked sense of humour: in 1919 he drew a moustache on a postcard reproduction of the *Mona Lisa* and wrote the letters LHOOQ underneath—said out loud in French this translates roughly as 'She has a hot arse'. There can also be no doubt that the man enjoyed the occasional pun. For example, the signature 'R Mutt'on the *Fountain* was inspired by the name of the foundry where it was purchased (Mott) but was altered to Mutt after Duchamp's favourite cartoon character at the time, from the serial *Mutt and Jeff*. Jeff was tall and skinny, whereas Mutt was short and fat, and therefore seemed like a good name for the squat, rounded form of the urinal. The initial R stands for Richard, which Duchamp explained is French slang for 'moneybags'. 'That's not a bad name for a *pissotiere*' (the opposite of poverty), he later explained. 'Get it?' It's not inconceivable that a person with that kind of imagination would enjoy the spectacle of gallery-goers and collectors falling over themselves to discover the 'meaning' of a randomly selected piece of plumbing.[3]

This is getting closer, although Duchamp was never that mean-spirited. What he had realised, staring at the snow shovel hanging from the ceiling of his studio, was that the meaning of a work of art is not made by the artist alone. In fact, even when the artist surrenders his work to the operation of chance (as with the stoppages), or short circuits his own taste completely by choosing an uninteresting object (as with the *Fountain*), the viewer will nevertheless create a meaning for the work. As Duchamp himself said in 1915, 'It is the viewers who make the painting[4]'.

Not that any of this would have cut much ice with the organisers of the 1917 Independents exhibition. After much heated discussion, the board decided that Mr Mutt's contribution would not be exhibited, since it was 'by no definition a work of art'.

35. BUSINESS ART AND THE ART BUSINESS

How Andy Warhol woke everybody up by putting them to sleep.

> Mechanical means are today, and using them I can get more art to more people. Art should be for everyone.
>
> **Andy Warhol, 1967[1]**

In 1913 Duchamp had painted a picture of a chocolate grinder, done in an unemotional 'technical' style—an early step towards his abandonment of aesthetics. Later, after the original *Fountain* went missing, Duchamp realised that, being a manufactured object already, there was no reason why it couldn't be mechanically reproduced by simply buying another one or, as he did in 1965, by ordering an edition of multiple copies from a factory.[2]

Andy Warhol, who had left a very successful career in advertising to go into what he called 'the art business', famously christened his studio 'The Factory' to show that *all* his art was being mass-produced. Instead of the individual, painterly mark-making of the Abstract Expressionists, Warhol produced his canvases using an anonymous commercial art process—silk-screening. And it wasn't nice, well-executed silk-screening either—Warhol's paintings proudly proclaimed their mass-produced nature by drawing attention to the lack of care that goes into the production of popular art. His multiple Marilyns, Elvises and electric chairs are full of over and under-exposures and bad colour alignments, and their origins in clippings from cheap, tacky magazines and newspapers are readily apparent from the huge ben-day dot patterns that become even more obvious by being blown up and repeated. A lot of the time, Warhol didn't even make the work himself, leaving it in the hands of assistants, as if to say that he didn't care too much how it turned out.

> If you want to know all about Andy Warhol, just look at the surface of my paintings and films ... there's nothing behind it.
>
> **Andy Warhol, 1966**[3]

Many people assumed at the time that Warhol and the other Pop artists like Roy Lichtenstein (who carefully handpainted subtly altered reproductions of romance comic strips) and Claes Oldenburg (who made giant hamburgers out of floppy, synthetic material) were making some kind of statement about the evils of Capitalism by rubbing all this banality in the art audience's faces. But for most of them, and certainly for Warhol, nothing could be further from the truth. In fact, Warhol frequently insisted that his art was about nothing, or at least nothing you couldn't see straight away. This was another trick he'd picked up from Duchamp: just as visitors to the *Fountain* had praised its aesthetic qualities—in spite of the fact that, for Duchamp, it had none—so the people who went to see Warhol's supremely blank paintings of soup cans and dollar bills felt as though they should say *something*, but what? Here, Warhol realised that he could put the public, and more importantly the media, to work for him in investing his art with significance. On TV, even more than in real life, the one thing you can't have is uncomfortable silence—so, if someone asked him what his painting was about and he didn't say anything interesting, pretty soon the interviewer would tell *him* what it was about.

> **Interviewer:** Andy, do you feel that pop art has sort of reached the point where it's becoming repetitious now?

Warhol: Uh, yes.

Interviewer: Do you think it should break away from being pop art?

Warhol: Uh, no.

Interviewer: Are you just going to carry on?

Warhol: Uh, yes.[4]

Warhol's shift from advertising to fine art coincided with his beginnings as a film-maker—his Factory would produce movies as well as paintings. In July 1963 he bought his first movie camera, and over the next two months he shot a film—*Sleep*, planned as an eight-hour movie of his boyfriend John Giorno, sleeping. Because of the technical limitations of his camera, Warhol had to settle for a finished product that ran for five hours and twenty-one minutes, and contained a few more edits than he would have liked, but he was pleased enough, and *Sleep* had its debut screening the following January at a small theatre on East 27th Street, run by the Lithuanian-born director of the Film-makers Coop, Jonas Mekas.[5]

In his book, *Popism*, Warhol jokes that one of the reasons he'd decided to make a movie about sleeping was because everyone he knew was doing so much speed that pretty soon sleep would become obsolete. Still, no amount of diet pills was going to help the patrons of Mekas's theatre make it all the way through Warhol's first opus. Perhaps Mekas should have taken a leaf out of Cage's book and offered a refund to the die-hards. In any case, Andy himself certainly didn't have that kind of time on his hands—he left after a couple of minutes, much to the annoyance of Mekas, who'd already tied one patron to a chair for attempting to leave.[6]

> Andy has fought by repetition to show us that there is no repetition, really, that everything we look at is worthy of our attention. That's been a major direction for the twentieth century, it seems to me.
>
> **John Cage, 1968**[7]

In *Factory Made—Warhol and The Sixties*, Steven Watson points out the similarities between the first screening of *Sleep* and John Cage's performance of *Vexations* the previous year.[8] Both involved long, repetitive events which, on closer inspection, were nowhere near as simple as they at first seemed, and both built on Duchamp's realisation that the audience is at least partly responsible for a work's meaning. It should come as no surprise then to find that John Cale, who had participated in the performance of *Vexations*, had by 1965 become part of an Andy Warhol production as a key member of the Velvet Underground. Here, Cage and Warhol's independent discoveries would converge, as Cale's long, static drones, derived from his experiences with Cage and his subsequent playing in La Monte Young's group, were heard simultaneously with Warhol's films in a sort of portable Happening that Warhol called *The Exploding Plastic Inevitable*. Suddenly, what had seemed like fairly weird avant-garde experimentation only a few years earlier now made a much more immediate kind of sense, and the sensory onslaught of the *EPI* (repetitive sound, near deafening volume, disorientating images and light show) would help to define the modern Rock spectacle for decades to come. As Lou Reed would later put it in an interview with Victor Bockris, 'Andy told me that what we were doing with music was the same thing he was doing with painting, i.e. not kidding around'.[9]

Warhol's own comments about *Sleep* are revealing: 'When people go to a show today, they're never involved anymore. A movie like *Sleep* gets them involved again.' While there's no question that Warhol was pleased with *Sleep* ('It's so beautiful!' he exclaimed as he watched the rushes), it's also true that he liked the movie *because* it was boring—in the way that a series of unedited out-takes or an overlong home movie is boring. For Warhol, this is the best possible situation to be in as a viewer, because instead of just sitting and watching, you're forced to contribute to the film in an imaginative way. For example, in *From A To B and Back Again—The Philosophy of Andy Warhol*, he describes watching an old Esther Williams musical number where a hundred girls are jumping off swings. What Warhol finds most absorbing in this scene is the idea that one of those girls may have lost her nerve and not jumped at the correct time. Somewhere, he fantasises, mouldering in a vault in Hollywood, is the out-take of that scene, where the girl fails to jump, and *that's* what he wants to see. Not because it's good—he knows it will be bad and awkward—but because it's given him an idea ... it can be *used*. In other words, in that moment, Andy Warhol is no longer just watching movies—he's making movies.[10]

36. THE APPEAL OF REAL

Why bad acting makes good art and how Andy Warhol and Jack Smith invented reality TV, forty years too early

Shortly before beginning work on *Sleep*, Warhol had himself been filmed shimmying on top of a giant Claes Oldenburg wedding cake for a scene in *Normal Love*, a movie by underground film-maker

Jack Smith. Warhol (or 'Andy Panda' as Smith sometimes called him) was immediately impressed by the director's style, and the two shared a love of celluloid trash. 'Trash', Smith announced in 1963, 'is the material of creators.'[1] This sensibility, the rarified enjoyment of the truly, heroically awful, would be defined for all time the following year by Susan Sontag in her essay, Notes On Camp:

> The pure examples of camp are unintentional; they are dead serious. The art nouveau craftsman who makes a lamp with a snake coiled around it is not kidding, nor is he trying to be charming. He is saying, in all earnestness: Voila! The Orient![2]

Smith was obsessed with B-movie superstar Maria Montez, a terrible actress who appeared in shabby exotica movies like *Ali Baba and the Forty Thieves* and *White Savage*. The film-maker had invented his own vocabulary to accommodate his almost obsessive love for Montez, where the 'exotic' was prized above all else ('pasty', 'moldy' and 'superstar' were a few of Smith's other coinages). He wrote short stories, too—lurid, Burroughsian fantasies of a decaying Hollywood backlot peopled by decomposing superstars and massive plaster edifices slowly crumbling into dust. It was in this imaginary pile of film refuse, what Warhol refers to elsewhere as 'leftovers', that Smith found the raw material for his films.

> Maria Montez was propped up beside the pool which reflected her ravishing beauty. A chunk fell off her face showing the grey under her rouge ... Best to fish the chunk out of the pool and pat it back into shape. It'll show as a blotch on her cheek, but we can shoot around that.[3]

At the heart of Smith's aesthetic is a reversal of the usual standards of good or bad taste that, according to Sontag, is the basic currency of camp. In a 'good' movie, millions of dollars worth of lights, camera and action are painstakingly combined to create the illusion of reality in a dark room for a couple of hours. This, Smith would argue, is inherently phony, or, to use his own custom-made vocabulary, 'moldy'. In a 'bad' movie, all of this falls apart. Instead of watching and enjoying the illusion, you suddenly find yourself watching the *reality* behind the movie—out-of-their-depth performers struggling to convincingly deliver bad dialogue amidst a bizarre assemblage of movie industry machinery. This failed attempt at phoniness, according to Smith, is compellingly real.[4]

'Real' was an important idea for Warhol. Even as his movies became more plot-oriented and character-driven, he continued to emphasise the fact that his superstars were 'real people' and therefore better than those phony Hollywood actors. Here Warhol was, as with many things, way ahead of the game. Toward the end of the 1990s, a powerful idea swept through the television industry. Network executives and heads of programming realised, seemingly as one organism, that despite all the money spent on scripts, actors, production values and special guest stars, what people really enjoyed watching on TV was real life. You know, those moments when the set falls down, somebody bursts into tears and we are suddenly confronted with human experience in all its naked glory—real people with real problems caught on camera. This idea has reached its pinnacle with the arrival of 'Big Brother: Up Late', a show which simply points cameras at people in a house doing stuff, while the audience waits for something to happen, something ... real. Warhol would no doubt be pleased to see that no one has to tie anyone to a chair anymore to make them enjoy being bored.

Warhol knew that the attention-seeking drag queens and speed freaks he was filming for his movies spent most of their time 'performing' anyway, so it's kind of hard to tell where the 'reality' in his movies stops and the acting begins. In *From A to B and Back Again* he recounts a conversation with his friend Damian—'She was being so serious, but it was just like a bad movie. I love bad movies. I was starting to remember why I always liked Damian.'[5] Again, all of this recalls Jack Smith's fondness for Maria Montez and her 'atrocious acting sighs'—they're so *real*[6]—as well as the adoration heaped on 'worst director of all time',

Edward D. Wood Jr. In Tim Burton's 1994 portrait of the director, *Ed Wood*, Wood's cast and crew wince visibly as George 'The Animal' Steele ('Lobo') struggles pathetically to get his enormous bulk through the door of one of Wood's moldy sets. When Wood announces that the scene is 'perfect' and that they can move on to the next shot, they look at him as though he's actually from outer space.

> **Bill:** Hey Ed, shouldn't we do another take? Big baldy got kinda stuck in the doorway.
>
> **Ed:** No, it's fine. It's real! In actuality, Lobo would struggle with that problem every day.[7]

Wood's movies satisfy Sontag's definition of 'naïve' camp—Wood was not trying to make films that were 'so bad they're good', he sincerely believed his films were great, and his sincerity is part of their appeal for the afficianado of camp. Likewise, the appeal of watching David Hasselhoff in 'Baywatch' or Tori Spelling in 'Beverly Hills 90210' lies in the fact that they are, as Sontag would put it, 'not kidding'.

37. THE FLANEUR

Walter Benjamin goes shopping with the Surrealists

> Go and see the worst pictures, they are sometimes sublime.
>
> **Ado Kyrou, *Surrealism au Cinema*, 1963**[1]

The fans of Hasselhoff, Ed Wood, Roxette and the Eurovision Song Contest might sometimes seem as though they've lost their minds, but in this they're in good company. Camp in all its manifestations, from your friend's indefensible passion for Jerry Bruckheimer movies, to Jack Smith's irrational attachment to Maria Montez's moldy epics, is a close cousin to Salvador Dali's paranoiac-critical method. Just as Dali had decided to look at the world in a 'mad' way in order that it might reveal to him the beautiful truths known only to the mentally ill, so Smith, in making the world's worst actress the sole object of his desire, was privy to rarefied pleasures that the uninitiated could not hope to understand:

> Those who could believe, did. Those who saw the world's worst actress just couldn't and they missed the magic. Too bad—their loss.
>
> **Jack Smith, *The Perfect Filmic Appositeness of Maria Montez*, 1963**[2]

This Surrealist appreciation of film can be traced back as far as Breton's war-time friend Jacques Vache, who would create his own unique movie collages by wandering in and out of different cinemas at five-minute intervals—channel surfing on foot[3]. The Surrealists loved going to the movies, and not *Un Chien Andalou* or *L'Age d'Or* either—the marvellous could be found in the most unlikely places, and bad movies were their favourites. Like Warhol with his Esther Williams musical, they weren't going to see art films, they were watching films as art—looking for the unintentional, the surprising, the raw stuff that film fantasies are made from. This approach to mass culture wasn't limited to the cinema—shopping could be a creative act, too. In the wake of Duchamp's snow shovel, the hardware store became alive with possibilities, the flea markets of Paris in the 1920s and 30s full of readymade sculpture for those of a paranoiac-critical frame of mind. 'I go there often', wrote Breton in 1928, 'searching for objects that can be found nowhere else: old fashioned, useless, broken, almost incomprehensible.'[4] It was here that Max Ernst found the materials for his disturbing collages of old Victorian engravings, and when Man Ray and Erik Satie had the idea to make a sculpture after an afternoon of drinking, they didn't pick up a set of chisels and start chipping away at a block of marble—they went shopping.

Paris was a good place to wander around in those days. It was laid out in a way that gave priority to the pedestrian, everything within easy walking distance, with plenty of opportunities to amuse or distract yourself along the way. The idler, or *flaneur*, could spend his time walking in and out of theatres, browsing through arcades and stopping in cafes, living in the city as though the city itself were his home. Into this city of dreams strolled the literary critic Walter Benjamin, who moved to Paris after fleeing his native Germany in 1933. For Benjamin, the Surrealist *flaneurs* seemed to represent a changing approach to art.

> Every day the urge grows stronger to get hold of an object at very close range by way of its likeness, its reproduction.
>
> **Walter Benjamin, 'The Work of Art in the Age of Mechanical Reproduction', 1936**[5]

Benjamin felt that the modern metropolis, with its shopping arcades and magazines, was bringing art closer to the people—you didn't have to go to a museum to look at Da Vinci's *Mona Lisa* anymore, you could buy a picture postcard of it for a few francs and stick it on the wall in your room. As Benjamin explained in his famous essay, 'The Work of Art in the Age of Mechanical Reproduction', the new technologies of photography and offset printing had the effect of making the original work less mysterious by making it available to more people, diminishing what he called its 'aura'. Not only that, but in photography and film there was no original work of art at all—it makes no sense to talk about the 'original' film—it's a mass medium. What Benjamin is saying is that this is a *good* thing, art is no longer a special and separate activity, it can be seen by many people at once, and can potentially be made by anyone at any time.[6] Now that you could have the *Mona Lisa* in your apartment, you could do whatever you wanted with it—hang it upside down, cut out her head and replace it with your girlfriend's, or draw a moustache on her and write something rude underneath. Now *you* are the artist.

Not that you need to read Walter Benjamin to know that it's fun to pick things up off the street or make collages out of old postcards and art books. Anyone who's ever enjoyed Monty

Python's *Flying Circus* would be fairly familiar with the idea that there are laughs to be had by mutilating old paintings. The enormous pink foot that descends from the heavens at the start of each episode was originally attached to a naked cupid in a painting by sixteenth-century Tuscan artist Angelino Bronzino, before being vandalised by Python animator Terry Gilliam more than 400 years later. In Gilliam's book, *Animations of Mortality*, Brian the Badger explains the thinking behind this method. 'Here we are in the Hall of Masterworks', he says, strolling past the *Mona Lisa*:

> Cheap foreign labour has always been a mainstay of Good Business Practice and we in the animation game are not about to be an exception. Wherever possible we try to use bits of these masterpieces. Not only is the workmanship far superior to that available today but, more importantly, the painters are all dead ... a great help to Mr Swinburne in the accounts department.[7]

What makes all of this possible is that the masterpieces in Gilliam's museum are reproductions. If he'd tried ripping the foot off a real Bronzino, he'd have been arrested, but the age of mechanical reproduction has turned the vandal into an artist. This, Benjamin would have argued, is real cultural democracy. Gilliam is not a respected master of Tuscan Mannerism—he's just a guy with some art books and a few ideas—but now he's more famous than Bronzino. Bronzino's foot is now Gilliam's foot—looking at the original painting, the foot is hilarious in a way that Bronzino would never have intended; it actually looks out of place, as though Bronzino has stolen it from Gilliam. Whatever symbolic purpose the dove in the bottom left-hand corner of the original painting might have been meant to convey is gone, replaced by the undeniable fact that it's sitting right underneath the famous foot from Monty Python, and, any minute now, that foot is going to come down, just like it does in the title sequence: SPLAT! History has been rewritten, with a camera and a pair of scissors.

As early as 1918, Hannah Hoch and Raoul Hausmann had noticed this kind of thing going on in a town on the Baltic coast where they were holidaying. Hoch remembers seeing, in a house they were visiting, a coloured souvenir print of Kaiser Wilhelm II surrounded by suitably patriotic imagery of healthy German oak trees and great soldiers proudly fighting for their country. On closer inspection, she noticed that one of these soldiers had the face of the household's landlord cut out and stuck in place underneath the helmet. Suddenly, by a simple intervention of photography, scissors and glue, the picture's meaning was changed, and Herr Felten the landlord became a part of German military history rather than just a footnote to it. By 1919 Hoch had taken her own scissors to a pile of magazines and catalogues, and produced *Cut with the Cake Knife*, a riot of popular images sliced into strange new shapes—Karl Marx's head grows out of the side of a piece of factory machinery, an elephant devours a swimsuit model, football players crawl up the Kaiser's nose, and a praying mantis looks on while a steam train roars past, leaving in its wake a single word Dada.[8]

38. NAVEL-GAZING VERSUS BELLY-DANCING, PART1

At the magazine rack with Hannah Hoch and Linder

Hoch and Hausmann were quickly joined by two more scissor-happy collagists, George Grosz and John Heartfield. They came up with a name for what they did—Photomontage—and a dress code—overalls—to show that they were not artist-geniuses but art-workers, people just like you and me who had risen up from the ranks of image-consumers to be image-creators. All of this must have appealed strongly to Richard Huelsenbeck who, after a stint at the Cabaret Voltaire in Switzerland, had returned to Germany in 1917 to open up the Berlin franchise of Dada—the anti-art movement that had been born in the heat of those rowdy nights of belly-dancing and simultaneous poetry in Zurich. Huelsenbeck would have seen in the Photomonteurs the same anarchic impulse that had inspired Tristan Tzara to create a poem by cutting up a newspaper and drawing the fragments at random out of a bag, and they certainly shared his intense dislike for the Expressionists, with their navel-gazing inwardness and escapism. So he put together a manifesto for Dada, Berlin-style, in which he called for an art 'visibly shattered by the explosions of last week', and the Berlin Dadas busied themselves creating an art of fragments from their ruined, hyperinflated city, a city, as Huelsenbeck described it, 'of mounting, thundering hunger'[1]. The aftermath of World War I had left the German government with a vast accumulation of war debts, which the German treasury attempted to pay off by simply printing more and more money. As a result, inflation soared. In *Modern Times, Modern Places*, Peter Conrad describes how, at the war's end, one US dollar was worth seventy-five marks. Four years later, that same dollar would buy you *four trillion* marks. 'Cups of coffee', writes Conrad, 'tended to treble in price while you were drinking them.'[2]

While their work was certainly motivated by a genuine disgust at the state of their country's affairs (Grosz's work in particular is a bitter indictment of the greed and wastefulness of the Weimar Republic), the Berlin Dadaists also took a kind of perverse glee in their rummagings through the wreckage of popular culture. If nothing else, they thought, it would annoy the Expressionists.

> I'd always loved magazines and I had two separate piles. One you might call women's magazines, fashion, romance, then a pile of mens mags: cars, DIY, pornography, which again was women, but another side. I wanted to mate the 'G-Plan' kitchens with the pornography, see what kind of strange breed came out.
>
> **Linder, quoted in Jon Savage's *Engand's Dreaming*[3]**

One of these strange new creatures reclines on the cover of the Buzzcocks' 1977 single, 'Orgasm Addict'. Linder, a Manchester-based artist who designed many of the band's early sleeves, posters and handbills, has successfully crossbred a clothes-iron with a porn star. The shiny new appliance now appears in place of her head, while smiling lipsticked mouths have been grafted onto her breasts. Linder loves her magazines, but, like the Dadaists, hers is an active, rather than a passive, way of consuming culture, and, as such, her work functions well as a case study for Benjamin's ideas regarding the 'democratic' nature of photography and mechanical reproduction. The magazines she used for her raw materials could be found at any corner shop, and manipulating them required no special training or technique—anyone could do it. This is why Linder's photomontage was such a natural fit for a Punk group like the Buzzcocks—it seemed to say that the means for making art were available to everyone, and this idea was, and still is, at the heart of what makes Punk Punk—do it yourself.

UK Punk, in which Linder, along with contemporaries like Malcolm Garrett and Neville Brody, was an instigator, was a product of similar social circumstances to those of the Berlin Dadas. In the 1970s, inflation and unemployment wracked the economy of a country that had never properly come to terms with its own war debts. In this context the shiny dreams of post-war consumer happiness peddled to Britons over the previous two decades began to turn sour. Linder's clothes iron, once a symbol of Futuristic promise, had become ridiculous, a piece of surreal junk, long before she attached it to the body of a centrefold. The only kind of art to be made in a landscape like this was an art of fragments, things scavenged from the scrap-heap of history, as Walter Benjamin would do, picking up worthless banknotes from the streets of Berlin, and finding in their garish designs what he described in 1929 as 'the revolutionary energies that appear in the *outmoded*'.[4]

39. BEAUTY IS IN THE STREET

Smashing the great deception with Guy Debord, Malcom McLaren, Jamie Reid and Jarvis Cocker

With the promises of late Capitalism exposed as a sham by Britain's ruinous economy and general bad mood, the Punks took it upon themselves to remove the last remnants of its disguise, exposing, once and for all, the boredom and repression that consumerism was designed to conceal. The Sex Pistols' graphic artist, Jamie Reid, appropriated images from a brochure advertising Belgian holidays for the sleeve of the band's 'Holidays in the Sun' single. In the original illustration, a holidaying young couple pose in front of a scenic view, the man's speech bubble announces: 'It's just a short excursion to see wonderful historic cities.' But in Reid's version, it's as if the man has been given a truth drug, or as if we have been given the power to see into his thoughts or the thoughts of his masters. 'A CHEAP HOLIDAY IN OTHER PEOPLE'S MISERY', he says, while his girlfriend smiles cruelly.[1]

This sleeve, as well as other Sex Pistols design solutions (like the tourist buses with their destination signs altered to read 'nowhere' and 'boredom' used for the promotion of *Pretty Vacant*), is an example of an artistic strategy perfected in the late 1960s by the Situationist International. The SI believed that late

Capitalism had transformed all of modern life into what they called 'The Society of the Spectacle', which reduced people to passive consumers, spectators in their own lives. As the movement's leader Guy Debord put it (paraphrasing Marx), 'all that was once directly lived has become mere representation'.[2] In the face of this overwhelming victory of the spectacle, the old art forms were next to useless. Indeed, the Situationists believed it was the inevitable fate of the artwork, no matter how radical, to be absorbed, or to use Debord's word, 'recuperated' into the spectacle itself. Debord could see that the techniques of the Surrealists, which had been designed to discredit and destroy reality, were now being used to prop it up. From the endless knock-offs of Dali and Magritte in the world of advertising (a cloud superimposed on a head is used to sell cold and flu tablets), to the Automatic Writing on the sleeve of a Bob Dylan album—all forms of radical art were subject to be transformed into commodities. In this way, the society of the spectacle de-fanged potentially dangerous ideas and domesticated them. Surrealism may have once promised to 'change life', but now it was just another lifestyle, which could be yours—for a price. Given that works of art were so easily susceptible to spectacularisation, Debord had to insist on a fairly strict 'no artworks allowed' policy for his art movement. In their place, Debord advocated new methods by which the SI might bring about the long-promised revolution of everyday life.[3]

One day in December 1968, the members of a UK offshoot of the SI known as King Mob, one of them disguised as Santa Claus, strolled into Selfridge's toy department and began handing toys out to children. 'Christmas was meant to be great, but it's horrible', they said, as the gobsmacked kids ran out of the store with their free toys. 'Let's smash the great deception.' Among those chased out of the store by police was a 22-year-old art student named Malcom McLaren. McLaren had just participated in what Debord would call the creation of a Situation, an interruption of the spectacle, an outburst of real life in a fake world—and it wouldn't be his last. While it might not have been planned as such, the Sex Pistols' appearance on Thames TV's 'Today' programme in 1976 can also be seen as a constructed situation, and McLaren would certainly come to see it that way, despite being terrified at the time that his hot new band had sabotaged their shot at the big time by saying rude words on live TV:

> **Bill Grundy:** Go on, you've got another ten seconds. Say something outrageous.
>
> **Steve Jones:** You dirty bastard.
>
> **Grundy:** Go on, again.
>
> **Jones:** You dirty fucker!
>
> **Grundy:** What a clever boy!
>
> **Jones:** You fucking rotter!
>
> **Grundy:** Well that's it for tonight.
>
> **Transcript from Thames TV's 'Today', 1 December 1976**[4]

McLaren and his obstreperous charges may not have immediately realised it, but in that moment they were operating in a tradition that, according to Debord, stretched back to early Surrealist heroes like Jacques Vache, as well as the inimitable Arthur Cravan. Cravan was a boxer, and not a particularly great one, but through a bizarre sequence of events, he'd found himself in the ring, squaring off against world champion Jack Johnson in 1915. Cravan lost, of course, but the legend of Arthur Cravan, prizefighter and poet, and sometime art critic, was born. In 1917 the Dada painter Francis Picabia invited Cravan to give a lecture on 'The Independent Artists in France and America'. Before the talk, Picabia and Duchamp took Cravan out for lunch and got him very drunk, and by the time he took the stage, he could barely stand up. In the end, according to Ruth Brandon, Cravan's 'lecture' consisted of a collection of curse words at least as bad as the stuff you might have heard on Bill Grundy's show in December 1976, accompanied by the undignified sight of the poet-boxer

removing his clothes ('It's so hot in here', he complained). The police dragged him away before the pants came off, but Duchamp proclaimed the talk a success. 'What a wonderful lecture', he said to Picabia.[5]

Debord, had he been there, would have concurred, just as he would have enjoyed Pulp singer Jarvis Cocker's impromptu derailment of the spectacle at the Brit awards in 1996. Cocker, as John Harris relates in his chronicle of Britpop, *The Last Party*, found himself armed with an 'access-all-areas' pass and a gutful of booze, at the side of the stage while Michael Jackson performed 'Earth Song' surrounded by a cast of angelic-looking children and representatives of all the world's major religions.[6] Disgusted by this pious and phony display, Cocker strolled out onto the stage, wiggled his arse at the TV cameras, and lifted up his shirt, before running away. It might not have been much, but in that moment Cocker had reversed the one-way flow of the spectacle and, however briefly, broken the spell.

That all of these 'constructed situations', The Sex Pistols' interview, Cravan's 'lecture', and Cocker's striptease, have alcohol in common as a catalyst is entirely appropriate. Debord, in his 1991 memoir, *Panegyric*, claimed that:

> Among the small number of things that I have liked and known how to do well, what I have assuredly known how to do best is drink. Even though I have read a lot, I have drunk even more. I have written much less than most people who write, but I have drunk much more than most people who drink.[7]

Apart from drinking and causing trouble, the other technique advocated by the SI as a way of bringing about the revolution was *detournement*, a kind of termite-art, whereby the products of the spectacle are altered and then sneakily re-inserted back into the world. One Situationist detournement uses an American sci-fi adventure comic featuring square-jawed superheroes in Futuristic radiation suits, but replaces their corny dialogue with excerpts from Situationist philosopher Raoul Vaneigem's *The Revolution of Everyday Life*. Now, instead of saying 'prepare the shuttle' or 'I've got a bad feeling about this', our hunky heroes are earnestly discussing the fate of revolutionary art movements in the society of the spectacle. 'We're playing into the hands of supersession', declares one of the adventurers, cradling his space-helmet in his arm, 'just as sometimes, a murdered man can be said to have played into the hands of his executioner.' Even the Chief looks worried at this grim prospect. Luckily, at that moment, the solution comes blaring from a speaker on the spaceship's intercom: 'From now on we must reassert all the essentially revolutionary demands abandoned by mass movements as they lost their initial revolutionary impetus.' What the ship's computer is saying is that the SI must try again to bring about the revolution promised by Breton or by the Dadaists, but avoid, at all costs, the possibility that the means used to achieve that revolution might be used to sell cold and flu tablets at any point in the future. Having accepted their mission, our heroes don their recuperation-proof goggles and set out, bravely, into the society of the spectacle.[8]

Jamie Reid had been introduced to the ideas of the SI while at art school with McLaren, and busied himself throughout the early seventies with various forms of detournement. In 1972, Reid designed a series of stickers in the style of a supermarket ad campaign, which he plastered on store windows up and down London's Oxford Street shopping district.

SPECIAL OFFER!
THIS WEEK ONLY
THIS STORE WELCOMES SHOPLIFTERS

According to Reid, many people took advantage of his special offer the day after the stickers went up. When the store detectives tried to apprehend them, they simply pointed to the sticker on the window.[9] This is a perfect example of what Debord would call 'realised art', art that keeps its promise to transform life, so that there is no longer any need for art. Reid's sticker is not an artwork as such—it's a detonator, a device to bring about a refusal of the spectacle.

Reid would later put these SI-inspired strategies to good use in his work for the Sex Pistols—the 'special offer' star motif was recycled for the band's slogans, such as 'CASH FROM CHAOS' and 'NEVER TRUST A HIPPY'. In Reid's most famous image, Her Majesty Queen Elizabeth II is detourned, transformed into a protest against her own jubilee with a flick of Reid's scalpel. Meanwhile, other Punk groups did it themselves. Leeds-based radicals Gang of Four released its first EP, *Damaged Goods*, in 1978. The group's proposed sleeve design used a found photograph of a bullfight, augmented with captions in which the bullfighter attempts to justify his position by explaining to the bull that he's just trying to make a living. 'I think', says the bull (an unwilling participant in the society of the spectacle if ever there was one), 'that at some point we have to take responsibility for our actions.' The same year (and on the same label), The Human League's *Being Boiled* arrived wrapped in a classic piece of SI-inspired design. On the front, a clip art couple, tastefully dressed in the style of the day, step out into a modern metropolis, ready for a fun night of dancing to the latest hit record by The Human League. But what's this they're dancing to—'Being Boiled'? 'Circus of Death'? It's as though the group have slipped something in their drink. As the couple dance and grin like happy consumers, the band's singer, Phil Oakey, is muttering horrible things over the electro-disco. 'Dominion is the name given to the fictitious drug administered by the ringmaster', he drones, 'to subjugate those who fall prey to his power.'[10]

40. CROSSING OVER

Going undercover in the society of the spectacle

The irony is that for all their attempts to undermine or subvert late Capitalism, *Being Boiled*, *Damaged Goods* and *God Save the Queen* are all, themselves, commodities—albeit painfully self-aware ones. In this sense, Punk and post-Punk would fall some way short of Debord's expectations. Debord often spoke of the importance of not turning the refusal of the spectacle into a spectacle of refusal[1], which is what Punk inevitably and almost immediately became. Punk, like Impressionism, Dada, Surrealism and Fluxus before it, has been recuperated, and Jamie Reid's style, as much as Johnny Rotten's stare and Vivienne Westwood's clothes, has become just another of the techniques available to the modern art director, another set of images, useful for selling certain things to certain people.

But while Punk may have failed by Debord's rigorous standards, the Situationist dream of destroying and discrediting the spectacle still lived at the heart of the Punk idea, and that dream was not easily abandoned. From 1977 onwards, Pop music (in the UK at least) became a series of attempts to undermine the spectacle by inserting oneself into it—to bring it down from within. Entryism became the new strategy of the 1980s, and many groups went so deep undercover in the society of the spectacle that they began to believe their own cover stories.

The cover of the Human League's *Dare* (1981) marks a turning point in this process. Where the sleeve of *Being Boiled* had given the band's audience a knowing wink, using the degraded imagery of Capitalism as a vessel to communicate the group's creepy message, *Dare* was something quite different. It wasn't a cut-up of a luxury perfume ad, such as Linder might have done for the Buzzcocks—it *was* a luxury perfume ad. The band had packaged themselves as an expensive commodity, complete with artfully applied make-up, a tasteful colour scheme, and a fancy-looking *Vogue* magazine type design[2]. The disguise was perfect—no-one would suspect that beneath this sumptuous packaging lurked the same group who used to sing about dead babies and killer clowns. The Human League had entered the market—and they weren't alone. As the eighties continued, many of the artists who had been inspired by the initial outburst of Punk, including the members of Cabaret Voltaire, ABC, Gang of Four and Scritti Politti, as well as John Lydon's new group Public Image Limited, embraced the act of selling out itself as an artistic strategy. 'Crossing over to the other side', sang Lydon excitedly on PIL's 'This is not a Love Song', 'I'm inside free enterprise!'[3] The idea was that it was smarter to submit to the corporate makeover, or at least do it on your own terms, and take on the spectacle from within, than to be left out of the conversation altogether, reduced to a cranky historical footnote, as, arguably, the Situationists would be.

But the problem with this is that the society of the spectacle makes no distinction between commodities and things which are cleverly pretending to be commodities, and, as the decade wore on, it became harder and harder to tell the difference between entryism and entrepeneurism. Was ABC's *The Lexicon of Love* a witty deconstruction of the use of language and imagery in the packaging of romance to the masses, or just a great romantic Pop record?[4] Was *Dare* a sinister joke about glamour seduction and money, or just glamorous, seductive and obsessed with money? The Human League had, by this point, simply become a Pop group—with no greater aims than to make people dance and cry and buy their records.

After a while, many of the artists themselves got tired of deconstructing fame and just started to enjoy being famous. The patron saint of the 1980s turned out not to be Guy Debord, with his cranky refusal of the spectacle, but Andy Warhol—who liked anything as long as it was popular.

41. NAVEL-GAZING VERSUS BELLY-DANCING, PART 2

Andy Warhol crashes the Abstract Expressionists' party

Andy Warhol: I'm starting pop art.

Al Kessler: Why?

Andy Warhol: Because I hate Abstract Expressionism—I hate it![1]

In the 1990 documentary, *Storming the Citadel*, art historian Jack Flam explains how the New York painters were specifically reacting against the prevailing tendency in American art towards scene-painting—pictures of the surface of life. 'Abstract Expressionist painting sought another truth', he says, 'that truth had to do with deeper values, a grander, nobler sense of reality.'[2] Pollock, Newman, Reinhardt, Rothko and co. also felt themselves to be against popular culture, a point of view that was born from years of being ignored by the media and the art-going public. So as you can imagine, the Abstract Expressionists didn't think too much of Warhol and his soup cans and coke bottles. Motherwell may, as he claims, have given the expatriate Surrealists their first taste of Coca-cola in the 1940s, but soft drinks still had no place in art. In *Popism*, Warhol tells the story of going to a party full of Abstract Expressionist painters with their 'anguished heavy intellects'. According to Warhol, the painter Mark Rothko took the hostess aside and whispered angrily, 'How could you let *them* in?'.[3] Meanwhile, the saloon doors swung in the breeze, and a tumbleweed blew by …

> How did people react? Those who had something to say about it tried to fit these new works into some historical scheme. Some shrugged it off and said, 'more of dada, we've seen this before; after Expressionism comes nonsense and anti-art, just as in the twenties'.
>
> **Leo Steinberg, 'Contemporary Art and the plight of its Public', 1962[4]**

This sense of opposition between the Abstract Expressionists with their higher truths and deeper values on the one side, facing down the Pop artists with their bad movies, magazines and consumer junk on the other, is one of the reasons why Pop, when it first appeared, was often referred to as Neo-Dada. In 1936 when Walter Benjamin wrote of the original Dadas that they achieved 'a relentless destruction of the aura of their creations, which they branded as reproductions with the very means of production',[5] he could almost have been writing about a Warhol painting. In his *Thirty are Better Than One* from 1962, Warhol took a single photograph of the *Mona Lisa* and repeated it, using the mechanical process of silk-screening, thirty times across the surface of a canvas, as though Da Vinci's famous portrait was a soup can or a box of cornflakes. Which, in a way, is exactly what Warhol was saying—as far as he's concerned, the *Mona Lisa* is just another thing you can buy, it's not special or unique, and what's more he *likes* it that way[6].

In his 1967 article, 'Understanding McLuhan', Hugh Kenner describes the media-ologist as the first 'Pop prophet', by virtue of the fact that no one needs to read his books to understand his point.[7] In the same way, Warhol is a Pop artist, because no one really needs to *see* an Andy Warhol painting in order to enjoy it. Not only is it true that Warhol's paintings can be appreciated without going on any kind of special art pilgrimage to see them (as you might with a Rembrandt or a Rothko), but also, standing in front of a Warhol 'original' is a totally ridiculous experience—it's probably the ultimate art anticlimax. A Pollock or a Van Gogh is always much better in the flesh—up close you can see all the nuances and textural subtleties, not to mention the true, brilliant tones of the paint itself that are inevitably lost in reproduction. A real Warhol, on the other hand, is always disappointing, since it's already a reproduction. It is, as Benjamin would say of the Dadaists' collages, 'useless for contemplative immersion'.[8]

It makes for some very awkward art gallery moments—what to talk about? You can't say the photo's good (he didn't take it) or that the silk-screening is well done (it isn't, and in any case, he didn't do that either). Warhol's work only really makes sense if you look at it from a McLuhan-esque point of view—that is, that the Medium (the mass-production system of Warhol's stencil factory itself) is the Message. The content of the paintings, Elvises, Marilyns, Electric Chairs, amounts to next to nothing. The real message of a Warhol is, to paraphrase Kenner, that there are Warhols, with all that that entails.

But what was really shocking about Warhol's art in the sixties was that it seemed to say that the days when art could change the world were over. If art is, as Warhol's *Thirty are Better than One* suggests, just another commodity, then why bother trying to say anything important? Warhol's Factory could take anything—movie stars, paintings, serial killers and cereal boxes—and reduce them to the same, endlessly repeatable form of brightly-coloured entertainment. But Warhol, as he knew, was just a specialist cottage industry, doing on a relatively small scale what the media does every day—TV had turned Mao Tse-tung into entertainment long before Warhol turned him into wallpaper.

42. MACHINE ART

The rise and fall of Constructivism

Back in the 1920s, the idea that art could not only make a difference, but actually help to build a better world, was strong enough for artists all over Europe to want to throw in their lot with Lenin—and, after 1924, Stalin—and embrace the coming revolution. Huelsenbeck, in his Berlin Dada manifesto, called for all German artists and intellectuals to pull together in order to bring radical Communism to Germany, and demanded 'the introduction of the simultaneist poem as a Communist state prayer'. Later, as we've already seen, Andre Breton was very keen to have Surrealism annexed to the French Communist party, and as late as 1930 he was sending telegrams to the International

Revolutionary Bureau saying that he and his comrades were 'at your disposal for mission needing intellectual role stop'.[1]

What Huelsenbeck and Breton found so exciting about Communism was that it seemed to offer a chance for artists and writers to be involved in the creation of a new society—from the ground up. 'Transform the world, said Marx; change life, said Rimbaud', Breton wrote, 'for us, those two watchwords are one.'[2] Where, under Capitalism, the art-worker was alienated from his fellow man by being pigeonholed as a creator of amusements for the middle-classes, the Russian artists of the 1910s and twenties were pitching in like everyone else—no different from the factory workers and the farmers. 'Let us tear ourselves away from our speculative activity', said the new Soviet art-workers, 'and find a way to *real* work!'[3] Artists could make themselves useful by helping to solve practical problems—using their talents to create buildings, furniture, magazines and ceramics for the newly reborn nation. While painting and sculpture would still go on, they would no longer be a means for

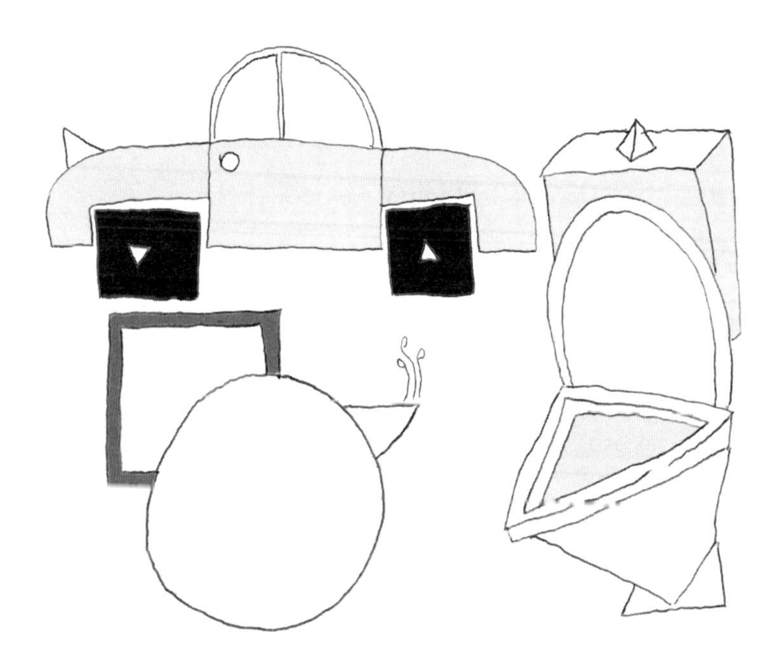

self-expression, but a kind of research project. This 'Laboratory Art', as the Russians called it, could assist the artist in discovering new forms by experimenting with different materials. The results could then be incorporated into designs for workers' clubs, posters and teapots—anything the people might need, artists would create.

In the years prior to the upheavals of 1917, the Russian avant-garde had absorbed the lessons of Cubism and Futurism, and both of these styles would inform the development of Russian art in important ways. From the Cubists they took the idea of the painter as scientist, breaking reality down to its building blocks as Picasso had done with his portraits and still lifes. The Futurists, meanwhile, with their mania for speed and modernity, had taught the Russians to love the factory and the steam train, and to find new ways to celebrate the union of man and machine that would, it was said, revolutionise society from the inside out. During what was called the period of 'heroic communism', prior to 1920, the Russians fused these techniques with the ideas of Marx and Lenin, and came up with 'Constructivist' as a name for the new art-worker. Armed with protractors and rulers, concrete and steel, Vladimir Tatlin, Aleksandr Rodchenko and El Lissitzky would redesign the world using circles, triangles and squares.

That was the idea, anyway. Anatoly Lunacharsky, the Soviet Commissar for Enlightenment, was initially supportive towards Constructivism—or had at least decided that the party should butt out of the in-fighting that characterised modern art at that point. 'As far as questions of form are concerned', he said, 'the taste of the people's Commisar and all other representatives of authority must be set aside. All persons and groups in art must be given freedom of development. No one movement must be allowed to suppress another.' But by the twenties, Lunacharsky had changed his tune, moving rapidly from a belief that the modern artist may need some 'guidance' from the party, to an insistence that the Commissar had 'the right to intervene in the course of culture'.[4] This spelt bad news for Constructivism, which was eventually written out of the revolution completely once Stalin came to power. In fact, with hindsight, the much-touted union of Communism and modern art seems to have been doomed from the start. As early as 1919, while Huelsenbeck was dreaming of an alliance between the Communists and Dadaists, Lenin was admitting that modern art left him cold:

> It is beyond me to consider the products of Expressionism, futurism, cubism and other 'isms' the highest manifestation of artistic genius. I do not understand them. I experience no joy from them.[5]

At the Dada fair the following year, Hoch and Hausmann went out under a banner that pronounced 'art is dead! Long live the machine art of Tatlin'. But although the Dadaists couldn't have known this (Hausmann admitted later to having only the 'haziest idea' of Constructivism),[6] machine art was not doing so well either. Between 1919 and 1920, Tatlin was busy designing models for his Monument to the Third International, a spiral tower of glass and steel, twice the size of the Empire State Building. Suspended within the tower were three separate structures, including an enormous glass cylinder that would rotate on its axis once a year. The fact that the thing was never built was only partly to do with a distinct lack of enthusiasm for Tatlin's project from the regime—Trotsky wondered whether the people's meetings really needed to take place in a giant glass cylinder, and, assuming that they did, whether the cylinder really needed to rotate. But the real problem was that there just wasn't enough glass and steel available in a country still reeling from the upheavals of a revolution and a civil war to realise Tatlin's grandiose scheme. Even the few Constructivist projects that were actually built often proved to be far less practical than all that rhetoric about 'machines for living in' suggested. The communal housing blocks, which had been designed for the newly revolutionised Russian workers, were too few and quickly degenerated into overcrowded vertical slums.[7]

43. THE SHARP EDGE OF THE WEDGE VS THE FRAYED END OF THE PAINTBRUSH

El Lissitzky's amazing adventure in the twenty-first century, featuring Franz Ferdinand

The Constructivists may not have done much constructing, but they did do a lot of designing, and are better remembered now for their posters than for their buildings. In 1925 Aleksandr Rodchenko created one of modern advertising's most memorable images with a poster for the state publishing house, *Gosizdat*, in which a woman in a headscarf puts a hand to her mouth and shouts a striking black triangle containing the word 'BOOKS'. As always with the Constructivists, the emphasis is on purity of form and simplicity of means, the shapes are geometric, the colours are flat and bold, and the typography is sans serif—serifs, like the ornamental trimmings on pre-revolutionary buildings, had no place in the new Soviet art. Rodchenko's poster also makes use of the Dadaists' photomontage technique, which the members of club Dada assert made its way back to Russia after El Lissitzky had seen one of their shows while in Germany in 1921.[1]

Like Benjamin and the Berlin Photomonteurs, Rodchenko was excited by the 'democratic' nature of photography—it was easy to do and, more importantly, it was easy to reproduce, and could therefore be made available to everyone. But Rodchenko's aims for photomontage were subtly different from those of Hannah Hoch and the Dadaists. While he did produce some strikingly odd images to accompany Mayakovsky's poem 'About This' in 1923, generally Rodchenko was not in the business of putting football players up the Kaiser's nose. His experiments, however radical, were always done with an aim to simpler, more powerful communication. As El Lissitzky put it:

> The frayed end of the paintbrush is at variance with our concept of clarity.[2]

Fast forward eighty years, and Rodchenko's happy Soviet worker is back, looking, if anything, a little younger than she did in 1925, more Beatnik babe than proud peasant. This time, she's traded the state publishing house for the more lucrative world of Rock and Roll, so instead of hollering 'BOOKS' her Modernist speech-bubble now reads 'FRANZ FERDINAND'. The Archduke who got shot in the event that triggered the First World War? No, the Scots post-Punk revivalists whose first self-titled album, featuring the hit 'Take Me Out', had made them the darlings of Indie Rock in 2004. Where the debut had featured a Futurist photomontage on the back and a Dada-esque type design on the front, their second album, *You Could Have it So Much Better*, is adorned with an explicit homage to Rodchenko's poster.[3]

How would Rodchenko feel about a Scots Rock band 'appropriating' his poster for its album cover? He'd most likely be surprised, and even slightly annoyed, at the way an image that was produced as part of the great social experiment of Communism had been turned into an advertisement, a symbol of Capitalism, the thing it had been designed to replace. Rodchenko was not without a sense of humour, and as Christina Kiar has pointed out, the products and processes of Capitalism held a sort of lurid fascination for the designer, and may even have influenced him in his search for strategies to spread Communist consciousness.[4] But even if Rodchenko's work was produced with a sharp eye on commercial culture, and was itself, in a sense, advertising, it was of a very different kind. His poster was meant to alert the viewer to the availability of state-published books, but those books were for everyone, and no individual stood to gain from the transaction, they were for the people.

Of course, assuming that Rodchenko had somehow managed to travel through time to arrive in 2006 and see a copy of the album sitting in the racks at your local music store, in the time that he was here, he'd probably learn enough about the world as it is now to make him *really* depressed. Communism in

Europe has collapsed, and the victory of Capitalism seems to be so complete that it's even capable of absorbing the imagery of the Communist revolution itself. Rodchenko might be pleased to learn that his radical experiments in the use of images and type virtually invented graphic design as we know it today, but he would also be treated to the undignified spectacle of Lenin's head being photomontaged onto a bus side and used to sell pre-mixed vodka drinks—and not in a good 'for-the people' way either.

And what about Franz Ferdinand? The band's statement about wanting to make 'music for girls to dance to' has a nice 'functional' feel to it, and suggests that the band members might see themselves more as art-workers than art-geniuses. Elsewhere, they've talked about wanting to play like machines, and Rodchenko, perhaps still seduced by the Communists' promise to revolutionise society through industrialisation, might like the sound of that too. Nice to see, also, that guitar solos have gone the way of the serif in Franz-rock—none of that bourgeois ornamentation for these young Modernists. If Rodchenko could take them with him back to 1920, they could be put to work writing slogans for the Agit-Prop radio station, or at the very least, providing 'music for girls to dance to' at the Vesnin brothers' Palace of Labour (another unbuilt Constructivist project).

Franz Ferdinand is by no means an ideology-free band, but the difference between the utopian enthusiasm of Rodchenko's *Gosizdat* poster and the cheerfully ironic gesture of Franz Ferdinand's album cover is a good example of what people mean when they talk about 'Postmodernism'. The sad fate of avant-garde art in Soviet Russia, which officially wore out its welcome in 1932 when Stalin threw out the Constructivist's proposed design for the new Palace of the Soviets in favour of a Neoclassical solution, accusing them, in a final indignity of being 'bourgeois', is just one of the contributing factors to a general loss of faith in the idea that art can improve the world.

44. CRAZY BALDHEADS

Walter Gropius, Johannes Itten and the early years of the Bauhaus

Because of the ongoing traffic of ideas between Russia and the rest of Europe in the early twentieth century, much of the rhetoric attached to Constructivism found an echo in the designs and philosophies of the Bauhaus School of Art and Design in Germany during the same period. Right from the beginning, the school's director Walter Gropius insisted that the artist must be put to work if art is to be anything more than a pastime for the idle rich. In the first Bauhaus manifesto of 1919, he boldly states that there is 'no essential difference between the artist and the craftsman':

> Let us therefore create a new guild of craftsmen without the class distinctions that raise an arrogant barrier between craftsman and artist! Let us together desire, conceive and create the new building of the future ... which will one day rise towards the heavens from the hands of a million workers as the crystalline symbol of a new and coming faith![1]

It starts out like a manifesto for a design school, but by the end, it sounds more like the kind of literature handed out by people who are trying to get you to join a cult. This, at least in the early days of the Bauhaus, was not too far from the truth. Gropius hired two types of teachers for his new school: the Workshop Masters, who would teach the students how to craft wood and steel, weave tapestries and throw pots; and the Masters of Form, who were mostly painters, and would instruct the students in the principles of colour and composition. One of the first Masters of Form to be hired, the Swiss painter Johannes Itten, steered the students in a quasi-mystical direction, bringing the influence of his chosen faith, a transcendentalist belief system known as Mazdaznan, to bear in his teaching programme. Itten encouraged

the students to shave their heads and wear custom-designed robes (as he did), and to embrace the Mazdaznan health regime of vegetable mash and regular enemas.

Not all of the students thought this was so great (especially after Itten took over the school's canteen), but, despite his eccentricities, Itten's ideas would have an enormous influence on the Bauhaus, and on the future of art education in general. In 1919, most first-year courses at European art schools had you studying the history of painting and reeling off the names of the Old Masters, but students who'd shown up for their first day at the Bauhaus had something quite different in store. Before they'd even opened a book or sharpened their pencil, Itten made the students do breathing and meditation exercises so as to improve their physical control and sharpen up their senses. 'Please stand up', he'd say. 'You must loosen up, get really loose, otherwise you can't work! Turn your head! So! Still further!'[2] His foundation course, in which students were encouraged to discover the inherent properties of materials like wood, steel, paper and cloth, and explore the relationships between colour and form in nature, made a dramatic break with earlier methods of art teaching, and in the process, virtually invented the modern art school, where courses like Itten's are still taught to this day.

But a key difference of opinion regarding the aims and purposes of the school eventually caused a serious rift between Itten and Gropius. By 1921, teacher Oskar Schlemmer was writing of a 'crisis at the Bauhaus'[3], which hinged on whether or not the school should accept commissions from Berlin businessmen and private industry. Itten the transcendentalist believed that such things distracted the artist-craftsman from his true purpose; Gropius the realist wanted to forge stronger links between the Bauhaus and the factory floor, and to have the school produce students that were ready for industry. While Gropius could see that Itten's methods were giving the students a finely honed visual sensibility, he was concerned that all that meditation and mystical hooey was having a bad influence. The world was changing, and Gropius didn't want to turn out a generation of backwoods craftsman quietly throwing pots and contemplating the universe—he wanted graduates who were prepared to go down into the world and design solutions for living in the twentieth century. In 1923, unable to resolve his differences with the school's director, the chrome-domed mystic split for a Mazdaznan meditation retreat in Zurich.

45. HOLY MAHOGANY

László Moholy-Nagy, Hannes Meyer and the Dessau Bauhaus

Itten's replacement was the Hungarian Constructivist László Moholy-Nagy, who, Gropius would have been pleased to note, arrived wearing not the robes of a mystic but the overalls of a factory worker. Moholy's arrival marked a major shift in direction for the Bauhaus, as he and Gropius virtually reversed the school's philosophy. If the Bauhaus had initially been in the business of creating objects that were useful because they were *beautiful*, now, under Moholy's influence, it would turn out objects that were beautiful because they were *useful*.

The pre-Moholy Bauhaus had, at its heart, the idea of the artist as an expressive medium—a special individual who translates his experience and unique vision of the world into concrete forms. For Moholy, this was nothing more than Expressionist hogwash, a romantic fairytale. Moholy believed that if there was even to be such a thing as art in the modern world, it had to be equipped to grapple with the problems of the day—like the Berlin Dadaists, as well as his Constructivist comrades Lissitzky and Rodchenko, he was for an *objective* art. After Moholy took over the foundation course from Itten in 1923, out went the breathing and meditation exercises and all that stuff about the higher, truer reality—and in came scientific rationalism. Moholy kept a close eye on all the latest developments in science and manufacturing technology and was, by Gropius's accounts, something of a gear-head. He relished his position as a heretic among the other Masters of Form, Expressionist painters like Paul Klee and Wassily Kandinsky, and never tired of annoying them by speechifying about the uselessness of subjective forms of art in the machine age.[1]

But Moholy's introduction of the Soviet machine aesthetic into the Bauhaus curriculum would have some unwanted side-effects. With the disastrous state of the German economy in the years following the war came a rise in the popularity of extreme political groups, as a desperate people cast about for solutions to the country's seemingly insurmountable problems. Forged in this super-heated crucible, Adolf Hitler's Nazi party managed to survive the recovery of the economy after 1923, and even the imprisonment of its leader during the following year, during which time Hitler set down his vision for Germany's future in his polemic, *Mein Kampf*. Support for the Nazis grew as the decade wore on, and in 1929, Wilhelm Frick became the first Nazi to hold a position in German politics as Minister of the interior in the state of Thuringia—the Bauhaus's home.[2]

Hitler appealed to Germans with a kind of radical conservatism, which favoured the 'natural' and 'healthy' over the 'foreign' and 'degenerate'. As former Bauhaus student Professor Kurt Krantz explained it, the Nazi aesthetic was often summed up in the phrase, *blut und boden*—blood and soil.[3] As far as the Nazis were concerned, the Bauhaus, by insisting on the machine over the oak tree, was culturally suspect. Calling for the school's closure in 1924, the party announced that 'our healthy instinct tells us that truly authentic art cannot consist of colour-composition alone, or of the filling-in of flat areas, or technical construction'. The Bauhaus, they claimed, was 'assisting the collapse of our culture'.

Hitler was no luddite—he understood the importance of automation and industry. But by making a fetish of the machine, and worse, mixing it up with painting and sculpture, the Bauhaus had fallen foul of Hitler's ideas (and he had plenty of them) about what constitutes good, healthy art for good, healthy Germans. The Nazis accordingly dismissed the products of the Bauhaus as 'degenerate', just as they would the Jazz and Swing music favoured by its students in the Bauhaus band.

The Bauhaus had always been something of a political football in Germany, and this had as much to do with the students as it did with Gropius or his staff. The students were devoted to the embattled Bauhaus, and were proud to be associated with it, but they did nothing to improve public relations between the school and its increasingly conservative hometown. Dr Alec Armstrong, who studied at the Bauhaus between 1922 and 1924, remembers wild nights of loud music, public nudity and wanton vandalism.[4] The boys wore their hair too long, the girls cut it too short. 'Don't look', said parents to their children as the students tore off their clothes and went skinny-dipping in the local baths, 'they're from the Bauhaus!'. The students' conspicuous bohemianism made the school an easy target for the Nazis, who constantly agitated for the school's closure. Eventually, Gropius denied Hitler the satisfaction, and relocated the school to the more liberal-minded area of Dessau.

Along with the new postcode came a brand new building, which Gropius designed himself. The new Bauhaus stood as a monument to the school's ideas, a strikingly simple arrangement of geometric forms in concrete, glass and steel, a building whose form was determined by its purpose, and a living, working illustration of Gropius's 1923 manifesto:

> We want a clear, organic architecture … unencumbered by lying facades and trickeries; an architecture whose function is clearly recognisable in relation to its form.[5]

While Gropius had spoken of building as 'the ultimate aim of all creative activity' since the school's early days, it was not until moving to Dessau that the Bauhaus had an actual architecture department. Hannes Meyer, a Socialist committed to improving the life of the common man through the design of functional buildings, was hired to teach the new course. Meyer's presence took the Bauhaus even further in the direction of scientific rationalism than Moholy had, and in the process, brought more unwanted attention from its enemies in Berlin, enemies who wasted no opportunity to write the school off as 'Russian', and therefore undesirable. The Nazis eventually forced the Bauhaus (now under the stewardship of its third and final director, the architect Mies Van Der Rohe) out of Dessau in 1932, and finally closed it down for good the following year. As a result, many of the school's most important teachers fled to the United States, where they took up infuential teaching positions—Moholy-Nagy founded the 'New Bauhaus' in Chicago in 1937 (where he would later invite John Cage to teach a course in experimental music)[6], and Gropius and Mies Van Der Rohe both taught in American universities. More importantly—they put up buildings. The United States had no shortage of concrete, steel, glass, and—most importantly—clients, to enable them to realise their vision of Modern architecture. Mies Van Der Rohe's dazzling 1958 Seagram Building in New York is the apotheosis of European Modernism in the New World, and just one of hundreds of glass, steel and concrete slabs to be erected in the name of Functionalism in cities like New York and Chicago.[7]

46. WORKER HOUSING

A brief history of modern architecture, from Mies Van Der Rohe to the PJs

Philip Johnson, an American architect who'd assisted Mies on the Seagram building, gave this new style its name. In 1932, while the Nazis were throwing students' work out the broken windows of the Dessau Bauhaus, Johnson was working as the director of the Museum of Modern Art's Department of Architecture, where he organised the exhibition that would bring the ideas of Mies, Gropius and other European Modernists like Le Corbusier to America. The show, which introduced New York gallery-goers to the Modernist principles of 'formal regularity' and 'the avoidance of applied decoration', was actually called 'Modern Architecture: International Exhibition'. But it's known today by the far catchier title Johnson and his collaborator Henry-Russell Hitchcock gave to its catalogue: The International Style.[1]

Thanks to the extensive rebuilding of European cities after the Second World War, as well as the booming post-war economy of the United States, the International Style soon lived up to its name, and became the dominant architectural approach of the late twentieth century. From the scores of glass-fronted skyscrapers built in Manhattan, to the worker's housing blocks thrown up in the UK, France and Australia, from schools to summer houses, hospitals to heliports, the International Style ruled the earth until it eventually became clear that people just didn't like living in huge concrete boxes or being towered over by faceless glass and steel monoliths, no matter how much integrity of form they might possess. This contradiction, the vast gulf between what Modernist architects and designers believed was 'good for the people' and what those people actually wanted, had existed at least since the days of the Bauhaus. In her 1924 treatise on 'Economic Living', Annalise Fleischmann, one of the school's star pupils, starts from fairly sensible principles, arguing that 'to gain four hours of freedom by means of economic house design implies a significant change in the pattern of modern life'. So far, so good—she goes on to say:

> The traditional style of living is an exhausted machine, which enslaves the woman to the house. The bad arrangement of rooms and their furnishings (padded chairs, curtains) rob her of her freedom, restrict her development and make her uneasy. Today the woman is a victim of a false style of living. It is obvious that a complete change is urgently required.[2]

Was it really possible that the proletariat's easy chair was making her un-easy? Modernist designers like Fleischmann sound as though they're trying to help, but beneath the rhetoric, there was little evidence that Functionalism made people happier. In his book, *Modern Movements in Architecture*, Charles Jencks quotes Philip Johnson's overview of architecture in Nazi Germany from 1933. 'The present regime', he writes, 'is more intent on leaving a visible mark of its greatness than in providing sanitary equipment for workers.' As Jencks points out, Johnson is writing about Albert Speer, but could just as easily be writing about himself or any one of his colleagues from the glass-and-steel-box brigade.[3]

In 1975 Jencks claimed that Modernist architecture had been more or less dead on its feet since the 1950s, a style without substance that preached the psuedo-science of Functionalism while blindly adhering to an aesthetic every bit as phony as the beaux-arts ornamentation it sought to replace. Meanwhile, the actual needs of the actual people were ignored. '"Modern Architecture"', he wrote in 1972, 'becomes the convention for "good taste", and an excuse to deny the plurality of actual needs.'[4] Jencks later pinpointed the exact moment at which the International Style bit the dust as 3.32 pm on 15 July 1972, when the Pruitt-Igoe housing project in St Louis, Missouri, was blown up with dynamite. Despite many attempts to fix the social problems in the towers, problems which could be found replicated all over the world in similar buildings from Manchester to Melbourne—and which had already become apparent in Russia half a century earlier—the city finally decided that it was the *building* that was the problem. Pruitt-Igoe was, as sociology Professor Lee Rainwater wrote in 1970, a 'federally built and supported slum', and its stark Modernist design amplified rather than diminished the difficulties in the lives of its 10,000 inhabitants. The concrete 'streets in the air' which connected the towers became breeding-grounds for crime and drug use, the elevators stopped working and were never fixed, and the thirty-five towers became infested with mice and cockroaches. According to the *St Louis Post-Dispatch*, a crowd gathered on nearby Dickson Street to watch the second day of the demolition. As the dynamite went off, and the tower imploded, the spectators let out a shout, like fans cheering a football match.[5]

The International Style had, it seemed, tried and failed to find a solution to the problem of what to do with all the people in the world. Modern Architecture was over—whatever followed would, inevitably, be Postmodern.

47. THE END OF MODERN ARCHITECTURE

Ducks, Sheds, and the Seven Crutches of Modern Architecture

> Architects ... It is more useful to imitate something 'old' but proven, rather than to turn out something new which risks causing people suffering.
>
> **Rob Krier, 'Urban Space', 1975**[1]

In the late seventies, with the dust still settling from the destruction of the Pruitt-Igoe project, Philip Johnson threw out the Bauhaus style guide and embraced lying facades and trickery all over again, when he gave AT&T's corporate headquarters in New York a funky retro-style top, inspired by a funky retro piece of furniture, the Chippendale Highboy. This might seem like heresy from a man who'd worked with Mies Van Der Rohe, but Johnson had been harbouring his doubts about Modernism in architecture, and the assumptions that had grown up around it, at least since the 1950s. Speaking at Yale in 1959, he identified what he called 'the Seven Crutches of Modern Architecture', including the Crutch of Comfort, the Crutch of Pretty Drawing, and the Crutch of Utility:

> They say a building is good architecture if it works. Of course, this is poppycock. All buildings work.

Even Mies understood the importance of beauty in architecture, but somewhere in all that rhetoric about 'form following function', the subtleties in the approach of the original Modernists had been flattened out and reduced to formalist doctrine—in other words, a crutch. Johnson fessed up to being guilty of leaning on these crutches himself from time to time, especially the Crutch of Structure—a crutch that may well have been manufactured in the Bauhaus wood-shop:

> Structure is a very dangerous thing to cling to. You can be led to believe that clear structure clearly expressed will end up being architecture all by itself.[2]

Johnson's about-face with the AT&T building amounted to a rejection of the sterility of Modern architecture in favour of Postmodern playfulness, or to use Jencks's term, 'camp'. Jencks defines camp in terms which would be familiar to Andy Warhol with his Esther Williams movies or to anyone who's spent time enjoying an Ed Wood film or watching the Eurovision Song Contest. Camp, according to Jencks, is a way of enjoying failure, by which he means all the things that are not aesthetically 'correct' (or 'cool') according to the tenets of modern architecture:

> (Camp) tries to outflank all the other stereotyped views of failure which are morbid or moralistic and substitute a sort of cheerful openmindedness. It is realistic, because it accepts monotony, cliché, and the habitual gestures of a mass-production society as the norm without trying to change them. Thus the epitome 'it's so bad it's good', which accepts the classifications of traditional culture but reverses the verdict.[3]

'Camp' architecture, unlike the Modernist white box, allows for the existence of the ugly and the ordinary. In 'Learning from Las Vegas', architect and theorist Robert Venturi makes a case for the decorated shed over the duck as the prototype for Postmodern architecture. The what over the what?[4]

The duck in question is 'The Long Island Duckling', a 7.5 tonne concrete drive-through structure, originally built in the 1930s by a farmer named Martin Mauer, who wanted to draw the attention of passing motorists to his fresh duck eggs. Venturi uses the Big Duck as an example of symbolic architecture—where the building is designed at the service of an idea (in this case, 'we sell duck eggs'). This is something you'll be pretty familiar with from long car trips—Australia in particular has a rich tradition of what Venturi calls 'building-becoming-sculpture'. Queensland's Big Pineapple is designed to communicate a message, and the message is 'We have pineapples'. All other considerations (the soundness of the building's structure, the comfort and well-being of the people who work there) are secondary to the building's overall symbolic function. This kind of thing might seem a long way from the International Style tower block, but Venturi believed that the

Big Duck 'pervades modern architecture'. Frequently, the modern building exists simply to communicate the idea that it is 'heroic and original', and, as such, it is insensitive to the needs of the humans who live and work in it.

As an alternative to the duck, Venturi offered the 'Decorated Shed'. Here, the building is designed according to the needs of the person who will use it—the shed is just the right size, shape and location for fixing a boat, potting plants, or recording an album. But having made your shed, you get to personalise it—you can grow roses up the side or decorate the inside with pornography. The 'ornament', as Venturi calls it, is applied independently of the structure. Where the duck is 'heroic and original', the decorated shed is 'ugly and ordinary'—and better for it. Significantly, Venturi backs up his assertion with a quote from the patron saint of the ugly and ordinary, Andy Warhol: 'I like boring things.'[5]

48. THE END OF MODERN ART

Art loses its aura; Walter Benjamin is not surprised

Just as the Modern architects had insisted that the form of a building should follow its function, with no tricky decoration to distract from the expression of its building-ness, so art critic Clement Greenberg had argued that it was the job of the Modern painter to isolate the painting-ness of painting, to discover what it is that makes painting—as opposed to literature or photography—unique. Where the architects had stressed the importance of letting materials be themselves, allowing the physical properties of concrete or steel to determine the shape and colour of their buildings, Greenberg had encouraged painters to let paint be paint, and emphasise the flatness of their canvases.[1] The Modernist painters were strongly advised against making pictures of people, no matter how much fun it might be. Not that there was anything wrong with imagery per se, but as Greenberg demonstrated, imagery, even a single teacup, inevitably suggested three-dimensional space, and three-dimensional space was out.

Breaking this rule could see you kicked out of the group faster than you could say 'Salvador Dali', as Roberto Matta discovered when he started including figures in his work again in the forties. 'I became sort of the fellow who wasn't accepted', he said in 1966. 'They were happy as long as my work expressed cosmic violence and whirlpools. I think it was a pity we didn't see more of each other.'[2]

Sounds like a lot of rules to follow, doesn't it? In architecture, it sort of made sense—if you're in the business of designing things that people have to live in, then its important to feel as though you're doing it the right way, at least until you're *proven* wrong. But painting is different—if you get it wrong, nobody gets hurt, so from our point of view it seems almost ridiculous that anyone could take it as seriously as the Modernists did. It was certainly ridiculous to Andy Warhol. In *From A To B and Back Again*, when his friend Damian says that artists take risks, it's all Andy can do to keep from laughing. For Warhol, the idea that artists take risks is an insult to people who really *do* take risks, 'like Evel Knievel'.[3]

In many ways, Greenberg and the Abstract Expressionists represent the last gasp of what Walter Benjamin called 'auratic' art—what art was like before mechanical reproduction and Capitalism changed it forever, a hang-over from ancient times when works of art were tied in to magic and ritual. Even as they strove to test its limits, the Modernists, by and large, took for granted the idea that artworks contained power: for them, art made a difference, it was as serious as your life. No wonder Pop Art annoyed them so much—'If this is painting', said one well-known Abstract painter to Leo Steinberg in 1960, 'I may as well give up.'[4] Pop was the first *post*-modern style of painting; just as Johnson had done with his decorated shed for AT&T, Pop Artists 'appropriated' imagery from outside art for their pictures—flags, hamburgers and movie stars—and in doing so they implied that there might not be that much difference between 'art' and 'non-art'. Now that the 'aura' of fine art had vanished, how was it different from any other kind of image? Roy Lichtenstein painted pictures of romance comics *and* Abstract Expressionist brushstrokes in a blank, mechanical style, which, like Warhol's, hovered in some mysterious zone of non-aesthetics, somewhere between enthusiasm and disinterest. This, of course, is exactly the same 'cheerful openmindedness'[5] Jencks wrote about in relation to architecture, the same easy-going acceptance of mass-production. To the Pop artists, everything was up for sale, but like Benjamin's *flaneur*, they were just browsing.

49. UP FOR SALE

Blondie, Bryan Ferry, The International Noise Conspiracy, and Postmodern Pop

> Henceforth, in what we may call post-industrial Capitalism, the products with which we are furnished are utterly without depth: their plastic content is totally incapable of serving as a conductor of psychic energy.
>
> **Fredric Jameson, *The Cultural Logic of Late Capitalism*, 1971**[1]

Not everyone was prepared to take the death of auratic art at the hands of Capitalism or the 'anything goes' attitude that followed it lying down—not Fredric Jameson, and certainly not Swedish band the International Noise Conspiracy (INC). 'Capitalism', the band members said in a 2006 interview, not mincing their words, 'is a *very* bad thing'.[2] At issue in their song 'Up For Sale'[3] is the way Capitalism reduces artworks (their own included) to commodities, which, having been duly barcoded and shelved along with all the other items in the mall, are subsequently robbed of their power to change the world. In this nightmare society of mirrors and images, nothing is itself anymore—only a symbol representing the thing it used to be. INC illustrates this frightening business with a clever audio version of Johnson's Postmodern skyscraper, where the band's towering Punk noise is the building itself, while the appropriated tallboy top is suggested by a naggingly familiar five-note riff, swiped, as it turns out, from Blondie's 'Hangin' on the

Telephone'. 'Hangin' on the Telephone' is now made to share space with the International Noise Conspiracy as though they were both nothing more than competing brands of toothpaste. But INC is making a point about what's being lost in this process, and the gesture is made with a sense of bitter sadness that's entirely absent from Warhol's silk-screens.

'Hangin' on the Telephone' is itself a cover, originally recorded by obscure seventies American Punk band The Nerves, and incorporated, like a hairstyle, a T-shirt or a badge, into the giant living Pop-art collage that is Blondie for its 1978 album *Parallel Lines*.[4] Blondie used 'Hangin' on the Telephone' as though it were a found object, just as the band would later use the Paragons' 'The Tide Is High'. Bryan Ferry's prodigious output of covers in the seventies applies the same method. When Ferry sings the Rolling Stones' 'Sympathy for the Devil' or Bob Dylan's 'A Hard Rain's Gonna Fall', he performs them the way Andy Warhol would paint the *Mona Lisa*, or the way Lichtenstein would paint an Abstract Expressionist brushstroke. All the sincere, direct, emotional nuances of the original are reproduced, but as a knowingly degraded, cheap and nasty knock-off of the real thing. Ferry, like Warhol, is keen to debunk people's ideas about the difference between high and low culture: on 1973's *These Foolish Things* he does made-to-order Vegas versions of last decade's radical protest songs (Dylan's antiwar diatribe reveals itself to contain the mother of all double entendres in Ferry's lascivious hands—'It's a hard, hard, hard ...') alongside classic Teen-Pop fluff like 'Baby I Don't Care' and 'It's My Party' as if to say, who cares, they're all hits![5]

In this, Ferry is showing his roots—long before he became a Pop Singer he was studying to become a Pop Artist. While at art school, Ferry had been taught by Mark Lancaster, one of Warhol's assistants on his Marilyn paintings, as well as the British Pop painter Richard Hamilton.[6] On Roxy Music's first single, 'Virginia Plain', Ferry's lyrics are constructed as a direct equivalent to Hamilton's famous Pop Art photomontage *Just What Is It That Makes Today's Homes so Different, So*

Appealing?, a gaudy, overstuffed riot of consumer trash, where a grinning muscleman brandishes a giant, shiny lollipop while his girlfriend preens on the sofa, surrounded by time-saving appliances and fashionable junk.[7] Likewise, 'Virginia Plain' is not so much a song as a shopping list, as Ferry imagines driving down a big American freeway in a big American car dreaming big American dreams.[8] As he passes advertising billboards on the side of the road, he immediately incorporates their messages into his song—Fun in Acapulco, Flying Down to Rio, Jane Holzer's big blonde hair, smoke Virginia Plain.[9] Hannah Arendt might claim that the American suburban sprawl is no good for the *flaneur*, who needs to wander through the city arcades on foot in his search for the Marvellous, but someone forgot to tell Bryan Ferry, who gleefully assembles his Surrealist collage of desire from the upholstered seat of his Cadillac, like a chrome-plated, fuel-injected Walter Benjamin.[10]

Roxy Music was, itself, a work of Pop Art. In their early publicity shots, the band seem to have crawled right out of one of Hamilton's collages with their ridiculous pile-up of sci-fi spacewear, fifties Rock and Roll flash and nonchalant 1920s glamour. Inside the gatefold of their debut album, Ferry is shown wearing a gold imitation tiger-skin jacket, with his hair sculpted into an improbable quiff. To his left is the band's synthesiser player and tape operator, fellow art-school graduate Brian Eno, wearing glitter make-up and sporting long, prog-rock style hippie hair. The album opens with the bewildering 'Re-Make Re-Mode',[11] whose chorus is the registration number of a car, and whose final sixty seconds sees the band twisting the dial on their car radio and picking up Little Richard, The Beatles, Duane Eddy, Schoenberg and John Cage—and digging it all. In this, Roxy set a template for the band-as-Pop collage that would be useful right through the seventies and into the eighties and nineties. A brief list of bands that followed the Roxy recipe would include The Cars, Duran Duran, Sigue Sigue Sputnik, Transvision Vamp, Pulp and, perhaps best of all, Blondie. Like Ferry, Blondie's Chris Stein was an art school graduate, and the band presented itself from the start with all the glossy impenetrability of a Warhol portrait. (Warhol, in turn, claimed that Blondie were, along with Duran Duran, one of his favourite bands.) Blondie, in their photographs, in their choice of covers, and in the disparate styles of their music itself (today Punk, tomorrow reggae, rap the next day, Disco the day after) were pure Pop Art, an accumulation of consumer desires (the blonde, the shiny car, the arty foreign movie, the teen-romance comic) that, like Roxy's billboards racing past the car window, were always up for sale, but always tantalisingly out of reach.

The Scissor Sisters' 2004 cover of Pink Floyd's *Comfortably Numb* (from 1979's *The Wall*) outdoes Ferry's *A Hard Rain* for sheer joyful Pop-art travesty.[12] The New York-based trashmeisters rip into the Floyd's Rock classic as though they were the Bee Gees labouring under the mistaken impression that they were singing Frankie Goes to Hollywood's *Relax*. In the process, they rehabilitate Floyd's brief flirtation with Disco on *Another Brick in the Wall Part 2*:

> It wasn't my idea to do disco music, it was Bob's. He said to me, go to a couple of clubs and see what's happening with disco music, so I forced myself out and listened to loud, four to the bar bass drums and stuff and thought, Gawd, awful!
>
> **Dave Gilmour, 2004, quoted in *Mojo* magazine**[13]

Now, more than twenty-five years later, the Scissor Sisters have forced Gilmour back into his dancing shoes and pushed him onto the dancefloor. As it turns out, not only do the Pink Floyd lads look good in white flares, but their existential gloom is a surprisingly good fit with disco's own brand of sublime pointlessness. In his eye-witness account of the early days of Disco in tiny gay clubs in the early seventies, Andrew Holleran describes a secret world of the 'comfortably numb':

> ... a core of people who seemed to have no existence at all outside of this room. They seldom looked happy. They passed one another without a word in the elevator, like

> silent shades in hell, hell-bent on their next look from a handsome stranger. Their next rush from a popper. The next song that turned their bones to jelly...They pursued these things with such a devotion that they acquired, after a few seasons, a haggard look, a look of deadly seriousness. Some wiped everything off their faces and reduced themselves to blanks.[14]

But what for the Scissor Sisters is a fun day out at the mall, making new meanings from the songs thumping out of the clothes boutiques and CD shops, is for some a textbook example of everything that's wrong with Postmodern Pop. The Scissor Sisters' *Comfortably Numb* was (judging by the number of people who called the radio station I worked at to complain about it) an infuriating listening experience for many, possibly for reasons Fredric Jameson had identified while comparing two very different paintings of shoes, one by Vincent Van Gogh and the other by Andy Warhol. Van Gogh's *A Pair Of Boots* is a rich, textured painting of a dirty pair of workman's boots—we know from looking at the painting that Van Gogh saw these boots, and that he has passionately and sincerely attempted to represent them for us, and perhaps even begin to tell us a story about the life of the person who wore them. On the other hand, Warhol's *Diamond Dust Shoes*, a 1980 silk-screen print of brightly coloured high heels, seems to tell us nothing more than 'I like shoes', or maybe even just 'there are shoes'. Perhaps even that is giving the painting too much credit—maybe, as Marshall McLuhan would no doubt assert, the image tells us nothing more than that 'there are mass-produced images', as if that is all late Capitalism has left us with. Jameson writes:

> (Diamond Dust Shoes) no longer speaks to us with the immediacy of Van Gogh's footgear; indeed, I am tempted to say that it does not really speak to us at all...(It marks) a new kind of flatness or depthlessness, a new kind of superficiality in the most literal sense, perhaps the supreme formal feature of all postmodernisms.[15]

Little surprise then—given their shared feelings about the fate of art in the age of consumerism—to find that Jameson is a featured musician on the International Noise Conspiracy's *Bigger Cages, Longer Chains* EP from 2002. Jameson plays 'Postmodernism or the cultural logic of late Capitalism' while Inge Johansson sings:

> I've tried all the ads and I tried the flavours yeah I tried it all
> This lack of substance and all surface makes me in need
> of help...
> Can't deliver satisfaction promised
> It's just a fucking bore.[16]

50. MODERN LOVERS

How a big night out helped the Futurists fall in love with the modern world

On 1975's *Roadrunner*, a Massachuset's-born Velvet Underground fan named Jonathan Richman sings a teenage hymn to the wonders of technology. He walks past the Stop 'n' Shop, then he drives past the Stop 'n' Shop. 'I liked that much better than walkin' past the Stop 'n' Shop', he explains, 'cos I had the radio on!' Richman's life has been improved beyond measure by his car and his radio—not just for the pleasures they offer in themselves, but for the way they seem to transform his experience of the existing world. 'I felt in love with the modern world', he sings, 'I felt in touch with the modern world.'[1] High on this feeling, with the radio on full blast, and the pine trees and neon lights zipping by, Richman decides to name his band The Modern Lovers—which is surely just another way of saying you're a Futurist.

> We affirm that the world's magnificence has been enriched by a new beauty; the beauty of speed. A racing car whose hood is adorned by great pipes, like serpents of explosive breath ... is more beautiful to us than the *Victory of Samothrace*.

FT Marinetti, from 'The Founding and Manifesto of Futurism', 1909[2]

Futurism, one of the key ingredients of the Constructivists' philosophy, was officially born in 1909, and the moment is captured with great panache by the movement's leader, the poet FT Marinetti. As Marinetti tells it, he and his friends had stayed up all night talking about whatever it is that artists talk about when they get together. By the early hours of the morning, this heady combination of sleep deprivation and artistic high-mindedness had them convinced that they were privy to insights so new, so radical, that they must be immediately announced to the sleeping world. 'Let's go!', yelled Marinetti, leaping into the driver's seat of his jalopy. 'We must shake the gates of life, test the bolts and hinges. Let's go!' So the Futurists tore around the pre-dawn streets in their 'snorting beasts' (that's cars) for a while, scaring dogs and old ladies. Marinetti is still yelling out the car window, 'Let's break out of the horrible shell of wisdom and throw ourselves like pride-ripened fruit into the ...', when suddenly he swerves to avoid a couple of cyclists, loses control of the car, and he and his snorting beast land upside-down in a ditch full of muddy water. Marinetti, however, is so in love with the modern world that the filthy factory muck he's swimming in is, to him, a delicious elixir. 'Fair factory drain!', he cries, 'I gulp down your nourishing sludge.' Revived, he emerges proudly from the wreckage of his car, with joy in his heart and a copy of the 'Manifesto of Futurism' in his trembling hand.[3]

The Futurist painters, following the commandments brought down from the puddle by Marinetti, set out to celebrate the newly electrified world in paint. Giacomo Balla's *Arc Lamp*, completed in the same year as the manifesto, is a hymn to technology, where the blinding light of a street lamp relegates the moon's dim glow to the scrap heap of history.

But the Futurists were not so much against nature as against antiquity and tradition, with it's stuffy reverence for the landscape and the nude. Marinetti, if he'd had his way, would have re-routed the canals to flood the museums, he'd cheer and honk his horn as all those Old Masters sank to a watery grave—after all, he asked, what's the difference between a museum and a cemetery? Marinetti was a young punk—'under thirty' as he often reminded his readers—and he wasted no opportunity to write off the mouldy 'filthy, worm ridden' artefacts of antiquity and had nothing but contempt for the retro 'hotchpotch of encrusted rubbish' that characterised Neoclassicism. In the 'Manifesto of Futurist Painting', Balla and his co-conspirators Umberto Boccioni and Luigi Russolo demanded a fresh start, declaring a ten-year moratorium on the painting of nudes, while insisting on 'sincerity and purity' in the representation of nature. 'Moving objects constantly multiply themselves', they wrote. 'A running horse has not four legs, but twenty.'[4] The Futurists had seen from the experiments of photographers like ET Marey just how many complex mechanical movements add up to something as simple as walking, why should an artist have to paint only one at a time? What they had in mind can be seen from Balla's *Dynamism of a Dog on a Leash* from 1912. There's nothing especially Futuristic about a dog, but Balla has shown that the way we look at a dog has been changed by technology—the dog's legs are painted like a multiple-exposure

photograph, and its wagging tail leaves a Doppler effect in the air as the street whizzes by at a pace set by the busy life of the city, the motor car and the steam train.

51. THE ART OF NOISES

How Luigi Russolo invented a cure for boredom in the concert hall, and might just have invented Rock and Roll too, had he owned an amplifier

Having woken painting out of its stupor, the Futurists turned their attention to the world of music, which, if anything, was in even worse shape. What was the point, wondered the painter Luigi Russolo, of twenty people sawing away at their violins when there was a symphony going on out there in the street? The Futurist had all the music he needed in the city's 'BACKFIRING MOTORS, CARRIAGES AND BAWLING CROWDS'. Compared with this, the stuffy boredom of the concert hall made Russolo sick:

> Let us now enter one of these hospitals for anaemic sounds. There: the first bar brings the familiarity of boredom to your ear and anticipates the boredom of the bar to follow. Let us relish, from bar to bar, two or three varieties of genuine boredom ...[1]

Clearly, music was in need of a shake-up. Would it be possible, Russolo wondered, in a letter to the composer Balilla Pratella, to bring the beautiful noise of the street into the concert hall?

What Russolo wanted was *not* to write orchestral music that imitated the noise of machines, as Mosolov would later do with his factory ballet; rather, he hoped to expand the palette of the existing orchestra to include all sound, including industrial noise, but also the sounds of the natural world. As with Futurist painting, Russolo was not about to use old techniques to represent the new; to him, the idea of an orchestra imitating a factory would be every bit as ridiculous as an artist trying to paint a car in the style of Rembrandt. The new music would need new instruments, devices capable of realising the rumbles, roars, creaks, whispers and tweetings that would constitute what Russolo called 'The Art Of Noises'. But here, Futurist music ran into a serious snag. Russolo had built ingenious little boxes called *Intonarumori* which, when cranked by hand, produced noises. They were divided into types—the 'bursters' produced a sound a bit like a car engine, the 'howlers' were like sirens, and the 'hissers' sounded like rain. The problem was that in 1913 there was no such thing as amplification—apart from the kind where you attach a big cardboard cone to the hole where the sound comes out, and hope for the best. This is more or less what Russolo had to resort to, the result being that, in performance, the *Intonarumori* were almost completely drowned out by the orchestra. Those who could hear them complained that, for all of Russolo's talk about the infinite variety of noises, all those little boxes seemed to produce the same, undifferentiated whooshing sound.[2]

'Ahead of his time' doesn't begin to describe Russolo's situation at this point. He had somehow hit on an idea that would inform virtually every important development in music over the coming century, including John Cage's imprecation to listen in *4'33"* but the machine that could enable him to realise it, the tape recorder, would not be perfected for another forty years. In the meantime, those who were interested in furthering the Futurists search for an Art of Noises had to make do with the technology of the day—gramophone record players.

52. LISTEN LIKE THIEVES

How Pierre Schaeffer and Grandmaster Flash put sound under the microscope

The gramophone had been around since 1890, but curiously, by mid century, not much had been done to explore the machine's potential for storing and manipulating sound. The Constructivist designer and Bauhaus teacher László Moholy-Nagy had made some tentative excursions into turntablism in the 1930s, following up ideas he'd first set down in a paper from 1923 titled 'New form in music: potentialities of the phonograph'. Moholy acknowledged the efforts of Russolo and the Futurists, and, with a sharp eye as always on the latest technological developments, wondered whether the improved amplification and recording systems of the modern phonograph might make it worth giving the art of noises another go. Looking the Bauhaus record player up and down, Moholy asked himself the following questions:

> What is this apparatus good for?
> What is the essence of its function?
> Are we able, and if so to what end, to extend the apparatus's use so that it can serve production ...[1]

By hinting that the turntable might be used for the *production* as well as the reproduction of sound, Moholy had hit upon an important idea, but the closure of the Bauhaus school in Germany by the Nazis brought his experiments to an end. John Cage, who later taught with Moholy at the Chicago School of Design, created his *Imaginary Landscape No. 1* for performers playing test-tone records on vari-speed turntables in 1939.[2] But the next real breakthrough in the development of noise-music began with a *scratched* record, that moment that every audiophile dreads.

In 1948, Pierre Schaeffer was working as a radio engineer at Radiotelediffusion Francais. One day in the studio, he scratched a record, but instead of leaping up off the couch to move the needle along, he *listened* to the scratch—the same sound, over and over again. Schaeffer called the resulting loop a '*sillon fermé*' or closed groove, and it changed the way he thought about sound forever. The closed groove, by endlessly repeating the same musical phrase, had put the music under a microscope. Because the music was no longer moving forwards in time, it became possible to hear it as pure sound, a collection of noises and textures with their own special and complex relationships.

For Schaeffer, the loop led to an entirely new method of musical composition called '*musique concrete*'. If music can be treated as pure sound, might not any sound become music?

Would it be possible, he wondered, to make a symphony out of sirens, coconuts and bicycle horns? Schaeffer went straight to work on the station's record collection, and later that same year he completed his '*Etude aux Chemins de Fer*' (railway study), composed by manipulating turntable recordings of steam trains. '*Etude*' features loops made from the clattery, metallic sounds of wheels over tracks, punctuated by bursts of steam-whistle and an odd piano-like sound, moving in the same rhythm as the train. Schaeffer wondered at the time whether it was even necessary for him to do anything to these sounds, whether it might be possible to broadcast three minutes of steam train on the radio, and have people enjoy it the way they enjoyed Mozart. Schaeffer saw himself more as a curator or organiser of sounds than as an artist—he only wanted us to listen, to hear the noise of the world the way that he had heard it that day in the studio with the scratched record, just as Russolo had hoped that his noise-concerts would one day help people enjoy traffic jams.[3]

Pierre Schaeffer might now look like some kind of pre-historic DJ, coaxing radical noises out of his turntables and reorganising his record collection into new musical forms with his primitive loops and samples—but he has nothing to do with the history of Hip-hop. Schaeffer, the original turntable scientist, never played a block party, and rap stars never give him props on their albums. Nevertheless, his *sillon fermé* is the basic currency of Hip-hop, and, because of the genre's enormous influence on Pop music in the eighties and nineties, at least half the music on the radio, from Beyoncé to Boards of Canada, is largely made up of loops. Thanks to the cast-iron imperatives of the dancefloor (keep the crowd dancing or lose the gig), the early Hip-hop DJs came to the same conclusion as Schaeffer by quite a different route, and, in the process, made it possible for any kind of noise to be understood and enjoyed as music, and did so on a scale that Schaeffer could only have dreamed of.

> Sometimes I'll put a loop on and let it play for, like, two or three days ... When you do something like that, you get to hear all the different parts and pieces and elements of it that you never really heard before ... It probably sounds strange to a lotta people, but you get to hear stuff that the musician didn't try to put in there. You know what I mean? It's just in there.
>
> **DJ Kool Akeim, quoted in Joseph G. Schloss,**
> ***Making Beats*, 2004**[4]

The loop is the basic unit of Hip-hop. Method Man's 'Bring The Pain' from his 1995 album, *Tical*[5] (to pick out one example of thousands), is mostly composed of a short loop from soul singer Jerry Butler's 'Mechanical Man'—a great loop, from an unexpected part of the song, where Butler hums wordlessly over the drum break. Caught in the loop of RZA's sampler, Butler's throwaway vocal mannerism is magically transformed into a funky earworm. Repeat, repeat, repeat.

Looping is the easiest thing in the world. It was fairly easy in Schaeffer's day, when it was simply a matter of cutting out a piece of magnetic tape and joining its beginning to its end, and it was even easier for the RZA, whose sampler would include a 'loop' function as part of its built-in features. If there were some way to compare timesheets, a log of hours spent in the studio by Jerry Butler and RZA respectively, to see who worked harder, Butler would come out on top by a long shot. And yet, to many people 'Bring the Pain' actually sounds better than the song it's excerpted from. It's as though RZA has taken a fragment of 'Mechanical Man's' DNA and from it bred a faster, stronger, more intelligent version of itself. Listening to 'Mechanical Man' now, it sounds OK, like one of any number of classic-sounding funky American soul records of the seventies. But the moment we recognise those four beats from 'Bring the Pain', the whole record springs inexplicably to life. Why does that little break sound so good? Because, thanks to RZA sampling it and looping it (and to Missy Eliot's use of the same loop on her cover of 'Bring The Pain' from her 2003 album, *Under Construction*),[6] you've heard it hundreds of times; you've become intimately acquainted with every second of that tiny fragment of music in a way that would have been inconceivable before the loop. RZA has made us dance—but he's also made us listen, as he does, to music on a microscopic level. The Hip-hop producer is alive to the minute possibilities of sound, steeped in arcane knowledge about snare sounds, producers and bpms, as well as the other, more mysterious qualities of a record, the stuff that, as Prince Akeim says, 'The musician didn't try to put in there'. This expertise, the ability to pick the right moment from the right record at the right time by weighing up and considering all these possibilities, is considered part of the job, and reflects the roots of the Hip-hop producer in the DJ.

53. TURNING THE TURNTABLES

Sir Jimmy Savile, Kool Herc and other prehistoric DJs

In the early 1950s, future 'Top of the Pops' presenter Sir Jimmy Savile had an inkling of the way things were going. Savile had been hosting 'record dances' since the forties, where he played Jazz and

Swing records on a gramophone hot-wired to a radio valve amplifier. After playing like this for a while, he decided to do something about the awkward silence that inevitably followed each record by ordering *two* turntables from his equipment suppliers. In an interview with Dave Haslam for his history of DJ culture, *Adventures on the Wheels of Steel*, Savile describes a hilarious exchange with the supplier's sales rep, who couldn't for the life of him imagine why anyone would need two record players:

> **Savile:** Ah, when one record plays, I'm getting the other one ready.
>
> **Sales rep:** Are they in that much of a hurry?
>
> **Savile:** Yes, my people are.[1]

In order to keep pace with these newer, faster people, DJs refined their craft over the next twenty years, driven, as always, by the need to keep more people on the dancefloor for longer. Soon they began to investigate the formal properties of the medium in which they were working, doing with record players exactly what László Moholy-Nagy had proposed back in 1923—turning the turntables into machines for production, not just reproduction. Some time in the mid seventies, a DJ from the Bronx in New York named Afrika Bambaataa began to notice that there were very few seconds, sometimes just a couple of bars of a records that *really* made people dance:

> I'd throw on Sergeant Pepper's Lonely Heart's Club Band—just that drum part. One, two, three, BAM—and they'd be screaming and partying.
>
> **Afrika Bambaataa**[2]

Bambaataa had started out as a DJ hosting parties in and around the Bronx River Housing Projects. The years after the Second World War, as we've seen, saw the rise of the Modernist tower block, and New York City, under the supervision of Construction Coordinator Robert Moses, had built 28,000 public housing apartments in the years between 1946 and 1959. By the 1970s, the long-term effects of low-income (mostly black) families being crowded into these high-rise apartments were becoming apparent, and the Bronx River Projects were wracked with violence and social unrest. It was here, in what Greg Tate has described as 'a crucible of Afro-diasporic rage, rampage and culture'[3], that Hip-hop was born. Many young people living in the apartments had joined local gangs like the Black Spades—these, if nothing else, gave kids a sense of purpose and belonging. Bambaataa had the idea of forming his own gang—but one with a positive role in the community—which he named The Zulu Nation, incorporating elements from the doctrines of the Nation of Islam, ideas he'd picked up from the 1964 Michael Caine film, *Zulu*, and the burgeoning neighbourhood pastimes of graffiti and breakdancing.

At the Zulu Nation block parties, Bambaataa refined his style of DJing, an approach that reflected his own diverse tastes, but that had originally been inspired by a Jamaican DJ named Kool Herc, who'd been hosting neighbourhood parties with his enormous Reggae-style sound system since around 1973. Rapper Percee P remembers growing up within earshot of Herc's sound system while living with his mother in the Patterson projects in the seventies. 'My building was right in front of the park', he told Emily Youseff in August 2006, 'so I could look out my window and see what people were doing and hear the music. Around my immediate area in the south Bronx, you could stand on the roof and see other projects two blocks away ... so just imagine—all those projects had jams in their parks, too.'[4] Herc had started out playing the Reggae records he'd brought with him, but soon switched to funkier stuff—The Incredible Bongo Band's cover of the Shadows' 'Apache', Babe Ruth's 'The Mexican', and Banbarra's 'Shack Up'. But, crucially, Herc didn't play the whole record—just the really good bit, usually the percussion breakdown, and this is what caught then 16-year-old Joseph Sadler's ear. 'I like what he's playing—but he's not playing it right',[5] said the future Grandmaster Flash. Flash spent close to a year closeted in his bedroom with a soldering iron and an odd assortment of hi-fi equipment perfecting the technique that would allow him to seamlessly mix from one breakdown to the next. Disregarding the Western classical tradition and virtually the entire history of Pop music to date, Flash would figure out how to take the musical fragments first identified and isolated by Herc, and mix them together for an hour of non-stop climaxes—percussion, air, disembodied shouts snatched from his favourite moments of his favourite records, crowd sounds, children's records, as well as brutal noises wrenched from the machinery of the turntable itself.

Flash was, as his name suggested, fast, and his impatience was key to his style and his success—perhaps because he knew that his audience was fast, too. Jimmy Savile's people had no time to wait for a DJ to change records between songs, but the crowds at Flash's shows didn't even want to wait for the song to finish, and neither did he. 'I'm fidgety', he told Bill Brewster and Frank Broughton in 2001. 'I can't wait for a record to go from the beginning to almost the end and then go into another record.'[6] The only song he allowed to play in its entirety was a synthesised hymn to the beauty of a steam train, the *Etude aux Chemins de Fer* of the seventies, Kraftwerk's 'Trans-Europe Express'. 'Leave that shit alone', he said, as the track's synthesised clickety-clack played on, 'that shit was cutting itself.'[7] While this is probably not exactly what was running through Pierre Schaeffer's mind thirty years previously—as he listened, fascinated, to his closed groove—the sentiment is the same.

54. DOING THE ROBOT

Kraftwerk, the Futurists, and the Man-machine

Walk in the streets and you have a concert, cars playing symphonies. Even engines are tuned, they play free harmonics. Music is always there, you just have to learn to recognise it.

Ralf Hutter, Kraftwerk, quoted in *Mojo* magazine, 1997[1]

'Trans-Europe Express' is one of a series of Futurist tributes to the beauty of technology that Kraftwerk recorded during its golden period, beginning with 'Autobahn', a joyous invocation of freeway driving that gave the band a surprise chart hit in 1975. But unlike Schaeffer's Railway Studies or Russolo's *Intonarumori*, Kraftwerk's machine music was intentionally romantic—closer in many ways to Mosolov's Industrial Ballet, where all the tricks of pre-modern classical music are pressed into service in order to produce a 'sound painting' of the modern world. This kind of thing, according to Russolo, is not OK; in fact, the whole business of 'imitative' versus 'pure' noise music would be a hotly debated topic in Futurist music, and would continue through the heyday of Musique Concrete as well.[2] Some found the whole business of manipulating recordings a little too 'impure', and after the invention of the synthesiser, a rival camp sprang up, insisting that only synthetically generated electronic sound was suitable for modern music.

Kraftwerk, being literally 'Postmodern', had chosen all its favourite ideas from this rich tradition of modern art and experimental music, without worrying too much about the ideological divides that separate them. In 1978, Kraftwerk released *The Man-Machine*, featuring a sleeve directly inspired by El Lissitzky. On the front, the Kraftwerkers line up on a metal stairwell whose angle is reinforced by a dramatic diagonal arrangement of Constructivist letterforms that spell out the album's title in French, German and Russian.[3]

> After the war, German entertainment was destroyed. The German people were Robbed of their culture, putting an American head on it ... we are the first German group to record in our own language, use our electronic background, and create a Central European identity for ourselves.
>
> **Ralf Hutter, interview with Lester Bangs, 1975**[4]

Growing up in West German in the 1960s, the members of Kraftwerk were confronted by the same set of circumstances that

Joseph Beuys had been dealing with in the field of visual art, and in his case as much as theirs, it's complex. When Kraftwerk talk about 'central European identity' they are referring to many things at once, but their Lissitzky-inspired sleeve is rich with clues as to what that might mean – not the least of which is the fact that they are facing ... east.

The Man-Machine had made his first appearance in Revolutionary Russia in 1912: Kasimir Malevich's *The Knife Grinder* shows the man and his machine as having already merged—it's hard to tell where the one ends and the other begins. The knife grinder's pumping legs are made of iron cylinders while his piston-like arm moves back and forth across the sharpening mechanism.[5] Malevich is so in love with technology that he makes his human subject more like a machine, as if to bring him up to date with the new century. This aesthetic revolution dominated the Russian avant-garde in the 1920s, and even found its way into music. The Constructivist composer Alexander Mosolov serenaded the beauty of factory work with his *Iron Foundry* ballet of 1927. Mosolov's strings hiss like steam-valves while the horns and percussion lock together like assembly-line workers, stamping out machine parts with mechanical precision.[6] The message of all this is clear—the new human being, assisted by his shiny new machines is, as Malevich himself put it, 'seizing the world from the hands of nature to build a new world, belonging to himself'.

Describing their Kling Klang studio to Lester Bangs, the members of the group evoke Malevich's Knife Grinder when they suggest that the whole studio, including all the equipment within it, is in fact one big machine, of which the group themselves are just another component.[7] In a move calculated to enrage advocates of real Rock—the kind of highly subjective Rock that puts a premium, above all, on personal expression—the members of Kraftwerk portrayed themselves as factory employees. Following this idea to its conclusion, they brought about their own obsolescence in 1978 when they introduced complete automation to their powerplant and replaced themselves with robots. These made their debut, according to former Kraftwerk percussionist

Wolfgang Flur, on a German TV show in May 1978. The robots performed the first song from the soon-to-be-released Man Machine album, featuring the lyrics 'ja twoj sluga. Ja twoj rabotnik', which in Russian translates as 'I am your servant. I am your robot'. 'It was obvious that we had to build this sentence into our show', says Flur in his memoir, *I was a Robot*, 'particularly after Ralf (who had once studied Russian at school) found out that "robot" translates in Russian as "rabotnik", meaning "worker"'.[8] Up until this point, being 'like a robot' was about the worst thing you could say about a pop performer—Kraftwerk would transform it into a compliment of the highest order. This is the very same reversal of the conventional standards of art (expressive, natural, human = good; artificial, manufactured, mechanical = bad) that caused such a stink when László Moholy-Nagy first showed up wearing his workers overalls at the Expressionist Bauhaus in 1923. A year earlier, he had written:

> The reality of our century is technology: the invention, construction, and maintenance of machines. To be a user of machines is to be of the spirit of this century. It has replaced the transcendental spiritualism of past eras.[9]

Moholy himself was, as we've seen, a product of his times, subject to the same historical impulse that had led the Futurists to make a claim for the car as being more beautiful than the oil painting.

The Futurists, had they heard it, might have written off 'Trans-Europe Express' as too imitative, with its 'clickety-clack' percussion, and they would have had even less time for the lyrics of 'Europe Endless'—'Parks, Hotels and Palaces'? Marinetti would have liked to see them all flattened by a bulldozer or a war. But 'Metal on Metal', despite being, in a sense, an update of Mosolov's factory music, would have turned Russolo green with envy. Here, Kraftwerk has created a symphony of noise from the Kling und Klang of steel girders—with a deftness that Russolo could only dream of—and, whether triggered from synthesisers in its live shows or blasting out of Grandmaster Flash's sound system at a New York block party, at a decibel level that would put the *Intonarumori* to shame.

Schaeffer, for his part, would have approved of Kraftwerk's meticulous recording and cataloguing of sounds—the group apparently 'researched' 'Autobahn' by making field recordings of engines, freeways and car horns,[10] but would have been nonplussed by its attempts to supplement these perfectly good sounds with synthesisers on the finished product. Listening to 'Trans-Europe Express' back to back with *Etude aux Chemin de Fer*, the difference is clear. Kraftwerk's train music uses the sounds and rhythms of the railway as a framework for a song, with a melody and lyrics over the top. In Schaeffer's Musique Concrete, the train *is* the music, the composer has arranged the sounds of machinery with an ear for melody and rhythm, in order to show us the melody and rhythm that exists in the sounds themselves.

Schaeffer, like Russolo, was writing music for technology that did not exist. Just as the Futurist was already dreaming of a way to collect and combine the noises of the world when recording was in its infancy and magnetic tape was just a gleam in an engineer's eye, Schaeffer, in 1948, was calling for the invention of a keyboard organ which would house within it all the sounds he'd been so laboriously cataloguing on tape, and would be capable of playing them back at the touch of a key—forward, backward and at any pitch he desired.[11] What Schaeffer wanted was a sampler, and it would be another twenty years before anyone figured out how to make one.

55. ZANG TUMB TUUM

The embarassing uncles of modern art

Producer and one-time Buggle Trevor Horn, flush with cash from his recent chart success with 'Video Killed the Radio Star', became one of the first people (along with Peter Gabriel) to own a sampler in 1983. By the following year he'd loaded it up with leftover drum tracks from the Yes album he'd been producing, along with a sound effect of a car engine starting and, with the help of a team of expert session musicians, had produced 'Close To The Edit'.[1] Here, Schaeffer's Musique Concrete met Flash's breakbeat research as the sharp cough of the car's ignition became abstracted through repetition and pitch-changing, while a crashing drum break and punchy horn stabs and vocal noises dropped in and out of the mix. 'Close To The Edit' became a huge hit with Hip-hop DJs, and pretty soon people were doing the robot to a symphony for automobile engines by a group called The Art of Noise.[2]

The Art of Noise's debut album was released on Horn's new label, ZTT, which stood for Zang Tumb Tuum—also the title of a poem by FT Marinetti, in which he serenades the beauty of modern warfare.

> Every 5 seconds siege-cannon riiip with a concerted ZZZANG-TUMB TUUM silenced by 500 echoes gnashed smashed scattered to infiniiity
>
> **F.T. Marinetti, 'Bombardment of Adrianople (Liberated Words)', 1911[3]**

The Futurist leader was a big fan of war—for aesthetic reasons, you understand. He liked its modern sounds, and smells, and set out to evoke them in his poetry by using his letters as expressive marks, such as the repeating row of i's in the poem's first stanza (which resemble rows of artillery) and with nonsense words and onomatopoeia—the title itself is a sound-picture of canon fire. 'Marvellous to hear smell all all taratatatatatatata of the machine guns', he wrote, 'shrieking at the tops of their voices beneath bites slaps traak-traak whip-slashes pic-pac-pumb-tumb jugglery clown leaps (200 metres) of the fusillade.' Marinetti's glamourisation of war can be seen as part of his desire to wipe the slate clean, to get the dead weight of European history off his back. Flooding the museums and burning the libraries was a start, but maybe what was really needed, to get rid of all those stuffy old professors and boring Neoclassical painters once and for all, was a good war. 'War', wrote Marinetti in 1909, 'the world's only hygiene.'

> We Futurists, Balla and Depero, will construct millions of metallic animals for the vastest war (conflagration of all the creative forces of Europe, Asia Africa and America, which will undoubtedly follow the current marvellous little human conflagration).
>
> **Giacomo Balla and Fortunato Depero, *Futurist Reconstruction of the Universe,* 1915**[4]

Five years later, Marinetti got his war, and—despite whatever aesthetic qualities it may or may not have had—it left Boccioni and Sant-Elia dead and Marinetti and Russolo badly wounded. Depero's 'marvellous little conflagration' completely redrew the map of Europe—without it the Russian revolution would not have taken place, and Germany's disastrous state of affairs at its conclusion directly created the conditions that would allow the Nazis to seize power, and for Fascism to take root in Italy. This was good news for Marinetti, whose talent for publicity found a new outlet when he threw in his lot with the Fascists and helped Benito Mussolini to assume power.

Marinetti's relationship with Il Duce, as well as the Futurists' sentimental attitude toward war, has left the movement tainted. They are, in many ways, the embarrassing uncles of modern art—invite them to the party at your own risk. In 1981, designer Peter Saville found this out for himself when he appropriated one of Fortunato Depero's designs for the cover of New Order's first album, *Movement.* Saville was a huge Kraftwerk fan, and his design for *Movement* is directly indebted to that group in the way that it combines a wistful nostalgia for the utopian dreams of the Modernists with a vague invocation of the totalitarian threat that lurked behind some of its more loony ideas. He'd originally planned to acknowledge his debt to the Futurists with a sleeve credit that read 'Designed by Peter Saville after Fortunato Depero', but the band's manager Rob Gretton nixed the idea[5]—although to be fair, it was a little late for Gretton to be worried about his band being associated with Fascism. Before the death of lead singer Ian Curtis the previous year, the band had been called

Joy Division, after the brothels of 'racially impure' women kept by the Nazis during the Second World War. Its new moniker was not much better; Hitler and Mussolini had spoken in the 1940s of bringing a 'New Order' to Europe, free of Bolshevists, Jews and other inferior types, who were, in any case, unfit to survive.[6]

While Mussolini could see the usefulness of a character like Marinetti for propaganda purposes, Hitler was determined from the beginning to destroy and discredit modern artists. The Fuhrer, as is well known, had originally hoped to become a painter, but was rejected from the Academy of Fine Arts in Vienna twice—'test drawing unsatisfactory' said the report card for his first application. As a result of this, as well as a subsequent series of attempts at watercolour painting and commercial illustration, he knew just enough about the subject of art to be dangerous. What he knew, beyond a shadow of a doubt, was that there was something wrong with Modernist painters—they were not right in the head. Who else but a degenerate or a mental patient would paint a sky green, when the sky is clearly not green? Either, he reasoned, they were suffering from an eye defect or some kind of hereditary stupidity, or else they were trying to deceive the German people for some more sinister purpose.[7]

56. DEGENERATE ART AND THE OBSTINATE COLOURIST

Why modern painters can't paint properly

Although he was lucky enough to be long dead (having shot himself in the stomach in 1890) by the time Hitler came to power, Vincent Van Gogh was exactly the kind of painter whose works the Fuhrer did not want in Germany. His paintings were full of distorted forms and 'incorrect' colours—the stars in *Starry Night* are too big, and blaze an unnatural yellow, and the artist seems to have mistaken the sky for the beach, it rolls and heaves like a heavy swell at sea. But while Van Gogh may have been mad—Hitler would have been pleased to note that the artist spent some time in a lunatic asylum in Saint-Remy just before he died—he certainly wasn't stupid, and he wasn't trying to fool anyone either. Van Gogh was trying to paint more *expressively*, to find a way to put feelings on the canvas as well as forms.

> ... I will paint him as he is, as faithfully as I can—to begin with. But that is not the end of the picture. To finish it, I shall be an obstinate colourist. I shall exaggerate the fairness of the hair, arrive at tones of orange, chrome and pale yellow. Behind the head—Instead of painting the ordinary wall of the shabby apartment, I shall paint infinity ...
>
> **Vincent Van Gogh, Letter to Theo Van Gogh, 1888**[1]

This was Van Gogh's breakthrough, but like most great leaps forward in art it was as much a development from the art styles of the recent past as it was a departure from them. While sharing an apartment with his brother Theo in Paris, Van Gogh saw his first canvases by the Impressionists, which had an enormous impact on his style. The Impressionists painted in clusters of dots or strokes on the canvas—up close they just looked like blotches of paint, but take a few steps back and they revealed themselves as vivid landscapes and scenes of city life. The Impressionists, as their name suggests, painted impressions—the effects of light on the retina, and by the time Van Gogh got to see them, they had developed an almost scientific approach to colour and light—especially artists like Seurat, who applied his coloured dots with the precision of a surgeon. This was the beginning of the slow dismantling of the idea that a picture is a window into space—like a little theatre—that would continue over the coming century. What the Impressionists had done was to start art down the road that would eventually lead to Clement Greenberg's concept of 'pure' painting. It was Van Gogh, who, having been given permission by the Impressionists to experiment with colour, took the next step.

In a series of self-portraits painted while he was in Paris, Van Gogh, who in his earlier work had mostly restricted himself to a palette of greys and browns, suddenly went colour crazy. In his hands, Seurat's dots turned feral, taking on a kind of writhing life, like tadpoles in a pond. In his *Self-Portrait in Front of an Easel* of 1888, the artist's face swarms with wriggly blotches of colour—bright greens, reds and blues run this way and that over his pale yellow face. Already Van Gogh had gone one better than the Impressionists: he was beginning to see that colour, having been freed from its usual role, could also be used to express invisible things like moods or emotions—an intense feeling associated with a time or a place. This is what his friend Gauguin meant when he said of *Van Gogh's Chair*, 'no one ever painted a chair like that before'. The hallucinatory brilliance of Van Gogh's colours and the subtle distortion of the chair's shape by the energy of his brushstrokes give the painting an almost ecstatic, religious quality.

This was no less than you'd expect from someone like Van Gogh, a man who identified with pain and suffering to an extraordinary degree, and whose bouts of crushing despair and madness alternated with moments of visionary ecstasy. It's those moments that are captured in paintings like *Van Gogh's Chair* or *Sunflowers*. But one of the problems associated with being an intense visionary madman is that, after a while, you start to get on people's nerves, and Van Gogh wore out everyone who knew him. His unpredictable and sometimes violent behaviour drove him out of the family home, thwarted his early ambition to become a missionary—the church recalled him from a stay in a poor mining town in Belgium, where Van Gogh had given away all of his money, clothes and food to the miners—and scared away several girlfriends. Van Gogh once showed up at the family home of his sweetheart, with whom he'd recently broken up, and loudly demanded that she come downstairs. Her parents told him she wasn't home, but Van Gogh saw that there was a place laid at the dinner table for her, and went nuts. Holding his hand over a lit candle, he insisted that he be allowed to see her 'for as long as I can hold my hand in this flame'. He never saw her again.[2]

Gauguin, whom he considered a good friend as well as a collaborator, came to stay with Van Gogh in 1888, and the two settled into a rhythm of feverish painting, heated artistic debate, and non-stop partying in the bars and brothels of Arles. After a

while the strain began to show, and their arguments turned ugly, Van Gogh threw a glass of absinthe in Gauguin's face at a café (Gauguin, in turn, tried to strangle the infuriating Dutchman), and only a few days later, attacked him with a razor. Gauguin managed to calm his friend down, but later, Van Gogh used the same razor to cut off part of his own ear, which he then gave to a prostitute he knew in Arles. 'Take good care of this', he told her.[3]

Even his long-suffering brother, Theo, could only take Vincent in small doses, and when Theo started a family, it became harder and harder for him to manage his difficult and demanding brother. It was this rift in his relationship with Theo that helped push Vincent over the edge. Theo was, along with Gauguin, one of the very few supporters of Van Gogh's art during his lifetime—he bought many of his brother's paintings, and constantly sent him money and art materials. But the owners of the art gallery where Theo worked remained unconvinced by his brother's works and discouraged him from showing them. Meanwhile Theo's baby was sick, and this put a strain on his household to such an extent that he needed Van Gogh to support *him* emotionally, something Vincent was in no state to do. Depressed about his prospects of making a living as a painter, and feeling as though he was a burden on his brother and society in general, Van Gogh could take no more. In an unsent letter to Theo, discovered after his death, Van Gogh wrote:

> Well, I have risked my life for my work, and it has cost me half my reason.[4]

Andy Warhol would have laughed out loud at this—an artist risking his life? Firemen risk their lives, motorcycle stuntmen risk their lives,[5] but is being an artist that big a deal? It's easy to say now that it is, because Van Gogh is one of the most famous artists in the world—he seems, somehow, to have been proven right. But if you knew him, or someone like him today, you'd recommend him to a psychiatrist and they'd put him on Prozac. He'd be calmer, better adjusted, he might even resolve the contradictions between life and art that he found so difficult and become a 'business artist' like Warhol—or like the later Salvador Dali, cranking out 'mad' paintings that risked nothing of himself but sold consistently well. They might lack the visionary brilliance of his earlier, pre-therapy work, but at least he'd be working, and his brother wouldn't have to send him money anymore. But this is not how it turned out. In 1889 'psychiatric treatment' meant being locked up with a lot of other mad people and given cold baths, and although Van Gogh emerged from the asylum at Saint-Remy feeling better, it was not to last. After completing one of his last paintings, the bleak, anxious *Crows in a Cornfield*, he returned to the place where he'd painted it and shot himself. [6]

57. SUICIDED BY SOCIETY

The fine line between madness and genius, and the fine line between Richard Dreyfuss and Vincent Van Gogh

In Steven Speilberg's 1977 movie, *Close Encounters of the Third Kind*, Roy Neary, an ordinary suburban American man who works for a power company, suddenly goes mad. His mind is filled with a mysterious vision of a mountain he has never seen, and he feels he has no choice but to give physical form to the picture in his head. Sitting at the dinner table with his wife and kids, he starts to play with his food, making a sculpture of the mountain with his mashed potato, raking it into shape with his fork and pushing it around with his fingers. As his family look on in horror, Roy breaks down in tears. 'Well', he says, his voice cracking from the strain, 'I guess you've noticed there's something a little strange with Dad ...' Next we see Roy building the same shape in the middle of his son's train set—he hurls great lumps of modelling clay at his sculpture and tears at its sides with his bare hands, before running screaming into the front yard, 'WHAT IS IT?', he demands of the suburban sky,'WHAT IS IT?'. Later, when he's driven his family out of the house with this insane behaviour, he will build an enormous model of the mountain in his living room. Shovelling dirt through the window of his house, covered with mud, he works and works at the obsession that drives him, circling around his monumental sculpture like a man possessed.[1] Roy, like Van Gogh at his most inspired, no longer has any concern for life as it's lived by ordinary people—friends, family, a job—none of this matters. All that matters is the work.

Roy isn't just like Van Gogh—he practically is Van Gogh. Directing Richard Dreyfuss in the role, Spielberg specifically modelled him on the painter in order to justify the awful sadness of Roy's abandonment of his family for his 'art'.[2] In the movie, the image of the mountain is an invitation from extra terrestrials, a message planted in Roy's mind by a higher intelligence, which he has virtually no choice but to obey—and for all the sense Van Gogh's behaviour would have made to the people who knew him and the doctors who attempted to treat him, he might as well have been talking to aliens. In *Close Encounters*, Roy is constantly being told to calm down, to take it easy, but how can he, when he has seen something indescribably beautiful waiting just out of reach? He's heard the call of another world, and a normal life will never be enough for him. At the end of the film, in a scene that recalls Van Gogh's hope that he might find peace in the afterlife 'on one of the numerous heavenly bodies', Roy leaves his family, his job and his planet forever.

> And thus, Van Gogh condemned himself because he had finished with living ... But above all, Van Gogh wanted to join that infinite for which, said he, one embarks as on a train to a star.
>
> **Antonin Artaud, *Van Gogh: The Man Suicided by Society*, 1947**[3]

The French poet and playwright Antonin Artaud believed that Van Gogh, far from being mad, was privy to insights so true, so profound, that society could not allow him to live. It's not that he thinks Van Gogh was murdered, but, as Artaud puts it, he was 'suicided' by society—his hand was forced by the world of sensible rational people who had told him, one too many times, to take it easy. Artaud knew the feeling—he had been in and out of mental institutions for most of his life—and he would later say that there were times when he knew that all it would take to push him over the brink was for one more doctor to say to him 'Monsieur Artaud, you're raving again'.[4] They were trying to civilise him, with their rational, clinical minds and their electro-shock therapy, and Artaud wanted nothing to do with civilisation. What good had come of it? Civilised men, those who sell out their dreams and deny their visions for a quiet life were, he wrote, 'pigs'. In 1925, Artaud put his name to a Surrealist manifesto that announced 'we are certainly barbarians, since a certain form of civilisation thoroughly disgusts us'.[5]

58. LET'S GO CRAZY!

Prince and La Revolution Surrealiste

You could fill a book with all the songs that have been written about going crazy as a good thing—'Stone Cold Crazy', 'Still Crazy After All These Years', 'Mama Weer all Crazee Now', 'Going Out Of My Head', 'Insane in the Brain'—and all of them relate in some way to Artaud's idea of madness as a form of insight, a better, purer vision of the world than the one perpetrated by 'civilised men'. In 1984's 'Let's Go Crazy', Prince cunningly disguises himself as a priest, that sworn enemy of the Surrealist revolution, and delivers a sermon to his congregation. 'Dearly beloved', he says, as the organ swells behind him, 'we are gathered here today to get through this thing called life.' Then Prince drops a bomb on the assembled faithful. 'In this life', he says, his voice starting to crack, 'you're on your own!' He's proclaimed the death of God, and trashed the solutions to Existential angst promised by Van Gogh's doctors—'When you call up that shrink in Beverly Hills', he intones mockingly, as the church organist throws away her sheet music and picks up a pair of drumsticks, 'you know the one "doctor everything-will-be-alright"'—but Prince is not done yet. 'When the elevator tries to bring you down', he says (and what better symbol of what Breton called 'the hateful prison of logic' than the elevator, which can only go up or down), then there's only one recourse ... 'Go Crazy!!!!'[1] They might drag you away and strap you into a straitjacket, but at

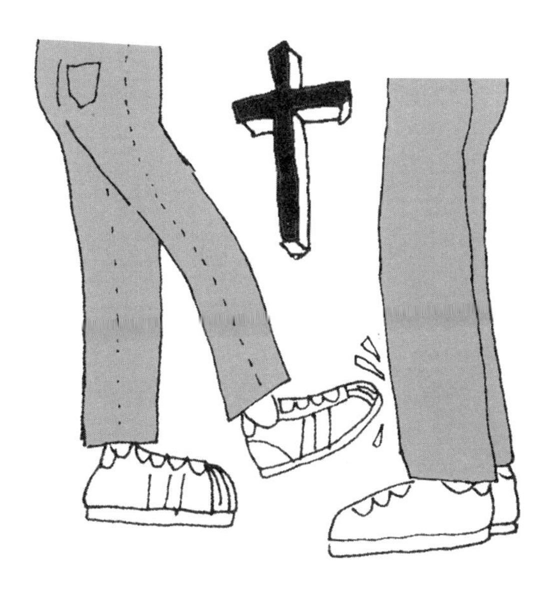

least you'd be in good company—after all, as Breton points out in his book, *Nadja*, 'They shut up Sade, they shut up Nietzsche'.[2]

In the 1920s, the Surrealists would play a game called 'Scholarly Notation', in which a list of people or ideas is drawn up, and the participants asked to give them a score between -20 and +20. In one such scoreboard, reproduced in Alastair Brotchie and Mel Gooding's *A Book of Surrealist Games*, 'logic' is given a -1 by Breton, and a -20 by both Tzara and Phillipe Soupault, while 'madness' is given a +19 by at least two of the participants, and an encouraging +4 by Breton.[3] Artaud was not present (possibly excommunicated by this point), but we can be fairly sure his scores would have followed this pattern closely.

Artaud believed that the artist should be a lightning rod for suffering, and the more directly that suffering is expressed, the better the art will be. What he disliked was art's tendency to tidy up the messy nature of experience, to impose structure and narrative where in reality there is none. But if Artaud had identified the problem quite early in his career, it would not be until 1931 that he would work out how to fix it. Walking around the Paris Exposition (an ancestor of today's world expos, where exotic displays from far-off lands were brought together in a kind of giant trade fair), he came across a display of Balinese Temple dancing. As he watched the ecstatic convulsions of the dancers, a light bulb went off over his head. Here was the kind of performance he was hoping to see, art and theatre no longer a distraction from life, a sideshow or light entertainment, but integral to life, tied up in ritual and magic, a pressure valve for the emotional needs of the society.[4]

This is what Artaud hoped to achieve with his concept for a new type of theatre, a 'Theatre of Cruelty'. He wasn't just talking about showing acts of cruelty on stage, or being 'cruel' to the audience—Artaud's theatre, rather, would be built on an acceptance of the fact that nature, life itself, is cruel, and that to impose rational sense and civilised values on it is absurd. 'Theatre will never be itself again', he wrote in 1932, 'unless it provides the audience with truthful distillations of dreams, where its taste for crime, its erotic obsessions, its savageness, its fantasies, its utopian sense of life and objects, even its cannibalism, do not gush out on an illusory, make believe, but on an inner level.'[5]

This is the common cause that Artaud shared with the Surrealists, although if anything he went much further in his attempts to get beyond reason. In his early days as a Surrealist poet, Artaud would complain that language failed him—like *Van Gogh's Chair*, his words and sentences could barely contain the intensity of feeling that he put into them, they writhed out of shape and split at the seams. Much later, in the year before he died, Andre Breton sat spellbound in the audience at the Theatre du Vieux Colombier as Artaud performed some of his new works, in which he often seemed to have abandoned language altogether, replacing it with shrieks, howls and guttural sounds—direct expressions of the poet's feelings, freed at last from the straitjacket of words.[6]

59. THE PING-PONG OF THE ABYSS

How a record stolen from a French radio station and a short spell in psychiatric care changed Allen Ginsberg's life

In 1947, Artaud recorded a play for French State Radio called *To Have Done with the Judgement of God*. As the broadcast date grew near, the controversy stirred up by his extraordinary performance at the Vieux Colombier reached the ears of the station's Director-General, who asked to hear a copy of Artaud's play—just to be on the safe side. He found what he heard so disturbing that it was pulled from the station's schedule on the same day that it was meant to go to air, and despite a hastily organised private broadcast a few days later, *To Have Done with the Judgement of God* was banned by the station that commissioned it for the next twenty years. But in 1961 the underground magazine writer and Surrealist acolyte Jean-Jacques Lebel snuck into the archives of French State Radio using a key obtained by his girlfriend who was working there at the time. There, in the locked cupboard marked 'not for airplay' he found Artaud's notorious recording on a vinyl LP, which he stole, not wanting to pass up what might be his only opportunity to hear the legendary play for himself. According to Barry Miles, Lebel, Allen Ginsberg and a few of their friends smoked some hash and sat around Lebel's apartment, listening, mesmerised, to a bootleg tape of what Artaud himself had described as his 'first rendering of the Theatre of Cruelty'.[1]

To this day, *To Have Done with the Judgement of God* has to be heard to be believed—it's so extreme, so uncompromising, that it's hard to imagine too many radio stations *today* that would consider airing it. Artaud and his actors tear the language to shreds and find, behind it, something much older and more primitive—an unformed vocabulary of screams and gibberish—pre-language. The voices are combined with a strange, atonal music of gongs, drums and tuned percussion which, while obviously inspired by the Balinese Theatre Artaud had seen in Paris, would no doubt have terrified the Balinese as much as it did the Director-General of French Radio.[2] But for all its strangeness, Artaud's play has a kind of physical immediacy that's hard to resist—you might not love it, but it's no more possible to ignore it than it would be to ignore a dying man. This was exactly the effect Artaud had been going for; he wanted a theatre that didn't need to be intellectualised in order to be understood, something that the audience could respond to with their nervous systems, like a hot potato being thrust into their hands. It's interesting, in this context, to note that Lebel originally played the tape of *To Have Done* backwards, and that the audience in his apartment that day in 1961 hadn't noticed anything wrong. The play's reputation as a radical work had preceded it, and Lebel and Ginsberg weren't too surprised at the unintelligible sounds coming out of the speakers. When they finally realised their mistake and flipped it over, they discovered that the forward version was almost as weird as the backward version, and decided they liked both of them equally. This, presumably, would have been fine with Artaud, who in 'The Theatre of Cruelty: First Manifesto' proposes a new language for the theatre which:

> Turns words into incantation. It expands the voice, it uses vocal vibrations and qualities, wildly trampling them underfoot. It pile-drives sounds ... It liberates a new lyricism of gestures which, because it is distilled and spatially amplified, ends by surpassing the lyricism of words.[3]

Ginsberg in particular was paying close attention. In 1955, he'd performed *Howl* for the first time at the Six Gallery in San Fransisco, a poem that mapped the no-man's land between genius and insanity, delivered in a style influenced partly by Surrealist automatic writing—'All you got to do is lay down on a couch', he later explained, 'and think of anything that comes into your head'[4]—and partly by traditional Jewish prayer singing, but mostly by Artaud's 'Van Gogh: The Man Suicided by Society'. Madness dominates *Howl*, from the opening line, 'I saw the best minds of my generation destroyed by madness, starving hysterical naked ...', to the ecstatic climax of its epilogue, 'the madman is holy as you my soul are holy!'[5] *Howl* was dedicated to Carl Solomon, whom Ginsberg had met in a psychiatric hospital in 1949. Ginsberg had pleaded insanity to charges of being an accomplice to a felony, while Solomon had been interred for stealing a peanut butter sandwich from the university cafeteria—although this mild Surrealist stunt concealed a more serious purpose. Two years earlier, Solomon had been in Paris, trying to see over Breton's large head as Artaud ranted and raved at the Vieux Colombier. He had walked out of the theatre deeply impressed, and decided soon after, having immersed himself in Artaud's writings, that the 'sane' world was not for him. When he met Ginsberg, he would pass on to him a copy of Artaud's 'Van Gogh' essay, where the author, visions of orderlies strapping him to a table and attaching electrodes to his head still fresh in

his mind, points his finger at the so-called civilised world for the painter's death.[6] 'Besides', says Artaud, 'one does not commit suicide alone.' Solomon and Ginsberg even shared an obscure Artaud-related joke, as Solomon warned the nurses that he would likely commit a crime the next time one of them said 'Mr Solomon, you're raving', although in his case the crime was nothing more serious than overthrowing the hospital's ping-pong table. But in *Howl*'s third section, Ginsberg refers explicitly to the time he and Solomon spent in the psychiatric institute, saying that Carl is 'madder than I am', and describing him as 'losing the game of the actual ping-pong of the abyss'[7]—a pretty fair description of what happened to Solomon. He may not have been mad when he checked into the hospital, but a few months of Insulin shock treatment at the hands of the Institute's doctors soon changed that.

Ginsberg was more fortunate, though he remained acutely aware that what happened to his friend could easily have happened to him. Thanks to his chance meeting with Solomon, he'd walked out of the institution with a valuable idea: that what society considers 'mad' could be the only reasonable way to act in a mad society, and, to Ginsberg, America in the 1950s seemed to be very mad indeed.

60. INVASION OF THE BODY SNATCHERS

America in the fifties, a nation besieged by Beatniks, Communists and other giant, carrot-shaped monsters

America you don't really want to go to war.
America it's them bad Russians.
Them Russians them Russians and them Chinamen. And them Russians.
The Russia wants to eat us alive. The Russia's power mad. She wants to take our cars from out our garages.

Allen Ginsberg, *America*, 1957[1]

In *America*, Ginsberg swaps places with America itself, to find out who's madder. Looking at himself (now not just a man but a whole country) in the mirror, he considers the coming war with the Communist East, and asks himself some tough questions, such as: if war is declared, what are his national resources? Emptying out his pockets he finds two joints of marijuana, a pile of unpublishable literature and twenty five thousand mental institutions[2]—somewhere in one of those is poor Carl Solomon. As for the unpublishable literature, that would be the work of Ginsberg and his contemporaries who, following the obscenity trial centring on the publication of *Howl*, and the success of Jack Kerouac's *On The Road*, were becoming known in households across America as the 'Beat Generation'. Soon, the Beats and their acolytes, having been told by their parents and professors one too many times to sit down and be quiet, would be overturning the ping-pong table on an unprecedented scale. By 1958, J. Edgar Hoover, then Director of the FBI, would announce to the nation that the three biggest threats to the American way of life were Eggheads, Communists and Beatniks. That the most powerful nation on earth should feel so threatened by a bunch of sandal-wearing philosophers who hung around Times Square smoking pot and filling their journals with poetry must have been flattering to the Beats.[3]

It also gives an impression of just how paranoid and fearful the intellectual climate was in America in the fifties. If Marshall McLuhan was right when he proposed that a society's repressed desires could be discovered by decoding its favourite movies and advertisements, the way a psychiatrist would analyse a patient's dreams[4], then the United States had, as they say, *issues*. In 1955, the same year that Ginsberg performed *Howl* for the first time, America's favourite film was *Invasion of the Body Snatchers.* Inspired by John W. Campbell's 1938 short story, *Who Goes There*, the movie was about an insidious alien invasion of Earth, where giant plants from outer space begin hatching perfect replicas of human beings, making it impossible to tell if your best friend was really your best friend or a sinister alien pod until it was too late. Campbell's original story stemmed from an early childhood trauma—his mother and her sister were identical twins, and he never knew who was holding him. But in the context of America's political climate, the idea took on another meaning. In the 1950s, Americans were terrified that their best friends and neighbours might not be what they seemed, not because they might have been turned overnight into alien pods, but because they might be Communists. In an irony that did not escape the more clear-minded commentators of the day, Senator Joe McCarthy's vigilant efforts to prevent the spread of Communism in the United States had led him to replicate a climate very similar to that of Stalin's Russia—inform, or be informed on. By day, Americans followed the progress of McCarthy's notorious HUAC hearings, where artists and writers were accused of trying to undermine Democracy by spreading Communist ideas in their work, having been ratted out by people they thought of as friends or colleagues, and often on the most flimsy pretexts. By night, they dreamed cinematic dreams of infiltration, assimilation and infection, as ordinary citizens were transformed from within by a creeping evil. *Invasion of the Body Snatchers* was the most well known of hundreds of alien-invasion movies—including *The Blob*, where the creeping menace from beyond took the form of ... a blob—that packed out the drive-ins during the McCarthy years, and not the first to be inspired by Campbell's *Who Goes There*. In 1951, Howard Hawks's *The Thing* whipped audiences into a paranoid frenzy, as the protagonists chase a giant, carrot-shaped alien around a terrified metropolis. In case you hadn't got the message yet, the film's final lines drive the point home in no uncertain terms: 'I bring you a warning', babbles Scotty, the reporter, 'tell this to everyone wherever they are ... watch the skies! Keep watching the skies!'[5]

61. BOMB CULTURE, PART 2

Beatniks and Sputniks

The Thing was released at the height of a rash of UFO sightings—all over America people were seeing strange lights in the sky and saucer-shaped objects hovering over cornfields. In his 1959 book *Flying Saucers: A Modern Myth of Things Seen in the Skies*, Carl Gustav Jung explained the phenomenon as a symptom of 'emotional tension having its cause in a situation of collective distress or danger, or in a vital psychic need'.[1] This makes sense when you consider that the flying-saucer craze began almost immediately after the end of the Second World War, a period marked by what Artaud would describe as 'a state of frightful hyper-tension'.[2] The complete destruction of Hiroshima and Nagasaki by atomic bombs made the possibility of instant death from above very real, and this collective anxiety stepped up a gear when the Soviets announced that they had developed their own atomic weapons in 1953. But when the Russians successfully launched the world's first orbiting, man-made satellite, *Sputnik 1*, in October 1957, fear gave way to what Tom Wolfe described in *The Right Stuff* as a 'colossal panic'. *Sputnik* didn't actually do very much besides orbit the earth and beep occasionally, but it was of enormous symbolic importance in the heightened atmosphere of the cold war. 'Now', said President Lyndon Johnson, 'the Communists have established a foothold in outer space.'[3]

The media frenzy over *Sputnik* also gave Americans a new suffix—'nik'—to be appended to anything that was suspected of being subversive or Communist. Beats and Commies were already linked in the public imagination as enemies of the state, so San Fransisco journalist Herb Caen was just putting two and two together when he came up with 'Beatnik' as a term for the scruffy bohemians who were beginning to make their presence felt in the North Beach area.[4]

So much for 'nik', but what about 'beat'? 'Beat' was actually a borrowing from underworld slang—the world of hustlers, drug addicts and petty criminals to which Ginsberg and Jack Kerouac looked for inspiration; a world that, with its extreme highs and lows of experience, its violence and ecstasy, was infinitely preferable to the paranoid, screwed-down nightmare that was Hoover's America. It was this alternate America that Burroughs, older and more worldly, had first shown them around in the forties, and it was here that they met a small-time thief and junky named Herbert Huncke who would give the Beat Generation its name. It was Huncke, in fact, who was responsible for the arrest that led to Ginsberg being committed to the psychiatric institute. Huncke had started using Ginsberg's apartment as a place to keep stolen goods, and Ginsberg, sensing the way things were going, decided to get himself and anything that might incriminate him out of there. Unfortunately, he decided to do it in a stolen car full of stolen clothes with one of Huncke's associates who, when the car was stopped by the police, floored the accelerator and led the cops on a high-speed chase over six blocks, until the car crashed and Ginsberg was arrested. Ginsberg seems not to have blamed Huncke too much for what happened, he even includes him in the litany of Beat saints in the footnote to *Howl*—'Holy Huncke!'[5]

> Huncke, whom you'll see on Times Square somnolent and alert sad sweet dark—holy! Just out of jail, martyred, tortured by sidewalks, starved for sex and companionship ... ready to introduce a new world with a shrug.
>
> **Jack Kerouac, *The Beat Generation*, 1959**[6]

When Huncke said 'beat', he meant 'beaten down'. Kerouac, in answer to another writer's asking him for a word to define the 'new vision' of writing that he and Ginsberg and their friends had been working toward, gave Huncke's word an Existentialist spin—to him it meant being at the bottom, but looking up. Kerouac especially would have plenty of time to ponder and refine the specific meaning of 'beat'. After the runaway success of *On the Road* in 1957, he, more than anyone, would be seen as the spokesman for the movement, and would be asked time and time again in TV, radio and print interviews to define 'beat'.

This is one of the things that made the Beats different to earlier barbarian invasions like Surrealism: It was the first literary insurrection to be broadcast into suburban living rooms via TV, radio and magazines—Beatniks were a mass media event. Most of the publicity was bad, the *Time-Life* story that Burroughs had been interviewed for on the day that Brion Gysin discovered cut-ups was, predictably, a beat-up, but this only helped their cause. The more the conservative pundits denounced the Beats as the wreckers of civilisation, the more young people across America started to feel that maybe civilisation ought to be wrecked, and that these Beatniks, 'waving their genitals and manuscripts' as Ginsberg put it in *Howl*,[7] might be just the people to do it. After all, if the Beats knew that society was sick, if they knew, as Artaud did, the truths known only to the insane and the inspired, then the establishment's attempts to silence them only seemed to prove them right. What did America have to hide? If J. Edgar Hoover thought they were dangerous, they must be on to something …

62. GO MAN, GO!

Poetry n' Jazz with Jack Kerouac and Patti Smith

Beat writing was tailor-made for the electronic age. It was, as Marshall McLuhan would put it, ear-oriented. The Beats' love of underculture, the secret America of hobos and hustlers, junkies and Jazzmen, had given them, among other things, an ear for *spoken* language. In his manifesto, *The Beat Generation*, Kerouac describes a wild night of music, dancing and excited talk, where 'everything is coming in from everywhere',[1] echoing the 'allatonceness' that McLuhan had identified as one of the hallmarks of the new ear-a. The best way to read the Beats is still out loud—Burroughs's wise-guy routines, Kerouac's locomotive prose and Ginsberg's rhythmical chanting come alive when rolling on the tongue and bouncing off the walls of a room. They knew this themselves, and all of the core trio of Beat writers gave live readings and made recordings throughout their careers, from Kerouac's recordings with Jazz pianist Steve Allen to Burroughs extraordinary run of recordings in the years before he died, collaborating with Michael Franti, REM, Kurt Cobain and 'Saturday Night Live' musical director Hal Willner. Ginsberg was still planning an appearance on 'MTV Unplugged' when he died in 1997.[2]

Because of its 'ear-oriented-ness', Beat writing was also a natural fit for musical accompaniment, and it's here that the tradition of poetry 'n' Jazz got started, as well as the traffic between Beat poetry and Rock and Roll that found its greatest expression in Patti Smith's 'Piss Factory' from 1975. Over a freewheeling R&B accompaniment, Smith relates a tale of urban, industrial alienation that sees her stuck 'workin in a piss factory inspectin' the pipe'. Smith's co-workers have been hypnotised by the lie of square society, 'too goddamn grateful to know they're gettin' screwed up the ass'.[3] She's beat—beaten down, but like her Beat forebears, Smith has heard the siren song of freedom in Jazz and R&B, and the piss factory can't hold her for long. To Smith, as for the Paris bohemians of the fifties, black music is Existentialism incarnate, life lived authentically, literally made up on the spot from moment to moment by the improvising sax player or Blues hollerer. She begins to fantasise about having a radio in the factory so she could listen to James Brown or Georgia Woods, longing for that moment experienced by Roquentin in Sartre's *Nausea*, where the emptiness of modern life is suddenly filled by music.

Just thinking about the promise of freedom in James Brown's voice opens a door in Patti Smith's mind—now she knows she will get out, 'I'm gonna go somewhere ...' she sings, as the band plays Jazz, a music described by James Campbell as 'the black man's mastercrime of cultural defiance ... the ultimate anti-bourgeouis art'.[4] Smith doesn't know where she's going—it hardly matters, the important thing is to keep moving, to keep making up your life as you go along, as Kerouac's Sal Paradise did while he zigzagged across the country in *On The Road*. 'Go' was a key word for the Beats; it was the title of John Clellon Holmes's first novel, and it's what Kerouac shouted out between the verses of Ginsberg's *Howl* as he read the poem for the first time at the Six Gallery—'Go, man, go!'[5]

This is why Ginsberg's *Howl* was so important—it was an old tradition in a radically new context. *Howl*, in performance, was a ritual of the kind that Artaud had admired in the Balinese Theatre, which gave precedence to sensation over meaning. In a 1959 recording Ginsberg's steady incantations build ever so slightly in intensity over the poem's eighteen minutes, until by the third and final section, his performance takes on a kind of ecstatic, religious quality.[6] Had Ginsberg been publishing his poetry in Surrealist magazines in the thirties, or declaiming it from the stage of the Cabaret Voltaire in Zurich in 1917, it would be read and talked about, certainly. But McLuhan's re-

tribalised world would pick up Ginsberg's message and send it around the globe as electronic gossip, disseminated and distributed through millions of record players, radios, TV sets and news stands. Soon, kids all across America and the world (including a young Robert Zimmerman, not yet Bob Dylan) would hear in Ginsberg's voice the same thing Carl Solomon had heard in Artaud's performance at the Vieux Colombier—the call of another world.

63. THE ID BEAST

Adventures on the Forbidden Planet starring Antonin Artaud and John Cage

When veteran sci-fi writer Frederik Pohl was first offered the job of novelising MGMs *The Forbidden Planet*, while it was still being made, he dismissed the project out of hand as juvenile trash. But when Pohl finally saw the finished product, he kicked himself. While the movie had its share of stock elements, including a loveable robot, a sexy space-babe and a mad scientist, *The Forbidden Planet* was something special—for a start it was a good deal more self-aware than most of its contemporaries. Where movies like *The Thing* or *The Blob* seemed like Freudian slips from the hysterical mind of McCarthy's America, *The Forbidden Planet* was more like a Dali painting, madness of a far more calculating kind. In the film, a spaceship lands on the planet Altair IV, which long ago had been inhabited by a race of super-intelligent beings, the Krell, whose advanced science had led them to develop a technology that could give tangible form to unconscious thoughts, no matter how deep, dark or repressed. The Krell's machines could strip away the layers of 'civilised' behaviour, and uncover, at the heart of it all, the primitive Id. Unfortunately, the Id was so powerful that, when the Krell gave it a physical form, it became a terrifying Id beast and destroyed them. Now thanks to Dr Morbius (mad scientist) the Id beast is on the loose again. Pohl was impressed, the movie was complex and well thought-out: it functioned perfectly well as a sci-fi adventure, but at the same time you didn't have to be Dr Freud to see the movie's subtext—that America's repressed desires would eventually return to tear it apart.

Scanning the credits, Pohl was surprised to see that the film's score had been composed by two of his old poker-playing buddies, the husband and wife team of Louis and Bebe Barron. Instead of 'music', the Barrons had been credited with 'Electronic Tonalities'.[1] The Barrons, contrary to standard Hollywood practice, had composed and recorded the entire score using electronic equipment at their home studio in New York, and as far as the musicians' union was concerned, that was no way to make music. According to the Barrons, you were generally expected to compose the score on the lot, in a little bungalow with a couch and a piano, but what they had in mind for *The Forbidden Planet* was not the kind of thing you could compose by writing down notes on a stave. Instead of the sawing strings and blaring brass that generally accompanied sci-fi adventures, the Barrons composed a Futuristic noise-scape of drones, shrieks and disembodied sound-events that actually felt like another world[2]—and while the musicians' union might not have liked it, Antonin Artaud certainly would have. In his manifesto for the Theatre of Cruelty, Artaud proposed music that would act directly on the sensibilities and called for the creation of new musical instruments, 'which can reach a new scale in the octave and produce an unbearable piercing sound or noise'.[3] The Barrons had, it seemed, using their advanced technology, given form to Artaud's raging Id beast.

Before coming to Hollywood, the Barrons had worked with John Cage on his *Williams Mix* in 1952. *Williams Mix* was another score composed using the *I Ching* to determine its lengths, but instead of being performed using musical instruments, the piece was constructed electronically, using the techniques of musique concrete. Tape recordings of hundreds of different sounds—talking, screaming, sirens, frogs croaking and pre-recorded music, including bits of Jazz and Beethoven—were spliced together according to the precise instructions of the score, they were in fact laid on *top* of the score, as though it were a dressmaker's pattern, with lines showing where the edits should be made and how long each piece of tape should be. It was backbreaking, painstaking work, and it took Cage and the Barrons a year to produce the resulting four-and-a-half-minute piece. During the long hours they spent working with Cage at his apartment, splicing tape with razor blades and occasionally applying talcum powder to their sweaty hands to stop them from slipping,[4] they may have noticed him reading a copy of Artaud's *The Theatre and its Double*.

> The idea I had from reading this book was that all the elements of theatre can be viewed independently one from the other, with none being subordinate to a narrative thread that runs through everything.
>
> **John Cage, quoted in Smith and Walker-Smith's *American Originals*, 1994**[5]

It was from Artaud that Cage got the idea of the simultaneous performance at Black Mountain, where poems, music, dancing and the playing of records all took place at the same time, without any narrative thread to connect them. Cage said that he believed it was important to be *bewildered* in both life and art, to not know what's going on, and soon, thanks to Cage's enormous influence as a thinker and a teacher, bewilderment was rife in the arts in the 1960s. As we've already seen, one of the knock-on effects of the Black Mountain event, as well as Cage's tenure at the new School for Social Research, was the advent of the Happening. As always, artists took what they needed from Cage—few were prepared to go as far as he was in allowing indeterminacy to take over and removing the composer from the process—but the kind of immersive, 'everything-happening-at-once' spectacle that Cage had presented at Black Mountain gave plenty of artists in New York the necessary permission to mount their own epics of bewilderment.

64. HAPPENING THINGS, PART 2

A Car Crash, an orgy and a lawnmower

In the back room of the Reuben Gallery in November 1960, Jim Dine staged a Car Crash. The room was dark, the walls and shelves were hung with plastic hoses and rolls of paper and cardboard—all painted white—and in a corner of the room stood an eight-foot tall girl wearing a white robe. From out of the darkness, came a man dressed in silver with a silver swimming cap on his head with lights attached—this was Jim Dine, in the role of the car. Soon, Dine was involved in a cat-and-mouse game with two other drivers, who chased him around the room with flashlights. Then the lights came on and Dine, standing in the middle of the room, made loud honking noises and blew up a white balloon until it burst. In the aftermath of the 'car crash', Dine stood at a blackboard, obsessively drawing cars with windshields as eyes and grilles for mouths, babbling and raving incoherently.[1]

Although Cage would no doubt criticise *Car Crash* for being too intentional, it's a good example of why many observers at the time thought that the New York Happenings might be the best realisation of Artaud's Theatre of Cruelty yet. Susan Sontag, who was once chased out of a gallery (along with the rest of the audience), by an artist wielding a lawnmower, cited the Happeners' desire to assault the audience as one example of the similarities between the two. But more importantly, she points out that the Theatre of Cruelty and the Happening share a 'disregard for the word'.[2] *Car Crash* is not 'about' a car crash any more than Artaud's lecture on 'Theatre and The Plague' was about the plague. Artaud more or less died of the plague in front of the audience—screaming, clawing at his skin, he worked himself into an almost delirious state. Like his *To Have Done With the Judgement of God*, it was weird, but in no way intellectual or theoretical. Any human being with a nervous system could respond to what Artaud was doing, and the early Happenings of the sixties were much the same.

Carolee Schneeman had Artaud in mind when she came up with the idea for her 1964 Happening, *Meat Joy*[3], which saw a stage filled with couples undressing each other down to feathered bikinis. As the orgy gets underway, a maid walks onto the stage and starts throwing raw fish, chickens and sausages onto the couples. After that, it's chaos, as the performers roll around the stage and on top of each other, rubbing each other with meat and paint. Who would have thought the Theatre of Cruelty could be this much fun? As it turned out, the fun was just beginning.

In 1961, having heard *To Have Done With the Judgement of God* both forwards and backwards, Allen Ginsberg made a couple of tape copies for some people he knew who would want to hear it.[4] These tapes would make their way, virus-like, through the culture, and eventually result in a mass outbreak of Artaud-plague towards the end of the decade. By the late sixties, the revolt against civilisation that the Surrealists had been plotting since the thirties actually looked as though it might come about, and the Rock ritual, the magical process whereby the singer becomes a lightning rod for his audience's anxieties, releasing them by acting them out, would be a key ingredient in this transformation of daily life.

65. ARTAUD ROCK

How Allen Ginsberg's Artaud bootlegs paved the way for the rise of the Lizard King

As early as 1955, the enjoyment of 'evocative gestures, emotive arbitrary postures' and 'the wild poundings of rhythm and sound'[1] had become the number-one favourite way for teenagers to spend their pocket money. In *Awopbopaloobopalopbamboom* (a word which could easily have been transcribed from Artaud's banned radio play), Nik Cohn traces the history of Teen-Pop back to Oregon-born singer Johnny Ray, who had his first hit in 1952 with 'Cry'. Ray didn't just sing about crying or wanting to cry—he re-created the act itself onstage. 'He contorted himself, he buckled and gulped, and that released an intensity of aggression that no one else had stirred',[2] wrote Cohn. The result was an extraordinary ritual release of anxiety and tension, and a nice vindication for Artaud, whose guess that the theatre of the future might provoke the audience's erotic obsessions as well as its taste for crime and cannibalism was proved correct. Johnnie Ray's audience screamed and sobbed along with him, but they also attacked Ray himself, ripping off his clothes and tearing at his skin as though they weren't sure whether they wanted to make out with him or eat him. By 1955, the Johnnie Ray phenomenon was so out of control that *The Sunday Pictorial*, in a story called 'Is Johnny Ray a Mass Hypnotist?' employed the services of a qualified 'Bobby-sox doctor' to get to the bottom of it. The doctor concluded that Ray had somehow 'short-circuited' the girls' intelligence, and had the power to release their 'hidden impulses'.[3] Amplified through the medium of the transistor radio and the portable record player, Artaud's Id beast was on the loose again.

> ... Recall this one guy used to sit there all day and night toking on his doob and intoning things like 'Genius ... is very close to ... madness ...' instead of doing his homework, and he had a very high appreciation of the Doors' early work.
>
> **Lester Bangs, 'Jim Morrison: Bozo Dionysus a Decade Later', 1981[4]**

It wasn't until 1965 that someone actually used the words 'Artaud Rock' to describe a Rock and Roll show, and when they did, it was in reference to the performance of a skinny wannabe Beatnik from Venice Beach named Jim Morrison, and his band, The Doors.[5] Morrison had actually received the Artaud virus from two sources, both directly traceable to Ginsberg's tapes of *To Have Done with the Judgement of God*. The first was sent to Julian Beck and Judith Molina, whose experimental theatre group, The Living Theatre, made the most comprehensive attempt to realise Artaud's ideas on the stage in the sixties with plays like *The Connection* and *The Brig*, both of which Morrison saw. The second tape went to Michael McClure, a poet who had been in the audience (and performed poems of his own) on the night when Ginsberg read *Howl* for the first time at the Six Gallery.

> Making images and pictures, even when speaking with melody, is not enough. There must be a poetry of pure beauty and energy that does not mimic but joins and exhorts reality and states the daily higher vision.
>
> **Michael McClure from the introduction to *Ghost Tantras*, 1963**[6]

McClure had been largely responsible for establishing the bohemian community in Venice Beach that Morrison found so intriguing as a film student at UCLA, and McClure quickly became a mentor for the aspiring young poet. McClure had been inspired by Artaud to test the limits of language, to uncover the primitive roars and grunts that hide beneath the civilised veneer of our speech. The result was what McClure called 'Beast Language', which he tested on actual beasts at the big cats' enclosure of the San Fransisco Zoo. In McClure's *Ghost Tantras*, Beast Language steps in at the point where normal language fails—'Tantra No. 39' is an elegy for Marilyn Monroe:

> I hope you have entered a sacred paradise for full
> warm bodies, full lips, full hips, and laughing eyes
> AHH GHROOOR. RHOOR. NOH THAT OHH!
> OOOH ...
> Farewell perfect mammal[7].

'Goodbye Norma Jean' it most definitely is not. Compare this with Jim Morrison's infamous Oedipal freakout in 'The End', from the first Doors album. Having uncovered an unspeakable, repressed desire, deep in his unconscious, Morrison reverts to Beast Language: 'Mother, I want to ... Aaaaaaaauuuugghh.'[8]

The Doors' heady mixture of Beat poetry, Artaudian theatre and Blues-Rock became a hit at the height of the summer of love, but their music and attitude were about as far from the incense 'n' patchouli aesthetic as it was possible to be. Morrison, like Artaud, knew that any worthwhile kind of public theatre had to acknowledge the existence of death, and famously said: 'I am interested in anything about revolt, disorder, chaos, especially activity that seems to have no other meaning.'[9]

66. MAYBE I'M CRAZY

Walking the fine line between madness and genius with Gnarls Barkley

My heroes had the heart
to lose their lives out on a limb
and all I remember, is thinking
'I wanna be like them'
Does that make me Crazy?[1]

In 2006, Gnarls Barkley, a duo comprising Hip-hop producer Danger Mouse and soul shouter Cee-Lo, had a UK number-one hit, with their song, 'Crazy'. After some time spent listening to Danger Mouse's pile-driving beat, Cee-Lo improvised a lyric inspired by the conversation in the studio that day. 'We just started talking about how fans have to think you're crazy to get into you as an artist', said the singer. 'It became this big conversation between us about who is crazy and who isn't.'[2] In the song, Cee-Lo wonders which comes first: madness or art? All his favourite artists seem to 'act crazy', and this seems to be integral to their art, perhaps even, as Artaud suggested, the source of their peculiar insight. This raises an important question in Cee-Lo's mind—is he crazy enough, and if he's not, is it possible to fake it? Salvador Dali would say yes, it is, as would the psychoanalyst Jacques Lacan, a big fan of Dali and the Surrealist writers, who insisted that their work was identical in every important way to the writings and drawings of the mental patients they so admired.[3] So, when Dali said 'the only difference between myself and a madman is that I am not mad', he was suggesting that there might be hope for Cee-Lo, that by exercising his paranoid-critical faculties he could re-create in his mind the state of derangement necessary for great art. As Dali wrote in 1930: 'I believe the moment is at hand when, by a paranoiac and active advance of the mind, it will be possible to systematise confusion and thereby completely discredit the world of reality'.[4] But 'discrediting reality' is more or less what Jim Morrison set out to do with his 'crazy act' on LA's sunset strip, and even though it was, as he once told Pamela Des Barres, just that—an act—by the seventies Morrison seemed to many to have gone genuinely insane. Cee-Lo, too, knows that experimenting with madness is like playing with fire, as he sings on 'Crazy':

> Ha ha ha
> Bless your soul
> you really think you're in control?
> Well, I think you're crazy.[5]

67. SHE'S LOST CONTROL

Joy Division's Theatre of Cruelty

There's a section of *To Have Done with the Judgement of God* known as 'sound effects and my cry in the stairwell', which would also do nicely as a description of Joy Division's second and final album, *Closer*. Thanks to producer Martin Hannet's use of cavernous digital reverbs and extreme mixing techniques, the Manchester band created an exquisite atmosphere of Existential loneliness on record, with Ian Curtis's haunting baritone (derived from Jim Morrison's singing style) floating above the band's tightly drilled racket. It was Curtis, whom Hannett once described in an interview as a 'lightning conductor', who made the band riveting in performance. In contrast to the way dancing usually functions at a Rock gig, as an expression of sexuality or a gesture of rebellion, Curtis danced as though there were something wrong with him or as if he were being compelled to do so by high-powered electric shocks. For Joy Division's fans, Curtis's twitching and flailing had an intense ritual significance, giving physical form to the anxious mood of Britain in the late seventies—particularly his native city of Manchester—which music journalist Jon Savage, looking back on the time he'd been living there, later described as 'bleak beyond belief'.[1]

When Curtis took the stage at the Rainbow Theatre in London in April 1980 and went into his trademark epileptic dance, nothing seemed out of the ordinary. The fact that his movements were a little more strained, his steps a little too quick, only made the performance more intense and powerful. Only Curtis's bandmates had the feeling that something was wrong. Having tried to wind up the song they were playing a number of times, the group finally ground to a halt, but Curtis kept dancing, faster and faster, until he collapsed into Steve Morris's drum kit and had to be carried offstage by the band. Again, this just seemed to make the gig better—a post-Punk update of James Brown's old routine where the shattered singer, having given everything he had to give, would be led off the stage by an assistant, only to have Brown throw off the cape that had been draped around his shoulders and lunge back into the microphone. Curtis would no doubt be back. But this was no stage routine—or if it had started out as one, it had escalated into something more serious—Curtis had had an actual epileptic fit.[2]

Curtis felt himself overwhelmed by problems in his personal life: he and his wife had recently had a child, but their relationship

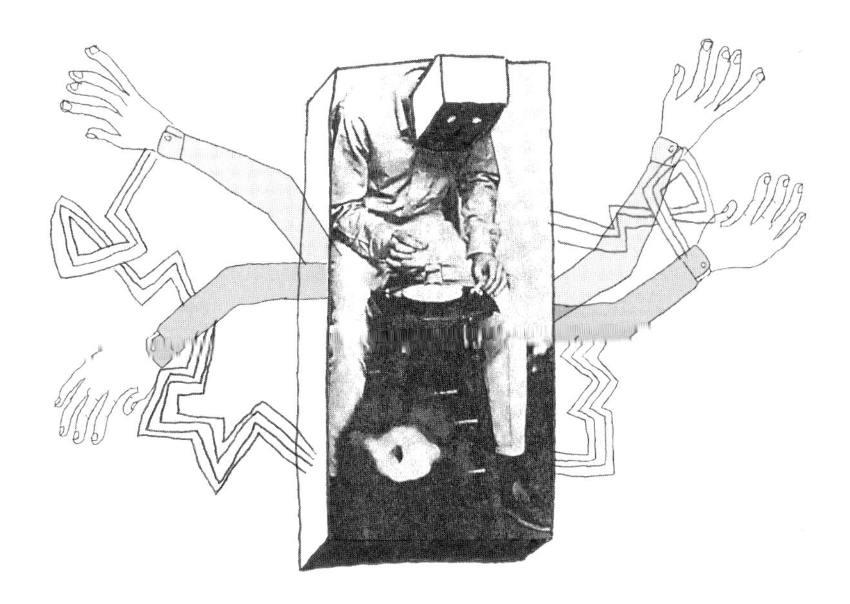

was in tatters thanks to Joy Division's punishing touring schedule, and Curtis had recently become involved in an affair with another woman. At the same time, Joy Division was poised on the brink of enormous success, but Curtis's epilepsy meant that he was being advised by doctors to lead a quiet life and avoid excitement. How could he, when his frenzied dancing and furious, pent-up energy were so much a part of why Joy Division was important for its audience? These factors—combined with the possibility of having to take medication for the rest of his life to control his fits, and exacerbated by the looming deadline of an American tour that was bound to put further pressure on his family life, as well as his worsening condition—tripped a wire in Curtis's fragile mind. He saw himself doomed to play out his audience's expectations for the rest of his life, going 'mad' onstage for their entertainment and exhibiting his illness like a carnival freak. He was, as Colin Wilson wrote of Van Gogh, 'A man who feels that defeat is inevitable, that life is a baited trap, who kills himself to escape the necessity of taking the bait again'.[3] Curtis hanged himself later that year.

68. ENTERTAINMENT THROUGH PAIN

How Throbbing Gristle tried and failed to save Fluxus by destroying it.

Curtis had always been attracted to the darker side of human nature—Bernard Sumner remembers that, from the beginning of their relationship, the singer was fascinated by anything to do with madness or death, and that this was reflected in his obsession with pre-Punk electronic pioneers Throbbing Gristle, an important early influence on Joy Division's sound.[1]

There's still no faster way to clear a room than to throw on a copy of Throbbing Gristle's *Greatest Hits*. 'Entertainment through Pain'[2] proclaims the exotica-styled sleeve design—Artaud would be proud. Even the late-nineties/early naughties resurgence of interest in all things cold, alienating and electronic failed to completely rehabilitate this extraordinary band, whose music, twenty years on, still sounds like a ritual purging of all of the human race's most shameful secrets, a weeping sore on the face of civilisation. 'Weeping' is in fact the title of one of Ian Curtis's favourite Throbbing Gristle (TG) songs. According to the group's singer Genesis P-Orridge, Curtis called him on the night he committed suicide and sang 'Weeping' down the telephone to him[3].

They'd been talking a lot on the phone over the past few years, and Curtis often expressed regret that his band wasn't more like P-Orridge's—which is to say, less like a Rock group and more like an outbreak of the plague—and this explains his interest in 'Weeping' not so much as a song about crying but rather as the act itself captured on tape. P-Orridge, for his part, liked the emotional directness of Curtis's performances, but felt that Joy Division's music was too thin and formulaic. The band's most extreme excursions into the Theatre of Cruelty were first principles for TG, the chilly industrial clankings and scrapings that flit around the mix of Joy Division's *Closer* LP could be the basis for a whole TG song and Curtis's doomy croon sounded like Sinatra next to P-Orridge's sickly-sounding intonations. 'See You Are', recorded live in Manchester in 1979, is about as direct an expression of psychic pain as you're likely to find outside of *To Have Done With the Judgement of God*. Over what sounds like the pulsing of a giant, electronic brain, P-Orridge utters sinister imprecations—his voice rendered inhuman and alien by the band's trademark 'Gristleizer' device—with the song's 'chorus' consisting of two protracted, bone-chilling screams.[4]

TG had evolved from a music and performance art collective known as COUM Transmissions. Starting in 1971 from a fairly mild revival of Dada combined with underground, improvised Rock, COUM became more radical as the seventies went on. A turning point came in 1973 when the group members became involved in the network of international Fluxus artists through their friendship with David Mayor, who had organised a travelling exhibition of FluxArt in the UK, known as FluxShoe.[5]

P-Orridge was concerned with the problem presented by the walling-off of art from the daily business of life in the Western world, and in this sense, the members of COUM were very much a product of the sixties, as they aimed for a kind of communal experience of art, a ritual outpouring of collective energy as opposed to a 'show' followed by a round of polite applause. So Fluxus—with its charter to de-specialise art, taking it out of the hands of geniuses and returning it to the community where it could be made by anyone at any time—was bound to appeal to them.

But by the seventies, something had gone seriously wrong with Fluxus. Despite its best intentions it had turned into something it was never meant to be: *an important art movement*. It wasn't the first time something like this had happened either. By this time you could already find Dada, Surrealist and Futurist artefacts safely filed away with all the other historically significant isms in the antiseptic cool of the Museum Of Modern Art in New York, where they could be appraised from a safe distance as 'masterpieces'.

But of all these, the absorption of Fluxus into the sinister blob of art history seemed to be the most offensive, and the most contrary to the movement's intentions. The idea of a crowd of gallery-goers respectfully shuffling past a photo of George Brecht playing a comb was obviously ridiculous. Surely the whole point of Fluxus was that you didn't need George Brecht to have art in your life—why pay through the nose to see the dead remnants of live Fluxus music when you could stay at home, pick up a comb, and make it yourself?

These were the questions running through P-Orridge's mind regarding the sad fate of Fluxus, and in 1973 he decided to do something about it. Writing to Fluxus archivist Ken Freidman, he declared his wish to 'rectumfy this downward path into obliviart history'—'rectumfy' presumably because he wanted to remove some of the deathly seriousness that had grown up around Fluxus by returning it to the original dictionary definition of 'a fluid discharge from the bowels'. To this end, P-Orridge proposed to

Friedman that he send his entire collection of Fluxus artefacts, valued at twenty thousand dollars, to COUM headquarters where they would be destroyed, thus sparing them from the sad fate of becoming masterpieces. After all, even the movement's leader, George Maciunas, had at one point entertained the idea of allowing Fluxus to self-destruct—he'd considered having all Fluxus documents, scores and artefacts printed in special ink which would disappear entirely after a couple of years. But the commodification of Fluxus was already too far gone for Freidman to allow COUM to harm his collection, and even if he'd been more amenable, it's unlikely that P-Orridge would have been able to come up with the twenty thousand dollars. In any case, the relationship between COUM and Fluxus ended badly.[6]

The recuperation of Fluxus continued over the following decades, to the point where Jake Platt, a visitor to a Yoko Ono exhibition in 1997, was ejected from the Cincinatti Contemporary Arts Center and fined $7500 for doing nothing more than trying to participate in an open-ended Flux artwork by drawing on it with a red pen. 'No one can tell you not to touch the art', said a text by Ono, printed on the gallery wall. But when the artist is one of the most famous people in the world, and the art in question is valued at $240,000, it turns out that there are plenty of people who can tell you not to touch the art. Events like this, as much as COUMs failed attempt to realise Fluxus by destroying it, have robbed Fluxus of much of its power. What was once a genuine invitation for all people to participate in creative life now seems like nothing more than a pose, as though the artist is saying, 'Hey, don't just stand there—come and join in' only to whisk the microphone out of your hand and have security throw you out of the FluxGig before you can make a sound. The furious spectator is left in a state of Fluxtration.[7]

> Somebody said to me during the peak of COUM, when it was so successful, 'That's all fine, but would you be able to do that in the local pub?'.
>
> **Genesis P-Orridge, 1998**

COUM became more and more fed up with the art world. It seemed that no matter how extreme their performances and provocations were, no matter how much paint, blood and nudity they flung at their audience, they just sat there and took it. In the photographs from 1975's *Studio of Lust*, the small crowd, watching P-Orridge, Peter 'Sleazy' Christopherson and Cosey Fanni Tutti simulating a sex act in the middle of the gallery while fake blood pours out of P-Orridge's mouth and tapes of obscene phone calls play in the background, look no more than slightly bemused. In an effort to get a rise out of these infuriatingly open-minded art people, COUM often went to extraordinary lengths. Reminiscing about COUM in 1983, P-Orridge recalled a performance at the Institute of Contemporary Arts in Los Angeles, 1976:

> I got a 10-inch nail and tried to swallow it, which made me vomit. Then I licked the vomit off the floor, and Cosey helped me lick the vomit off the floor. And she was naked and trying to sever her vagina to her navel ... and she injected blood into her vagina which then trickled out, and we then sucked the blood from her vagina into a syringe and injected it into eggs painted black, which we then tried to eat. And we vomited again, which we used for enemas.[8]

Here, at least, people walked out. But what COUM was hoping for was something closer to what Artaud had glimpsed in the Balinese Theatre or the mass fit of screaming hysteria that took place at a Rock concert, where a real exchange of social energy seemed to be taking place. At a Doors gig (P-Orridge listed The Doors as one of his favourite groups in 1979) or even better, a performance by The Stooges, the audience seemed poised on the verge of devouring their idol in some bizarre ritual sacrifice, but if COUM's Studio of Lust was awakening any deeply repressed desire for crime or cannibalism in its politely deferential audience, they weren't letting on. So P-Orridge, Tutti, Sleazy and new recruit and electronics whiz Chris Carter moved their operation out of the art gallery and into the world of Rock and Roll, which was, it's fair to say, completely unprepared for Throbbing Gristle.

TG began its mission just as Punk Rock was rearing its head in the UK in the late seventies, but Punk didn't go nearly as far as P-Orridge would have liked in rewriting the rulebook on Rock and Roll. P-Orridge was one of the few to see beyond the 'here are three chords now form a band' rhetoric of the early Punk movement. What was really being promoted was not a new approach to music at all, but a retrograde return to some sort of lost Rock utopia, an era of short hair, short songs and leather jackets. P-Orridge, with his head full of John Cage, Fluxus and the more extreme manifestations of performance art, was having none of it. Why use three chords? As far as TG was concerned, you didn't need any chords at all. This is one of the things that made TG's music so uniquely powerful—they refused to play their instruments properly. 'I just bash it around', said Cosey of her guitar in 1983, 'I don't play it sussed. I just get what I can out of it.'[9] Gen and Cosey's totally unconventional approach to the bass and guitar respectively resulted in a uniquely physical way of playing which, in its strongest moments, totally upended the tricks and clichés of the previous thirty years of guitar playing in Rock. This is what P-Orridge meant when he said you didn't need any chords to form a band. It could take a good musician a lifetime to scrape away all that accumulated tradition and technique—you were probably better off not learning it in the first place.

The untrained artist has no choice but to distort—she doesn't know how to do it any other way. But the trade-off is that she achieves an honesty, a directness of physical expression, that the professional, overwhelmed by a lifetime of learning and centuries of received tradition, would never be able to produce. When the Fluxus artist Al Hansen showed up for his first day at John Cage's experimental composition class at the New School for Social Research, Cage quizzed him on his musical ability. Did Hansen play an instrument? Could he read music? Did he understand the rules of harmony or the notes of the scale? Hansen answered no to all of these questions, feeling as though he was about to be thrown out of the class on his ear. After what seemed like the hundredth 'no' in a row, Cage finally broke into one of his trademark grins and exclaimed, 'You're a completely blank slate! There's nothing for you to unlearn!'.[10]

69. THE HUMAN HONK

Going to the bathroom with Captain Beefheart

> **Q.** Have you ever had somebody you idolized or looked up to as an artist?
>
> **A.** Can't think of anybody, other than the fact that I thought Van Gogh was excellent.
>
> **Q.** How about in music?
>
> **A.** Never in music, I never have. A hero in music. No, fortunately.
>
> **Lester Bangs, 'Captain Beefheart's Far Cry', 1980**[1]

When Don Van Vliet, AKA Captain Beefheart, began composing the music that would appear on his 1969 album *Trout Mask Replica*, he had very little to unlearn. Beefheart had released a series of increasingly strange albums with his Magic Band since 1964. He was a good Blues harmonica player and a talented singer with an enormous natural range, so he was by no means a musical ignoramus, but he was also something of a control freak and a megalomaniac, and he was determined that his new album would be written entirely by himself from start to finish, something he was, by any objective standards, unqualified to do. Or was he? Later in the same interview with Bangs quoted above, Beefheart does own up to one musical influence: 'a gander goose could be a hero, the way they blow their heart out for nothing like that.' What Beefheart is saying here makes a lot of sense: he doesn't need to be taught composition or learn to play an instrument any more than a goose needs to go to school to learn how to honk. He's a human animal, and somewhere in him is a sound, a human honk, if you like, which is entirely his own, it just needs to be given form.

Beefheart wrote the music for *Trout Mask Replica* at the piano, which he absolutely did not know how to play. But in a remarkable triumph of stubborn self-belief over actual ability, he demanded that his spontaneously arrived-at note clusters and weird arhythmic rhythms be reproduced *exactly* by the band, and left them to figure out how to do it. As Mike Barnes relates in his biography of Beefheart, this was easier said than done. Some of the tapes of his piano playing may have involved him hitting a ten-note cluster on the keyboard, which guitarist Bill Harkleroad would then be obliged to play, despite the fact that his instrument only had six strings. It was incredibly hard work for the band, and Beefheart was not at all interested in helping them work out how to do it—he just wanted it done. He has, in the past, compared the creative act to 'going to the bathroom', and saw no reason to sift through his own excrement once the act was completed. But if Beefheart had, to extend his own metaphor, presented the band with a spontaneously produced turd, he was now effectively asking them to reproduce every last detail of its form in a twelve-foot tall marble sculpture.[2]

In this sense, Beefheart's compositional process was not unlike one of the methods Marcel Duchamp used in creating *The Large Glass*. Duchamp dropped one-metre long threads from a height of one metre and glued them exactly where they fell. He then had the wobbly shapes created by this random event made into beautiful, machine-tooled wooden rulers which he used to 'rule' the lines in the section of the glass known as the 'network of stoppages'.[3] For Duchamp's chess buddy John Cage, the results of his random processes had to be adhered to with an even greater degree of exactitude. Once the score for *Williams Mix* had been worked out, with Cage deferring all the important decisions to the *I Ching*, his collaborators had to follow the score to the letter. When Bebe Barron heard the results of the months she and her husband had spent chopping and splicing tape at Cage's house, she wondered what the point was. Surely it would have been more fun, more satisfying for the people working on the piece, if they'd been allowed to improvise a bit in putting it together—a little bit more of the frog noise here, move some of the sections of the Beethoven and Jazz excerpts around so they sounded better. What would be so wrong about that?[4]

But the problem with musicians having fun, as anyone who's watched a Rock band jamming for more than ten minutes would know, is that they tend to fall back on old musical idioms—which is no good when you're trying to invent a completely new vocabulary for music.[5] This is why Cage had a strict 'no ego' policy when it came to people reproducing his scores, and Beefheart was the same. Any comfortable, familiar runs or riffs he might find his musicians breaking into were immediately quashed. As with Cage and Duchamp, Beefheart was suspicious of anything that smacked of habit or preconceived ideas of good taste, and rightly so—to a certain extent, things that 'sound good' to a musician's ears sound that way because they've heard them before.

For all its uniqueness, *Trout Mask Replica* does have musical influences, most obviously Blues (in particular Howlin' Wolf, whom Beefheart has expressed his admiration for) and Free Jazz. But Beefheart's way of playing 'free' is quite different to the way a musician like Eric Dolphy or Ornette Coleman does. These players arrived at the atonal sheets of noise and animalistic cries of their mature work through a long process of 'paying their

dues', playing standards in nightclubs, and making their way through all the developments and innovations of post-war Jazz. In other words, they had learned the rules in order to break them. Beefheart, on the other hand, had almost no idea what he was doing, and arrived at a similar result. (Interestingly, many of the new-wave groups that cited Beefheart as an influence in the late seventies, including Throbbing Gristle, assumed that the Magic Band's lurching, atonal racket was merely the work of inspired amateurs, rather than, as was the case, the work of incredibly skilled musicians sweating blood to realise the complex arrangements of an inspired amateur. But as with Beefheart's good-natured misunderstanding of Free Jazz, the result was often not too dissimilar.) The difference was that the Free Jazz players usually knew where they were going and how to get back from there. Beefheart, on the other hand, having no technique to fall back on, could be either disastrously bad or, as on one memorable occasion in San Rafael, California, in 1970, inspired, when in what Mike Barnes describes as a 'ritual exorcism of grief', Beefheart eulogised one of the century's greatest musicians. In bidding a fond farewell to Jimi Hendrix, who had died that morning, Beefheart resorted to the 'Beast Language' of Michael McClure's *Ghost Tantras*.[6] Just as McClure had found words inadequate for the task of paying tribute to Marilyn Monroe, his lust and grief pouring out in animalistic growls and roars, Beefheart cried his heart out for Hendrix on his saxophone with a great Existential honk into the void.

Hendrix's death was all the more tragic considering that his career seemed to have taken off only very recently. In fact, he'd officially made the transition from underground phenomenon to worldwide Rock star just three years previously, at the Monterey International Pop Festival. Monterey marked the moment that the San Francisco bohemian community that had grown up around figures like Michael McClure was transformed into a global youth craze. Only now they weren't Beatniks, they were Hippies, another term coined by Herb Caen—who seemed to have a knack for these things. Beefheart himself would have played at the festival, if his increasingly erratic behaviour hadn't discouraged his management from booking him,[7] but Hendrix played an extraordinary show at Monterey, which included adaptations of songs by Howlin' Wolf and Bob Dylan, as well as material from his recently released debut album, *Are You Experienced?* He closed his set, and the festival, by setting his guitar on fire, lifting it over his head and smashing it to pieces on the stage.[8]

70. AUTO-DESTRUCTIVE ART

A short history of violent catharsis in twentieth-century art, featuring Nam June Paik, Gustav Metzger and The Who

> Auto-destructive art re-enacts the obsession with destruction, the pummelling to which individuals and masses are subjected ...
>
> **Gustav Metzger, 'Auto-Destructive Art', 1959**[1]

In 1962, five years before Hendrix's appearance at Monterey, Korean-born artist Nam June Paik took the stage at a Fluxus gig in Dusseldorf to perform his *One for Violin*. Paik stood before the audience, gripping his violin by the neck with both hands in front of him, as though he were strangling a chicken. At first it must have seemed as though he were doing nothing at all, but the audience would soon become aware that Paik was ever so slowly raising the violin above his head. Having brought the violin as high as it could go, Paik, in one swift, violent movement, brought it crashing down on the wooden table in front of him, smashing it to pieces.[2]

When Fluxus came to the UK in 1964, the destruction continued. Robin Page booted a guitar out the front door of the Dover Street Gallery and, audience in tow, proceeded to kick it around the block.[3] Meanwhile, German-born painter and theorist Gustav Metzger smashed a bass guitar in front of a crowd of gob-smacked art students as part of a lecture on Auto-destructive art.

Attending Metzger's lecture that day was one Pete Townshend, guitarist with The Who, who was already putting Metzger's theory into practice.

One night that same year, during a particularly lacklustre gig at the Marquee Club, Townshend snapped the neck of his guitar on the venue's low ceiling. After such a lousy night, this was the last straw, and the guitarist took out the evening's frustrations on his now useless instrument, smashing it to pieces. *Now* the audience were getting interested—the violent, direct action of Townshend's *One for Electric Guitar* had moved the bored crowd in a way that an hour of well-rehearsed, energetically played Rock and Roll had not. The Who quickly incorporated Townshend's spontaneous guitar-smashing into its stage show, almost instantly, in fact—that same night at the Marquee, new drummer Keith Moon, having seen what a great reaction Townshend had got, straightaway laid into his kit with even greater ferocity. By 1965 Townshend was ramming his guitar straight through the front of his amp while singer Roger Daltrey swung his mike around his head like a lasso before letting it fly into the drum kit. Meanwhile, the PA exploded in a shower of sparks and smoke, and the crowd screamed for more. 'By the end, the stage would look like a battlefield', wrote Nik Cohn, 'all strewn with drum kit and busted guitar and bits of shattered amp, covered with smoke. Everybody sweated. The Who were wild in those days.'[4]

For the band, and its audience, The Who's ritualised destruction served as a pay-off for the implied threat of violence in the music itself, as if the tension derived from all that beating, thrashing and screaming could only be resolved in an act of violence. So when Townshend saw Gustav Metzger do his routine with the bass guitar at Ealing College, he knew what to call the thing he'd accidentally set in motion at the Marquee—Auto-destructive Art. (Townshend would later describe Metzger as his favourite guest lecturer during his time at art school, and would even blur the truth slightly by implying that it was Metzger who had inspired The Who's stage show in the first place.)[5]

While Metzger's lecture at Ealing College might have shared some similarities with Paik's *One for Violin*—or other instances of instrument abuse in Fluxus from Joseph Beuys attacking a piano with a pair of shoes to Ben Vautier's attempts to eat a record—Metzger had something more serious than 'art-amusement' on his mind.

Metzger had been a member of the Committee of 100, one of the main organising forces behind the annual march from Aldermaston to London to protest against the proliferation of nuclear weapons. It was here, in the bohemian milieu of the Aldermaston march and the Campaign for Nuclear Disarmament, that the tone of British underground art in the early sixties was established. In 1959, Metzger had the idea for a new kind of public art—monuments for a society that seemed hell-bent on its own destruction. In his manifesto of Auto-destructive Art, Metzger proposed a form of painting and sculpture that destroys itself while you wait. 'Auto-destructive monuments', he wrote, 'contain the brutality, the over extended power, the nausea and unpredictability of our social systems.' Like the happy consumer

of post-war Capitalist society, Auto-destructive Art would work overtime to bring about its own demise.

On 3 July 1961 Metzger demonstrated his *Acid Action Painting* for the first time, in front of a slightly nervous crowd of onlookers at London's South Bank. Like a poisonous Pollock, he flung hydrochloric acid at a series of monochrome canvases, and within fifteen seconds of his 'paint' hitting the surface, the canvases had been eaten away to nothing. Another work, *Construction with Glass*, comprised large sheets of glass held precariously in place by adhesive tape. When the structure could no longer hold, it collapsed under its own weight.[6]

Auto-destructive Art was protest art, but not the kind that necessarily made you feel bad. Metzger's *Construction with Glass* appeals to the same part of our nature that enjoys watching disaster movies or footage of buildings being dynamited (remember that the crowd watching as Pruitt-Igoe was blown to bits let out a cheer). It's the same impulse that motivated thousands of Britons to tune in to the BBC home service every Monday and Wednesday night to hear The Goons blow themselves up.

71. MUD, BLOOD AND IDIOCY

Babbling incoherently with Spike Milligan

Just as it had in the United States, the bombing of Hiroshima and Nagasaki in 1945, and the subsequent beginning of the Cold War, had a profound effect on creative life in the UK in the postwar years. Now that it was obvious that modern consumer society was simply a money-spinner for the arms race, it was the task of the UK's outraged bohemian community to mount some sort of response to the seemingly unstoppable growth of the death industry. But how to do it? What sort of monuments can you create for a culture that could blow itself up at any moment? What, if anything, would be an appropriate tribute to idiocy on this scale?

The answer, of course, was more idiocy, and you could hear great steaming heaps of the stuff every Monday and Wednesday night from 1951 to 1960 on the BBC's 'The Goon Show'. The original Goons—Spike Milligan, Peter Sellers, Harry Secombe and Michael Bentine—had all served in the armed forces during the Second World War, and for Milligan, who wrote the vast majority of the show's scripts, the War was the single greatest influence on his work. 'The Goon Show' often revolved around military themes—in 'The Jet Propelled Guided NAAFI', Britain's war-time government hatches a cunning plan to fire airborne missiles, each containing ten pianos, twelve tons of buttered crumpets and sixty thousand gallons of good old brown army tea, into enemy territory. Once deployed, these terrifying weapons could be serving hot tea and crumpets to an unsuspecting populace up to six thousand miles away in a mere sixteen seconds. 1954's 'The Dreaded Batter Pudding Hurler' sees the elderly residents of Bexhill-On-Sea terrorised by flying puddings that strike without warning in the dead of night. The show also features a running gag, where poor old Henry Crun and Minnie Bannister have their knees blown off by missiles fired by the Germans from across the English Channel every time someone lights up a match.[1]

Even when the scripts weren't actually about war, the show echoed the shocks and dislocations of modern warfare through its extraordinary sound effects:

> Colossal explosion. Followed by piles of bones falling to the ground.
>
> **'The Battle of Spion Kop', 1958**

> Explosion. Eccles and Moriarty yell and scream into the sky. The explosion goes at normal speed but Moriarty and Eccles speed up from normal.
>
> **'The Scarlet Capsule', 1959**

> Thud of body & bits of body scattering, ball bearings marbles roll along floor. Hand full of forks, metallic resonant nuts and bolts falling.
>
> **'Ned's Atomic Dustbin', 1959**[2]

The effects themselves were ingenious—the sound of a Wurlitzer organ being driven across the desert at terrifying speeds in 'The Mighty Wurlitzer' being a particularly good example—but often the Surreal results achieved by Milligan in combining concrete sounds with script cues were even better, as in this exchange from 1959's 'The Spy or Who is Pink Oboe'.

> **Jympton:** Have you ever heard of a German spy called (sings) 'la da die dum die dum, lum da die dum'. Have you heard of him?
>
> **Seagoon:** How do you spell it?
>
> **FX:** SERIES OF STRANGE SOUNDS PLAYED AT SPEED
>
> **Seagoon:** I think I'd recognise him if I saw him.[3]

Sometimes 'The Goon Show' descends into a kind of Expressionistic gibberish reminiscent of Artaud's *To Have Done With the Judgement of God*, and with similar purposes in mind. As early as 1949—two years after the non-broadcast of Artaud's play—when The Goons were not yet a radio show, just a bunch of idiots playing the piano and doing impersonations at Jimmy Grafton's pub, this meta-language was already taking form. 'Why talk?' said Milligan to a visiting reporter at the time, 'why speak words? Everybody speaks words.'[4]

'The Goon Show' made no sense, but the last thing Milligan wanted to be was sensible. As Roger Lewis relates in *The Life and Death of Peter Sellers*, sensible men had put Bentine to work in the RAF planning the dropping of tin toilets over Berlin and helping prisoners escape from POW camps by hiding radio components in jam. Sensible men had put Milligan himself in a straitjacket in a psychiatric hospital after the mud, blood and idiocy of war had reduced him to a crying, shivering mess.[5] And across the Atlantic, those same sensible men, or men like them, had ordered the complete annihilation of Hiroshima and Nagasaki using a weapon whose destructive force they barely comprehended—and were now sensibly stockpiling and testing newer, faster and deadlier versions of those same weapons. So Milligan wasn't kidding when he told a radio interviewer that he thought 'The Goon Show' was an accurate representation of the world.[6] As far as he was concerned, given how Surreal reality had become, it was practically a documentary:

> **FX:** ATOM BOMB
>
> **Harry:** Look Mum, another Atom Bomb.
>
> **Peter:** You lucky boy, that means Daddy will be home early from work.
>
> **'Ned's Atomic Dustbin', 1959** [7]

The big explosion was the ultimate Goon punchline, as though Milligan saw no other way for the hyper-tense idiocy of the human race to play itself out than in apocalypse, and that this, when it came, would be a blessed relief. In fact, the word 'catharsis' is apt in more ways than one here: one of The Goons' best-loved monstrosities was the retired 'military idiot' Major Denis Bloodnok, and inside the major's tortured intestines, a military conflagration far worse than any of the action seen in north Africa or the Pacific theatre seemed to be in progress. Milligan (and the BBC Radiophonic Workshop, who assembled the mortar fire, explosions and obscure plumbing noises required for the effect), by re-creating the war in miniature in Bloodnok's stomach, was suggesting that relief would only come from some final, explosive movement of the bowel: catharsis—in the old-fashioned sense 'pertaining to an evacuation of the bowels'. That this also recalls the dictionary definition of Fluxus is entirely appropriate.

In his chronicle of the post-war underground in Britain, *Bomb Culture*, Jeff Nuttall describes The Goons as an important bridge between the seemingly disparate worlds of the protest movement, the artistic avant-garde and the Pop charts. For the members of the Campaign for Nuclear Disarmament, the show's depiction of war as an absurd farce perpetrated by sinister bureaucrats would have appealed for obvious reasons, and Milligan himself (who was heavily involved in the protest movement, and a founding member of the Committee of 100) become something of a hero for the peace movement. The art students, meanwhile, saw in The Goons the same sense of disgust at Western civilisation that had erupted at the Cabaret Voltaire in 1917, and recognised many of the same techniques at work. It's only a short walk, after all, from Milligan's 'ying-tong iddle I po' to 'hihi yabomm hihi yabomm'. Tzara, Huelsenbeck and Janco's simultaneous poem, *L'Amiral Cherche une Maison a Louer* sounds uncannily like The Goons, as does Tzara's description of the piece as 'a contrapuntal recitative in which three or more voices speak, sing, whistle, etc. at the same time in such a way that the elegiac, humorous or bizarre content of the piece is brought out by these combinations'.[8]

As for the teenagers (still a relatively new phenomenon in the 1950s), 'The Goon Show' gave form to many of the anxieties that had driven them away from their parents and teachers in the wake of Hiroshima, in what came to be known as the 'generation gap'. 'Dad', as Jeff Nuttall wrote in 1968, 'was a liar. He lied about the war and he lied about sex. He lied about the bomb and he lied about the future. He lived his life on an elaborate system of pretence that had been going on for hundreds of years. The so-called "generation gap" started then and has been increasing ever since.'

For those on the younger side of this gap, The Goons' absurd slapstick sent a giant raspberry in the direction of all those authority figures they'd been misled into believing, the sensible grown-ups whose world was now not only discredited, but in immediate danger of being destroyed by their own hubris. For John Lennon in particular, The Goons would remain an important influence for the rest of his life, and the singer would make personal connections with a number of Goon-related figures at important moments in his career, including Peter Sellers and film-maker Richard Lester. The baton was officially passed from The Goons to The Beatles on the day of the band's audition at EMI studios in 1962, where they met producer George Martin for the first time. Lennon, being a smart young Punk, immediately told Martin that he didn't like his tie,[9] but the ice was quickly broken when Lennon discovered that the producer had worked on The Goons' records. Martin's experience of working with Milligan, Sellers and Secombe had given him an 'anything's possible' attitude to recording—having worked with a writer who thought nothing of handing his producer a request for a Wurlitzer organ racing across the desert, surely there was nothing a Rock and Roll band from Liverpool could throw at him that he couldn't take in his stride.

72. ROCK CONCRETE

Fluxus makes the Billboard charts

At this stage Martin's job amounted to getting a good, commercial Pop sound out of an energetic young Rock band, and as time went on, Martin encouraged The Beatles to broaden their musical palette—he famously twisted McCartney's arm into agreeing to a string quartet for 'Yesterday'—'not that Mantovani rubbish! This is a Rock group!'—and talked them into including a harmonica break on 'Love Me Do'. The Beatles, emboldened by the success of these and other experiments, started writing more challenging arrangements. By April 1966, when The Beatles were recording 'Tomorrow Never Knows' for their *Revolver* album, Lennon would be asking the unflappable Martin to make his voice sound like the Dalai Llama and a thousand Tibetan monks chanting on a mountaintop, and it was in situations like this that Martin's apprenticeship in audio surrealism with The Goons really began to pay off.[1]

Martin taught The Beatles that the recording studio could be a creative tool, a musical instrument in itself, and nowhere is this more evident than on 'Tomorrow Never Knows'. Inspired by McCartney's growing interest in electronic music and tape composition,[2] the song grafts Pierre Schaeffer's Musique Concrete onto Rock and Roll to spectacular effect, as the band spins tape loops of orchestral music, sped-up goonish laughter and what sounds like a speeding Wurlitzer organ over Lennon's ecstatic chanting. For all its spiritual preoccupations, 'Tomorrow Never Knows', like other Beatles psychedelic investigations of the studio such as 'I Am The Walrus' and 'A Day in the Life', is animated by a taste for sonic chaos first awakened in Lennon by 'The Goon Show'.

In 1968, The Beatles went into the studio to record a laid back, Bluesy shuffle called 'Revolution', which would appear, complete with rasping horns and 'shooby-doo wah' backing vocals on their self-titled double LP of the same year. The original take of the song had been much longer, the band jamming on the song's riff for a good ten minutes while Lennon abstracted the word 'alright', from it's original context in the song's chorus—'Don't you know it's gonna be, shooby doo, alright'—into an animal howl. Having been excised from the song, this improvised freak-out would become the starting point for a whole new composition, and The Beatles' most extreme excursion into avant-garde music: 'Revolution 9.'[13]

Lennon's 'alright's can still be heard in the finished version of 'Revolution 9', but without the band playing around him, his strangulated yelps and moans have become eerily disembodied—less James Brown and more like the ghost of Antonin Artaud, shrieking in the stairwell at Abbey Road studios. Now, Lennon's vocals flit in and out of an eight-minute montage of music and noise that begins with a loop of a crying baby playing in the left channel and a short fragment of choral music in the right, while a serious voice says 'number nine' over and over again. Bits of piano music appear and disappear without warning, as do the voices—flat, oddly menacing voices, sometimes too low in the mix to be understood, but occasionally leaping forward to deliver strange sentences: 'they are standing still', 'the watusi, the twist', 'take this, brother—may it serve you well'. Towards the end, the feeling of nightmarish unease erupts into violence, as flames leap across the stereo field, and rioting crowds and the sounds of war rise up over slithering, backward Rock and Roll. As 'Revolution 9' winds up, we're back at Abbey Road, listening to a bad recording of people talking in a room, with an oddly claustrophobic piece of music droning on in the background. A woman's voice says, 'You become naked'—it's Yoko Ono.[4]

Five years previously, no one who listened to Rock and Roll had even heard of Yoko Ono. Likewise, none of Ono's friends in the cluster of lofts and galleries in downtown New York, or the members of the international Fluxus movement in which she was an important catalyst and contributor, would have predicted that she would appear on an album by the world's most famous Pop group. In 1964, a vast gulf seemed to separate Ono performing *Cut Piece* at a Fluxus concert from The Beatles playing 'I Want To Hold Your Hand' for a mass of screaming teenage girls, and the chances of George Brecht getting to play the comb on the Ed Sullivan show seemed slim to none. But when Lennon met Ono at London's Indica bookshop in 1966, a process was set in motion that would see Fluxus thrust into living rooms and student dormitories all over the world in a most unexpected way.

To say that the vast majority of The Beatles' audience was unprepared for the mind-bending shock of 'Revolution 9' when they dropped the needle on the last side of The Beatles' *White Album* in 1968 is an understatement. There was no precedent for it in the history of Pop music. 'Tomorrow Never Knows', for all its sonic adventurousness, was still based on the chord of 'C' and kept a beat, but *Revolution 9* only made sense as music if you'd managed to come to grips with John Cage's assertion that 'everything we do is music', something that Ono, having worked with Cage a great deal in the sixties, understood implicitly.

73. FLUXUS BEACH PARTY

Yoko Ono and The B-52's

The Beatles' fans were in for more shocks when Ono began singing on solo albums and collaborations with Lennon in the seventies. Ono's voice, again, had no precedent in Rock—she wasn't a strong folk singer like Joan Baez or a powerful Blues shouter like Janis Joplin, she wasn't innocent and waif-like or seductive and coquettish. The sounds she produced ranged from a quavering, untrained sing-song, like a nervous child singing at a school eistedfodd, to noises that were closer to talking, screaming or crying or the sounds made by an animal in pain. Of course, Ono would have heard weirder things than this any night of the week at George Maciunas's Fluxus concerts, including the psychic horror-show of La Monte Young screaming at a plant until it died. Singing in Fluxus was, like anything in Fluxus, non-specialised. It didn't have to be 'good' singing, in fact, it was better if it wasn't. Good, professional singing, like good, professional art, only served to put up walls of expertise and technique between the artist and the audience. This is why Ono's singing is so unsettling in a Rock context—it's a real voice—untrained, unpolished, raw and cracking. In other words, it's impossible to ignore.

Yoko Ono's infuence has turned up in some unlikely places. In 1980, Athens, Georgia band the B-52's had a hit with 'Rock Lobster', a novelty surf-Rock number which contrasts the happy-go-lucky atmosphere of a fifties beach party with the threat of danger lurking beneath the waves. While the humans play happily on the shore, trouble is boiling over in the underwater world. Catfish chase dogfish, and piranhas snap hungrily, while a hapless underwater diver narrowly escapes the clutches of a giant clam, only to come face to face with the horror of ... the bikini whale![1] Like a lot of the best chart-topping hits, OutKast's 'Hey Ya', New Order's 'Blue Monday' and Gwen Stefani's 'Hollaback Girl' being other examples, 'Rock Lobster' is both irresistibly catchy and unspeakably weird. In fact, it's catchy because it's weird, its avant-garde oddball-ness is what hooks you into it, gives you a reason to keep listening to this song above all the other songs on the radio. The intrigue in 'Rock Lobster' comes partly from its unusual subject matter (it is, as far as I know, the only song about a Rock Lobster), partly from its musical onomatopoeia (the descending line of the guitar as Fred Schneider takes us, like some demented Jacques Cousteau, 'Down! Down! Down!' into the ocean), but mostly from the extraordinary vocalisations of Cindy Wilson and Kate Pierson, derived, as it turns out, from Yoko Ono's singing with the Plastic Ono Band.[2] 'Some people don't appreciate it', said Pierson in a 2002 radio interview, 'but we do.' Wilson and Pierson had always enjoyed making strange noises with their mouths and vocal chords, but it took Ono's example for them to entertain the idea of putting those noises in a Pop song. In much the same way as Louis and Bebe Barron would use the unfamiliarity of electronic music to conjure the strangeness of outer space in their soundtrack for *The Forbidden Planet*, Wilson and Pierson put the avant-garde to work in 'Rock Lobster', as Ono's more extreme shrieks, wails and yodels are used to paint a sound-picture of the scary world that lies beneath the surface of the waves.

By this point, Ono's singing had inspired a whole new generation of female vocalists (including Cyndi Lauper, who claims that Ono's book *Grapefruit* was one of the few items she took with her when she left home at seventeen)[3], encouraging them to scrap the conventional models for female vocalists and make whatever noise they felt like making. The No Wave bands that appeared in New York in the late seventies provide the missing link between Fluxus and Punk—anything that sounded 'good' or 'professional' was out, anything untrained, ugly and real was in. In this context, Ono's body of work was one of the few real precedents (along with Beefheart's *Trout Mask Replica*) for the de-specialised version of Rock practised by groups like Mars, DNA, Teenage Jesus and The Jerks,[4] and later, Sonic Youth.

> I thought John and I were punk before punk! I was very thankful the B-52's owned up. They said, OK, we were inspired by Yoko Ono.
>
> **Yoko Ono, *Mojo* magazine, 2002**[5]

In the interview quoted above, Ono draws up a list of her favourite songs, with an eye to setting the historical record straight. Here she claims, if not to have invented, then to have anticipated most of the major musical developments of the last thirty years, including Punk, Sampling and Rap. While the idea that Yoko is the original Rapper probably wouldn't find too many defenders (everybody knows it was Debbie Harry, right? Just kidding), the Sampling thing is less bizarre than it might first seem.

74. SONG OF THE YOUTHS

Stockhausen, Can and the shortwave band

Ono's involvement with Lennon, and her role in his artistic development, was, to say the least, a point of contention in the late sixties and seventies.[1] But not everyone saw Ono as simply a weird foreign woman who'd broken up their favourite band and stolen 'our John'. As Julian Cope reminds us in his peerless study of German underground Rock, *Krautrocksampler*, in Germany, Ono was well-known as an avant-garde artist in her own right before she even met Lennon. Ono's involvement in Fluxus came about partly through her relationship with the West German composer Karlheinz Stockhausen, as part of a scene that included John Cage, La Monte Young and the Korean-born Nam June Paik. For the Germans, Ono's appearance on the *White Album* heralded the beginning of a new correspondence between the underground and the Pop charts[2], making good on the promise of 'Tomorrow Never Knows' by implying that The Beatles were ready to engage with the avant-garde in a more committed

fashion. As Cope says: 'For many artists in W. Germany, that was reason enough to form a rock 'n' roll group.'

Stockhausen is a key figure in all of this. Electronic music-makers today might talk about being scientists of sound, but only Stockhausen would spend six months slaving over a tape recorder and sine-wave generator in order to produce five minutes of music, and that's what the composer did in his study for what would eventually become *Gesang Der Junglinge* (Song of the Youths) finally completed after eighteen months of editing and mixing in May 1956.[3] Splicing together pure electronic tones with white noise and a manipulated recording of a boy soprano, Stockhausen created one of the most exciting electronic compositions of the twentieth century—a work with roots in the European classical tradition derived from Schoenberg, which nevertheless pointed firmly towards the future. Stockhausen's work during this time has interesting parallels with Cage's—both worked extensively with tape composition as well as with electronic music systems for live performers. But Stockhausen would have no truck with Cage's 'disinterestedness'; he may have paid lip-service to the idea of 'ego-transcendence', but he was basically a genius in the old-fashioned mould. When Stockhausen wrote a score for a musician to play the short-wave radio (as he did with 1968's *Kurzwellen*), he was never going to be content to simply let the sounds be what they were—he had something more grandiose in mind:

> We have come to the edge of a world which offers us the limits of the accessible, the unpredictable; it must be possible for something not of this world to find a way through, something that hitherto could not be found by any radio station on this earth. Let us set out to look for it![4]

Likewise, when Stockhausen set to work on a collage of musical quotations from around the world in 1966, his intentions were a long way from the random slice and dice of *Williams Mix*. By electronically combining the sounds of the planet in *Telemusik*, Stockhausen was trying to artificially accelerate the development of McLuhan's Global Village to create 'a music of the world, of all cultures, all races'. In the end, however, it was not this kind of talk that eventually led to Stockhausen's split with Cage and the New York branch of Fluxus—rather it was the German's highly suspect attachment to such specialised, elitist practices as harmony and rhythm: hadn't he read the bit in the Fluxus manifesto about 'dilettantes' and 'professionals'? But while Ben Vautier and George Maciunas were handing out anti-Stockhausen flyers in New York ('PICKET STOCKHAUSEN CONCERT! THE DOMINATION OF WHITE PLUTOCRATIC ART HOLDS YOU IN BONDAGE!')[5], a couple of the composer's students were preparing to realise his vision of electronic world music in ways he could scarcely have imagined—on music TV, and in tight leather pants. But even here his ideas would prove to be contentious:

> **Holger Czukay:** I have radio sets, tape recorders, tapes, and on these, everything you can hear in the world is stored ... musicians from abroad that I receive by shortwave transmitter.
>
> **Interviewer:** Does that mean that Can is trying to electrify on a greater scale?
>
> **Irmin Schmidt:** Maybe Holger—but not us, no.[6]

It's 1977, and Can has just finished playing an improvisation based on a song from its 1972 album *Future Days*. By this time, Can's second vocalist, Damo Suzuki, had left the group, so there's no singing on this version of 'Moonshake', but there are voices. As the band cooks up a unique brew of twitchy European funk—somewhere between the Velvet Underground and the more Minimalist excursions of Miles Davis—Holger Czukay tunes in guest vocalists from his odd collection of tape machines and radios. As he sweeps up and down the band, urgent shortwave chatter dissolves into abstract easy-listening croon, then a swarm of twittering interference. As the song winds up, he even takes a telephone call. 'Hello?' says a woman's voice through the static, unaware that she's just become a guest vocalist—Czukay mimes confusion, 'How did *she* get in there?'.

Czukay and keyboardist Irmin Schmidt were both students of Stockhausen, but it was one of Czukay's own music students that encouraged him to start a Rock band, after playing him a copy of The Beatles' 'I Am the Walrus.'[7] A psychedelic Pop song built around the descending drone of a police siren, and incorporating a 'solo for radio', as a quick scan through the dial turns up a broadcast of *King Lear*[8], 'I Am the Walrus' seemed to Czukay to point the way forwards. After a couple of years during which they merely talked about starting a Rock band, Czukay and Schmidt finally recruited Jazz drummer Jaki Liebezeit and Czukay's pupil, guitarist Michael Karoli, and by 1967 Can was born. Originally, Czukay played the bass, but his expertise with electronics made him valuable in other ways. Most of Can's music was created during marathon group improvisations, playing until, in Czukay's words 'you have a track that retains a secret'.[9] Czukay would then whittle these monster jams down into carefully structured audio sculptures, which, while they rarely adhered to anything as simple as a verse-chorus-verse structure, obeyed their own curious logic. On 1971's 'Oh Yeah', Czukay splices together multiple takes, first spinning in vocalist Damo Suzuki's vocals backward over dreamy organ drones, then, after a dramatic edit punctuated by a bent zither note, the vocals right themselves, while the cymbals travel backwards, eventually colliding with the thunderclap that began the song in the first place.[10]

Czukay's sonic fictions could incorporate outside sources as well, the squelch and sizzle of his shortwave can be heard flitting in and out of the mix on *Future Days*,[11] and as with Stockhausen's hybrid of human voice and electronics on *Gesange Der Junglinge*, it was sometimes hard to tell where the radio ended and Suzuki's vocals began. But by the mid seventies, the rest of the band was becoming less and less interested in cultivating this kind of confusion, resulting, eventually, in the tense situation captured on the German music TV show quoted earlier, where Schmidt and new bassist Reebop Kwaku Baah appear more than a little embarrassed by Czukay and his collection of crazy gear. Later that same year, Czukay told *The Wire* magazine, the band unplugged his mixer on stage, and Kwaku Baah punched him in the face, accusing him of 'stealing musicians' souls'.[12]

75. WAR AND PEACE IN THE GLOBAL VILLAGE

Tuning in the noise of the world with Brian Eno, David Byrne, the Bomb Squad and the Beatles

> (Fourth World Music) is music that is done in sympathy with and with consciousness of music of the rest of the world ... It's almost like collage music, like grafting a piece of one culture onto a piece of another onto a piece of another.
>
> **Brian Eno, interview with Charles Amirkhanian, KPFA, 1980**[1]

In 1979, trumpeter Jon Hassell, another ex-student of Stockhausen's who had also played in La Monte Young's group, began talking to Brian Eno and Talking Heads singer David Byrne about an album of what they called 'Fourth World Music'. With this Futuristic melange of sounds from around the globe[2], Eno, Hassell and Byrne hoped to reincorporate the ritual significance of music in the developing world into contemporary Pop, using modern production techniques. Hassell, for some reason, bowed out of the project, but Eno and Byrne ploughed ahead, inspired by Holger Czukay's recently released solo album, *Movies*. Here, Czukay finally got to create the shortwave Disco he'd always threatened to make in Can, without worrying about the band turning him down or unplugging him. On *Movies*, the radio is loud and proud, blaring over the top of synthesised Funk tracks and Czukay's own, slightly camp singing. 'Cool in the Pool' and 'Oh Lord Please Give Us More Money' are crammed with hundreds of edits and loops, tubas, sped-up Arabic singers, explosions and voices from Hollywood movies are fused together in unlikely hybrids by Czukay's mixing-desk expertise.[3]

This kind of thing is commonplace now; The Avalanches (another group cited as a favourite by Yoko Ono in the 2002 interview) are just one of many groups to create entire albums out of tiny fragments of found sound. Their *Since I Left You* LP stitches together riffs, beats and random bits of ambience from Madonna, Kid Creole and the Coconuts and John Cale, to name but three of hundreds, to evoke a sort of fantasy cruise-liner party band, playing a non-stop soundtrack to a bittersweet holiday. DJ Shadow, RJ D2 and The Dust Brothers have created similar Frankenstein monsters out of re-animated audio, but in 1979, Czukay was the only person doing it on record, mainly because it was so damned tricky. In another seven or eight years, samplers would become cheap enough to make the cut-and-paste collage a more accessible form (resulting in records like MARRS' *Pump Up The Volume* and Bomb the Bass's *Beat Dis*), and more than a decade later, the artificially accelerated culture of Hip-hop turntablism would give rise to superhuman feats of live mixology like Kid Koala's *Carpal Tunnel Syndrome* and DJ Disk's *Ancient Termites*, but for now, Czukay was on his own.

But Eno was listening. One track on *Movies* in particular seemed to give a clue as to how his and Byrne's Fourth World Music might be realised, side two's 'Persian Love'. Over a sparkling guitar solo, Czukay tunes in the voice of a Persian singer, her voice floating eerily over the track, sometimes lining up, sometimes slipping into odd, unpredictable syncopations and weird harmonies. No one would have chosen to sing like that over that piece of music, but Czukay had made use of chance in a way that Stockhausen himself would have been pleased with, using electronics and live instruments to create a futuristic new hybrid. 'What happens consists only of what the world is broadcasting now', he said, speaking of *Kurzwellen* in 1968. 'It issues from the human spirit, is further moulded and continually transformed by the mutual interference to which all emissions are subject; and finally it is brought to a higher unity by our musicians in their performance.'[4] It was this higher unity that Byrne and Eno were chasing as they began work on the album that would eventually be released as *My Life in the Bush of Ghosts* in 1980. The record was made in New York and Los Angeles, but thanks to Byrne and Eno's radios and record collections, its reach extended much further, taking in the Sea Islands, Georgia ('Moonlight in Glory'), Egypt ('A Secret Life') and Lebanon ('Regiment'). As work on the project progressed, Byrne and Eno began to see its meaning in different terms. They found that they were naturally more attracted to more extreme, passionate vocal samples, and that these tended to come from people with extreme, passionate beliefs. Ecstatic chanters, fire-and-brimstone preachers, irate talkback callers and exorcists all make guest appearances on *My Life in the Bush of Ghosts*, and each, in their own way, had some of the quality that attracted Eno to Rock and Roll in the first place.

Eno, whose background is in the visual arts, made his musical debut in 1967, performing a version of La Monte Young's Fluxus score, *X for Henry Flynt*, where the player is instructed to produce a single unspecified sound over and over for an unspecified period of time (Eno slammed his forearms on the keyboard of a piano once a second over the course of an hour). But prior to that, Eno had been through another musical epiphany, involving piano-pounding of quite a different kind.[5] At an early age, he was captivated by what he once described as the 'idiot energy' of singers like Elvis Presley and Little Richard, both of whom, interestingly, were influenced by the fiery, declamatory styles of black preachers in the American south. Richard would find religion himself in 1957 (after an epiphany triggered by the launch of *Sputnik*, Richard claims to have seen a ball of hellfire over the stage), denouncing the sinful ways of Rock and Roll much as the Reverend Paul Morton does on Byrne and Eno's 'Help Me Somebody': 'Talkin' funny and lookin' funny! You need to take a good look at yourself, and see if you're the kinda person God WANTS you to be!'[6] By channelling these passionate, declamatory vocal performances into their futuristic Funk, Eno and Byrne were drawing a diagram that traced Rock's history back to religion and ritual, while pointing towards its future in Hip-hop, World Music and electronics.

By the late eighties, Hip-hop's own collage aesthetic (itself part of a continuity of African–American culture which values the creative re-interpretation of existing elements in new works) had met Byrne and Eno halfway. Public Enemy's production team, The Bomb Squad, had acknowledged the influence *My Life in the Bush of Ghosts* had on its dense, layered music.[7] 'Incident at 66.6 FM', from 1989's *Fear of a Black Planet* is a close cousin to 'My Life...'s Mea Culpa', where the contrasting vocal textures of a talk-back radio show are used as a kind of readymade call-and-response vocal. 'Incident' ... is edited straight into the beginning of 'Welcome to the Terrordome', whose chorus is entirely composed of found sounds—horn stabs, snatches of movie dialogue and old funk records are spliced together to form an impossible band, punctuated by odd bursts of guitar twang and industrial noise.[8] As with Czukay's 'Persian Love', you can bet that even if you had managed to get James Brown, Martin Luther King, Luigi Russolo and Prince into the studio together, they'd never come up with anything as exciting as the sonic fiction assembled by The Bomb Squad at the mixing desk on *Fear of a Black Planet*. Later, on *Anti-Nigger Machine*, Public Enemy use the radio itself as a sound source, looping sweeping sine tones and waves of static over the beats. Listen closely and you can hear the sound of a world at war with itself, or perhaps, as John Lennon said of 'Revolution 9', a sound-painting of a revolution.

Play 'Revolution 9' back to back with John Cage's *Rozart Mix*[9] from 1965, it's hard to tell where the one ends and the other begins. *Rozart Mix*, was, like *Williams Mix*, a tape composition—although in this case the score is for eighty-eight tape loops rather than one long series of edits. Cage made no decision about what was on the tapes, and instructed his assistants not to listen to them before they cut, preferring, as usual, to let chance (rather than personal taste—his or anyone else's) dictate the structure of the piece. While they didn't take indeterminacy as seriously as Cage, The Beatles were, by 1968, embracing 'randomness' in a big way, partly as a result of the avant-garde ideas they were beginning to absorb from Cage via Ono, partly from McCartney's interest in Stockhausen and Musique Concrete[10], but mostly through a natural inclination toward noise, chaos and distraction which—as Ian MacDonald points out in his exhaustive study of The Beatles' recordings, *Revolution in the Head*—had as much to do with their youth as their influences.[11] When Howard Luck Gossage observed with wonder that the teenagers growing up in Marshall McLuhan's Global Village could 'listen to the radio full blast, study, and put their hair up in curlers at the same time', he was describing something of the state in which The Beatles liked to work—all channels open—as well as the state of mind in which a piece like 'Revolution 9' would be received by its audience.

Now that The Beatles had helped make the introductions, it was becoming clearer that Rock and Roll and Fluxus might have more to talk about than they first thought. Both were (at least in the early days) strongly anti-elitist: The Flux artists' hope of wrenching art from the hands of specialists was echoed in the lives of The Beatles and other groups like The Rolling Stones and The Who, who had risen from the ranks of the Rock and Roll audience to become stars themselves—the message, heeded by thousands of teenagers from Stockholm to Sydney, was that anyone could do it.[12] And while it might have been hard to see in 1964, weren't *Cut Piece* and 'I Want To Hold Your Hand' two sides of Artaud's coin, both stirring, in their different ways, their audience's erotic obsessions, fantasies and taste for crime?

76. DANGER MUSIC

The Destruction in Art Symposium and The Flaming Lips

In 1966 Gustav Metzger invited an international consortium of artists working in all media whose work was in some way concerned with 'aggression and destruction in society' to contribute to his Destruction in Art Symposium. Participating artists included Fluxus alumni Al Hansen and Yoko Ono (it was as a result of this trip that she had her first exhibition in London, and it was here that she met John Lennon) as well as the Cologne-based happener Wolf Vostell, whose 1963 *De-Collagen 9* called for a train to drive at full speed into a car. Highlights of the festival included: Vostell drilling a hole so deep in the basement of Barry Miles's Better Books that he struck water; Puerto Rican artist Ralph Ortiz taking an axe to a piano; and Hermann Nitsch's extraordinary *Abreaktionspiel*, which at one point involved one of the performers stuffing the entrails of a lamb down his trousers and then pulling them out of his unzipped fly—later, a film of a penis being jerked around on a cord was projected onto the lamb's mutilated carcass.[1]

This stuff might seem unpleasant and dangerous, as did many other works of the day including Nam June Paik's instruction to 'crawl up the vagina of a living female whale' or the later Fluxus score that called for the performer to drive a motorcycle off the stage into the audience. But as Flux artist Dick Higgins explained in 1966, 'Today, a sense of risk is indispensable, because any simple piece fails when it becomes facile'.[2] This, when you think about it, is fair enough—waiting to see if Paik was going to get out of the whale OK is already ten times more exciting than a Ben Vautier piece, in which the artist announces that he will eat an egg every day at a certain time.

So far, the thing with the whale has never been attempted. But the audience at a Flaming Lips show in 1989 will never know how close they came to being run over by a motorbike. At this time, the Oklahoma band were, in their own description, a crappy, scrappy, no-talent version of The Who, in love with The Who's sense of danger, excitement and almost religious significance, but lacking all but the most rudimentary clues as to how to create this experience in their own work. At this particular show, Mark and Wayne Coyne had the idea of enlisting their older brother Marty to 'play' a 500cc Kawasaki as part of the evening's musical performance, with a microphone pointed down its tailpipe to further amplify its revs and roars. According to a friend of the band, speaking in the Lips documentary *The Fearless Freaks*[3], Marty Coyne confessed to him after the show that he was seized with an almost irresistible urge to pop the clutch and let the thing roar out into the audience, in a sort of Rock and Roll version of

Andre Breton's simplest Surrealist act—a revolver fired at random into a crowd. Leaving aside Marty's state of mind at the time (there were a lot of fumes in the room), the story raises some interesting questions. If the Lips had simply wanted the sound of the motorbike in the song, there were easier ways to do it, but they specifically chose to have a real bike—a huge, heavy piece of powerful, dangerous machinery which, if the slightest thing were to go wrong, could cause untold damage in the club's tiny space. Young and stupid? The band members happily admit that they were, but the motorbike story also reveals the beginning of an ongoing desire on the part of the band, and particularly its singer Wayne Coyne, to create a mood of Existential exhilaration, the cool feeling that comes from resigning yourself to the fact that you and everyone you know will die—maybe sooner than you think.

> I was waiting for a moment but the moment never came
> All the billion other moments were just slipping all away
> **The Flaming Lips, *Ego Tripping At the Gates of Hell*, 2002**[4]

Before their surprising twenty-first century flush of success, the Lips, like many other music industry second-stringers, toiled in day jobs to keep themselves in guitar strings and pay the rent. Throughout these wilderness years, Coyne held down a job as a fry-cook at a pirate-themed fish and chips restaurant called Long John Silvers (an experience which, among other things, made him qualified to contribute a song to *The Spongebob Squarepants* movie—when Coyne sings of the little sponge 'workin' like a dog at the Krusty Krab', you can tell that he's been there). In *The Fearless Freaks*, Wayne tells the story of a hold-up that took place at the restaurant. He and the cashier were herded into the back room by a couple of guys with 'really big guns', yelling, 'get on the ground motherfucker!'. Suddenly, Coyne was faced with the immediate possibility of death, in a way that had simply never occurred to him before. 'I thought, this is really how you die', he says, re-enacting the experience with the help of two Vietnamese kids on the site of the original Long John Silvers, now a noodle restaurant. 'One minute you're cooking up somebody's order of French fries, and the next ...'[5]

> I've been very near death. And you can't imagine the wild elation of those moments—it's the sudden glimpse of the absurdity of life that brings it—when one meets death face to face.
>
> **Andre Malraux, *The Royal Way*, 1935**[6]

In a sense, most of the music and performance done by the Lips since is an attempt to re-live this moment of Existential terror, the feeling of being a lone, ridiculous human being staring into the void, and finding in that moment, freedom—the freedom Sartre felt living close to death during the Nazi occupation of Paris (Sartre's definition of liberty after this was 'total responsibility in total solitude') or the freedom Camus alluded to in his entry in Yves Klein's visitor's book, 'with the void, a free hand'. Luckily for us, the band no longer does this by actually endangering themselves or the audience as they did in their early days (not just with the motorbike, but with frequent displays of 'intimate pyrotechnics' which, on one occasion, caused bassist Michael Ivins's hair to catch fire). Nowadays, the effect is achieved by a kind of Artaudian acting-out, a cathartic ritual celebrating the cruelty of life with bright lights, shocking films, deafening sound and fake blood—lots and lots of fake blood.

In the video for 1991's 'Everyone Wants to Live Forever'—which can be found on the Lips' recent video collection, tellingly titled *VOID*—a 'fat wrestler spasm guy' covered in fake blood throws himself at the band's feet.[7] As they play the song, he rolls on the floor in front of them, smearing himself and the stage in red paint as though performing a one-man version of Carolee Schneeman's *Meat Joy* (which, coincidentally, is the name of a band who once shared a bill with the Lips, briefly glimpsed in one of *The Fearless Freaks* many fast montages of old flyers, posters and handbills). In 1999's 'Waitin' for a Superman', Coyne appears for the first time in his now famous Beige Suit. The suit is the very embodiment of 'civilisation', a cheesy refusal of the possibility of death, rendered absurd by the fact that Coyne is bleeding from an enormous head wound. This costume, which the singer still wears on stage, seems to say he is determined to live with the feeling he experienced in that moment at Long John Silvers, when a scared drug addict pointed a gun at his head while he stood staring at a basket full of French fries. Now, Coyne's job is to entertain people, but he could just as easily die singing on a stage with a megaphone and a dancing pink rabbit in a nice beige suit, as in a family restaurant wearing a pirate eye-patch and a bird on his shoulder. In an instant, the room could be splattered with red, as it is in the 'Everyone' video, where a bucket of red paint is poured over an electric fan. But in the meantime, there is the possibility of living one's life authentically, and this is what Coyne is trying to communicate through his band's 'radical, Existential protest Rock'—without actually having to set anyone on fire.[8]

77. ACID

Turning on and dropping out with Mark Boyle and The Soft Machine

After his explosive performance at Monterey, Hendrix was immediately back on the road, touring the US with The Soft Machine[1], a group that came with its own lightshow, courtesy of Mark Boyle. Boyle was a visual artist who created Assisted Readymades from twisted junk found at bomb test sites, and had staged one of the most memorable works of the 'Destruction in Art' Symposium with his *Son Et Lumiere for Bodily Fluids*. Here, Boyle had projected the materials of his own body, including saliva, snot, earwax, sperm, blood and vomit, onto a wall while a pair of strangers made love, their heart rates and the pulsing of their nervous systems translated into visual waveforms and projected as part of the light show.[2] Later, Boyle and The Soft Machine built up a working relationship through their collaborations at the UFO nights at London's Blarney Club, and the artist's melting blobs of colour and blazing chemical burns became an important part of the band's live show. By this time, Boyle had swapped the blood and bile for more hygienic, but also far more dangerous, materials like oils, dyes and coloured acids—but the idea was the same. The light show, as the sleeve notes for the Soft Machine's debut album explained, 'divert(ed) the eye from the mind to the bodily functions'.[3] By immersing his audience in the messy stuff of existence, Boyle was making a case for the sensual world over the sensible world.

By this point, as we've seen, The Surrealists' Freudian reading of de Sade—the belief that a society that represses the real desires of its citizens is headed for trouble—had been transmitted to the sixties underground through figures like Artaud, Girodias and Ginsberg, and given added momentum and urgency by the nuclear arms race and, later, the Vietnam war. The only hope for such an uptight world, it was felt, lay in its citizens openly exploring their real desires, by breaking the taboos of social behaviour and sexual relations. So Boyle could afford himself a pat on the back when one art critic walked out of *Son Et Lumiere for Bodily Fluids*, denouncing the show as 'an insult to civilised man' and a failure as a work of art.[4] If civilised man couldn't even cope with a good, honest look at the contents of another human being's nasal passage, much less begin to see it as a work of art, then both civilisation and art could go jump in the lake. It was time to turn off your mind, and just in the nick of time, the right drugs became available to help you do it.

It was at the UFO that many in the British underground, including Pete Townshend, had their first taste of LSD. Suddenly, the question 'is it art?' had never seemed more beside the point. For the kids at the UFO, or enormous all-night raves like the 14-hour technicolour dream, the immersive experience of watching Boyle's swirling, bubbling colours while listening to the avant-garde pulsings of Pink Floyd or The Soft Machine subverted the rational mind—it didn't have to *mean* anything, it just *was*. When Lennon sang 'Turn off your mind' on 'Tomorrow Never Knows', he was referring specifically to the state of egolessness brought on by psychedelic drugs, the feeling that the boundaries between your sense of yourself and the world have disappeared.[5]

This 'uncensored experience of reality', as Ian McDonald describes it, gave many LSD users a short cut to the Zen-inspired philosophy of John Cage, and his call to 'wake up to the very life we're living', or so it seemed. In the fifties, Cage had some trouble persuading artists of his generation to turn off their minds. The sculptor Richard Lippold found Cage's insistence on egolessness so infuriating that he virtually stopped talking to him. 'Once he said to me, "Richard, you have a beautiful mind, but it's time you threw it away". To me, that's like saying, Richard, you make beautiful sculpture, why not cut off your hands?'[6] But as LSD became more widely distributed and publicised in the sixties—thanks to the missionary zeal of Dr Timothy Leary and his acid tests, as well as the large-scale manufacture of the drug in the UK by underground chemist Augustus Owsley III—this resistance began to dissolve, as people began to discover how much fun they could have if they checked their ego at the door.[7]

When I find myself becoming confused, I drop out and take a dose of acid. It's a short cut to reality; it throws you right into it. Everyone should take it, even children ... Human beings need total freedom. That's where God is at. We need to shed hypocrisy, dishonesty, phoniness and go back to the purity of our childhood values.

Joyce Francisco, quoted in Hunter S Thompson's 'The "Hashbury" is the Capital of the Hippies', 1967[8]

While a few of the originators of America's bohemian uprising embraced the psychedelic revolution as the final step towards liberating their uptight country from repression—including Allen Ginsberg, who recommended that all adult Americans should take at least one trip, in order to see their country as it really is—for many of the previous generation, the original Beats of New York and San Fransisco, and the veterans of the London to Aldermaston protest marches in the UK, the apparent descent into self-absorbed navel-gazing that had overtaken the counterculture as a result of the widespread use of LSD represented a betrayal, or at the very least, a gross misunderstanding of that culture's original aims. As Hunter S. Thompson, observing the growing rift between the politically radical Beats and the Hippies in 1967, wrote: 'the Hippies were more interested in dropping out of society than they were in changing it'.[9]

Many believed that the 'enlightenment' brought on by LSD was a cheat, derived from the effects of a chemical on the brain rather than from any real understanding on the part of the user. For John Lennon, the effects of this were almost catastrophic, as his habitual use of the drug in the mid-sixties (The Beatles were among the first in the UK to have access to LSD) almost completely dissolved his sense of self—and not in a good way. For Cage, with his careful and methodical exploration of Zen, the question 'Why?' could always be answered with 'Why not?,'[10] which is to say, he continued to engage with the world while at the same time realising the foolishness of trying to impose your will on it. Lennon, on the other hand, like many habitual users of LSD, had glimpsed the meaninglessness of the Western idea of individuality without having any alternative philosophy to replace it, and as a result, he no longer saw the point of doing anything at all.[11]

78. PERCEPTUAL INSTABILITY

Stanley Kubrick and Bridget Riley

> **Interviewer:** Have you ever used LSD or other so-called consciousness-expanding drugs?
>
> **Stanley Kubrick:** No, I believe that drugs are basically of more use to the audience than the artist. The artist's transcendence must be within his own work; he must not impose any barriers between himself and the mainspring of his subconscious.[1]

Kubrick himself may have just said no, but by 1968 he had created what underground magazine *Rat* was calling '*the* head flick of all time' in *2001: A Space Odyssey*. The magazine's reviewer noted the strong whiff of cannibas coming off the audiences for

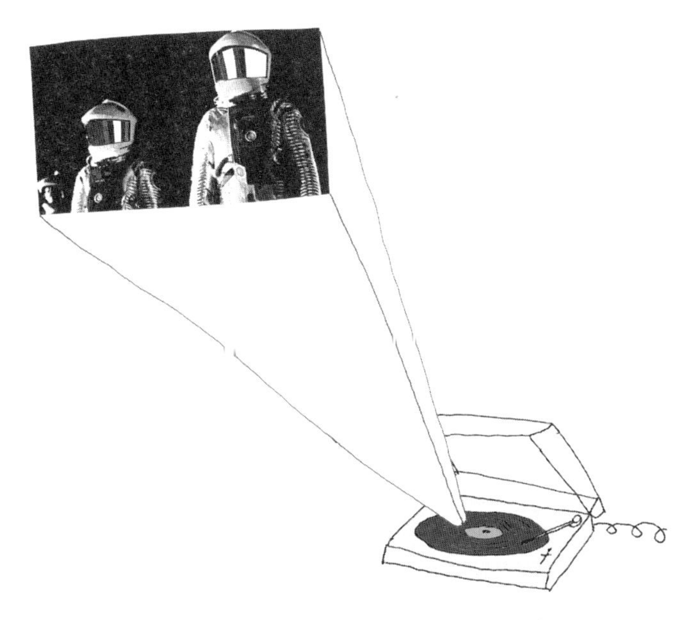

Kubrick's new opus, as well as a slightly more frenzied rush for the snack bar at intermission than was usual. Even when the film was over, there always seemed to be one or two trippers left in the theatre, solemnly contemplating the curtain.[2]

Many older viewers found *2001* hard going—it was too slow, too long, but most of all, too weird. But, as *The Village Voice* pointed out, for the kids, Kubrick's film was for 'groovin', not understandin''. The hook for the psychedelic explorer was the film's legendary 'Star Gate' sequence, a ten-minute lightshow depicting astronaut Dave Bowman's journey 'beyond the infinite'. To create the sequence, production artist Roy Naisbitt compiled a vast collage of high-contrast black-and-white artwork, which was subsequently fed through a process called 'slit-scan' photography to create the other-worldly corridor effects seen by Bowman on his journey to another dimension. In Jerome Agel's *The Making Of Kubrick's 2001*, Naisbitt can be seen leaning over a light-box, sifting through a stack of black-and-white negatives, including images of printed circuits, architectural plans, electron-microscope photographs and paintings by the British Op Artist, Bridget Riley, who was, if anything, an even more reluctant recruit to the psychedelic cause than Kubrick.

> I was surprised to be seen as a representative of the 'psychedelic' culture. It was a collision between my intentions as an artist and the cultural context in which I found myself. I remember being told as though it was some sort of compliment that it was the greatest kick to go down and smoke in front of my painting, 'Fall'.
>
> **Bridget Riley, William Townsend Memorial Lecture, 1997**[3]

Bridget Riley's paintings were, despite her objections, a hit with the 'heads'. Her works of the mid-sixties are mostly composed of black lines or dots on white grounds, arranged in repetitive geometric patterns. In *Fall*, wavy black lines are stepped across the canvas, pulling in tighter at the centre. The painting itself is very mechanical: there's no trace of the artist's 'hand', no visible brushstrokes, but the effect is, nonetheless, startlingly dynamic.

One glance at the painting, and the entire surface seems to jump out at you, look again, and the structure seems to swarm with activity, like a beehive, or bacteria in a petri dish. Other works, such as 1962's *Blaze*, an arrangement of zigzags moving in an ever-tightening spiral towards the middle of the canvas, seem to play host to flashes of non-existent colour.[4]

Riley's works were great fun even if you weren't on drugs. In fact, Op Art, as her style came to be known, was one of the few twentieth-century art movements to be almost immediately embraced by a large audience. Even people who wouldn't sit still for Andy Warhol's Pop Art could find something to like at a Bridget Riley show, as they shuffled from one geometric zigzag to the next, eagerly awaiting the thrilling shock of her next optical illusion. 'Did you see it?', they'd ask, nudging one another, 'Did you *see* it?' This is the coincidence between Riley's painting and the drug culture of the late sixties—they were both, broadly speaking, concerned with the business of perception. Like LSD, her paintings seemed to short-circuit the rational mind, and after all the bewilderingly heavy theory of post-war painting (even Pop Art for all its 'for-the-people' rhetoric, had a certain ironic coolness about it that many found perplexing) this was a relief. Op Art, at least, was guaranteed to work, regardless of whether or not you 'got' the theory behind it.[5]

This led some art pundits to wonder whether Op could even be called 'art' at all—it was, as one critic complained, too 'easily experienced' (can you imagine?). It was widely seen as a gimmick, like 3D glasses in movie theatres. Sure, the monster seemed to 'jump right out at you', but did that really make it a good monster movie?

Other critics looked for a lineage for Op in Marcel Duchamp's machine-art. Like Duchamp, Riley was doing her best to get away from the phony gestures and mannerisms of 'expressive' painting. Duchamp spoke later of 'forgetting the hand completely' when developing the 'mechanical' style of *The Chocolate Grinder*, and, later, *The Bride Stripped Bare*.[6] Riley, in her 1997 lecture, quotes the critic Félix Fénéon, praising the lack of 'bravura' in the work of the Impressionist painter Seurat: 'Let the hand be numb, but let the eye be agile, perspicacious and cunning.' (Riley was taking no chances; having carefully worked out what her paintings would look like, she delegated the actual painting to assistants, in case her hand turned out to be not quite as numb as she'd like.) Riley, like the Dadaists, was wise to the dirty little secret of Expressionist painting—that it doesn't necessarily express more emotion than any other way of painting; in fact, at its worst, it expresses nothing other than the fact that the artist is expressing herself.

Riley may have shared Duchamp's distrust of painterly style, but unlike him, she did have things on her mind that she wanted to express through painting. According to the artist, she was, at the time of painting *Fall* in 1963, 'having an extremely immature affair with a very nice man who was older than me'.[7] When the affair ended, Riley, feeling that her attempts to communicate with words were bound to fail, resolved to paint a picture that would *show* her ex-lover how she felt. But if Riley had an angry painting in mind, she was also determined to avoid the histrionics of Expressionism—the mistaken assumption that equates jagged brushstrokes and blacks and reds with 'angry'. Riley had something more focused in mind, and she turned for inspiration to the precise, rigorous art of the late Impressionists—specifically, the carefully placed dots of Seurat. It was Seurat, as we've seen, who gave Van Gogh the permission to treat paint as paint, to free him from the need to represent things as they are, and start thinking about what it is that the painting needs, and how he might best communicate feeling to the viewer through the medium, and Riley is very much like Van Gogh, in that her work balances a rigorous commitment to the tradition and craft of painting with an intense desire to share emotions and personal experiences with the viewer in as direct a manner as possible.

This is why Riley was so infuriated with the runaway success of her art, both in the psychedelic underground and in the world of advertising and fashion where her style was very much the flavour of the month in the mid-sixties. 'Here's how the *In* Birds will play the Pop Art game, GEARWISE' announced the caption from a fashion spread in *Music Parade*, 1965: 'Crazy circles, ill-assorted diamonds, zany zigzags ... remember—Black and White is THE colour.' Two years later, designer Rich Carter superimposed an Op-Art spiral over a silhouette photograph of the Rolling Stones to create a swirling, psychedelic poster for the band's upcoming shows.[8] Meanwhile, magazines advertised mail-order 'Hypno-Mandala' posters featuring zig zags and leaping interference patterns straight out of Riley's recipe book.

Had she chosen to do so, Riley could have created a business-art empire to rival Andy Warhol's based on her Op Art paintings. But Riley was horrified by the popularity of her work, and had no intention of licensing her patterns for use as fabric prints for mini skirts or psychedelic album covers to be pored over by stoned Hippies.[9] She felt as though the vast majority of the people who were enjoying her art had no appreciation of the rigorous process that informed it, or the serious engagement with the history and future of painting that it represented—and she was right.

This was a problem faced by a lot of 'perceptually unstable' art in the sixties—Minimalist music, in many ways an aural equivalent of Op Art, being another example. But unlike Bridget Riley, the Minimalist composers were, by and large, OK with people liking their work—whatever their reasons. In fact, for the Minimalists, being likeable was actually a form of revolt, a decision to opt out of the perpetual series of revolutions that characterises Modernism. If, as Wallace Stevens wrote, 'incessant new beginnings lead to sterility', then the Minimalists would set out to surprise themselves by doing the same thing over and over.

79. BEING BORING

Steve Reich and the joy of repetition

In her memoir, *I'm with the Band*, super-groupie Pamela Des Barres recalls a night spent at the house where Captain Beefheart and the Magic Band were in the process of creating *Trout Mask Replica*:

We smoked a lot of pot and Don put on a record. We lounged around the living room while a guy with a really deep voice repeated this phrase overandoverandover until it turned into many different ideas. When the record was over, the needle skipped and skipped, so we listened to that for a while too.[1]

The record in question was Steve Reich's *Come Out*, created in 1966, and one of the founding statements of the Minimalist style. *Come Out* is based on a recording of nineteen-year-old Daniel Hamm saying the words 'come out to show them'. Hamm had been arrested for murder in the Harlem riots of 1964 and, as Reich tells it in the sleeve notes for a 1987 re-release of *Come Out*:

... the police were about to take the boys out to be 'cleaned up' and were only taking those who were visibly bleeding. Since Hamm had no actual open bleeding, he proceeded to squeeze open a bruise on his leg so that he would be taken to the hospital.[2]

The complete phrase—which appears at the beginning of the piece—is, 'I had to, like, open the bruise up and let some of the bruise blood come out to show them'.

Reich made the piece using tape loops, the same technique employed by The Beatles on 'Tomorrow Never Knows' that same year. Two identical loops of Hamm's phrase were played on two identical tape recorders, and as they played, slight fluctuations in the motor speed of the two machines caused the loops to go 'out of phase' with each other, and Reich exaggerated the effect further by occasionally putting his thumb on one of the machines to slow it down further. Gradually, Reich added a reverb effect to the two loops, and then later on, he doubled the whole thing up, so that by the end of *Come Out* there are eight loops of Hamm saying 'Come out to show them' running in and out of phase with each other.

Come Out is an extraordinarily simple piece of music—there's no band or orchestra, no singing and no score. It contains only one element, the short fragment of Hamm's speech played, as Miss Pamela had observed, 'overandoverandover'. So much for the description—listening to the piece is something else again. It's no more possible to precisely define the experience of hearing *Come Out* than it is to pin down the kaleidoscope of visual effects created by Riley's black and whites, since most of these effects are not 'in' the work itself, but occur at the level of perception, between the eye and the mind of the viewer, or in the case of *Come Out*, between the ear and the mind.

As Pierre Schaeffer had already observed with his *sillon fermé* in 1948, any looped sound will inevitably become abstracted from its source. His *Etude Pathetique*, produced in a hurry that same year, is a virtuoso display of this transformative process. Grabbing whatever records were lying around the studio that day, Schaeffer assembled a 'remarkable ensemble' of coughs, spoken phrases, rattling saucepan lids, accordian runs and harmonica riffs. All these sounds were looped, using turntables, and in the process take on a curiously abstract quality. The scratchy voices lose their meaning, and become sound objects.[3]

Forty years later, when Chuck D recorded his vocals for Public Enemy's 'Rebel Without a Pause', he rhymed over a 4-beat loop of the introduction from the JB's 1972 Funk anthem, 'The Grunt'. The song begins with a very fast run on a saxophone ending in a high, squealing note. 'I spent a day, locked myself in my mom's house', Chuck recalled in 2003. 'I was writing to a tape with the Grunt sample, and my moms thought it was a tea kettle going off. She was, "You got some tea on the stove?"'[4] Chuck's Mom is hearing things, just as DJ Kool Akeim, after listening to the same loop for two days straight, would start to have audio hallucinations, hearing 'things that the musician didn't try to put in there'.

This process of abstraction through repetition is the first thing you notice in *Come Out*, and it's probably the reason that Beefheart could dig the needle stuck in its rut at the end of the record as much as the record itself; now that Reich had magically turned speech into music, the same process could transform a skipping needle into a beat. But this is by no means the only thing going on in Reich's piece. As the loops go out of phase, subtle rhythms are set up, only to disappear as the phase relationship changes: what at first sounds like the echo of a fairground PA turns into a more musical rhythm at around the two-minute mark. Then, just as this has begun to settle into a groove, it changes again, into a more 'swung' pattern, like a fast Blues shuffle. At this point, the reverbs appear, and the swarming density of the sound begins to throw up aural phantoms—the vowel sound in 'come' has become the steady plunking of a giant rubber band, the 't'sh' in 't'show them' is a hissing ride cymbal. Non-existent words and phrases begin to appear on the edge of hearing. By the last three minutes, the density of the sound is such that Hamm's simple phrase has been transformed into a swarm of electronic tonalities—the 't'sh' has become the chugging of a futuristic freight train, the 'o' in 'come' has multiplied across the sound field into an alien throb.

Unlike Pierre Schaeffer, Reich wasn't all that interested in tape manipulation itself—tape was simply a means to an end. The mechanical logic of the tape recorders used in *Come Out* had, once Reich had established the parameters, determined the result of the piece, without much subsequent interference from the composer. If you're thinking this sounds a little like John Cage trying to remove his ego from his music, well, it is and it isn't. Cage was an important influence on Reich, as he was to a whole generation of composers. Smiling beatifically, telling students and journalists that 'everything we do is music' and that we must 'let sounds be themselves', Cage was a liberating force in the sixties, a get-out-of-jail-free card for the restrictive theories of Serialism—more about which later. But for all of the persuasiveness of his ideas, it had not escaped Reich's attention that a lot of Cage's music didn't *sound* very good. Whatever fascinating procedure had led Cage to the final form of *Williams Mix* or *The Music of Changes* was inaudible to the listener, and the end result was, to many ears, simply bewildering and unmusical. This, from Cage's point of view was an ideal situation, he has often spoken of the importance of being 'bewildered' and if people found his work 'unmusical' that was because they were still clinging to an old-fashioned preconception of what music is. In other words, his stuff was good for you, but not much fun.

So Reich's early tape works were, to a certain extent, a reaction *against* Cage. Where in Cage the process is hidden in the music, in *Come Out* the system is right there in front of you. Anybody could hear immediately what was going on, in the same way that everybody knows what's going to happen if you turn an hourglass upside-down—the system will run its course, the sand will eventually fall to the bottom of the glass, just as Reich's tape loops will run out of phase and then come back to each other with the same inevitability. Reich called this 'Music as a Gradual Process'[5], and it finds its clearest expression in 1968's *Pendulum Music*. As Reich tells it, he was working on a Happening in Colorado when the idea for the piece came to him:

> I had one of those old Wollensack tape recorders with a microphone plugged in and the speaker turned up. Being out west, I let it swing like a lasso. As it passed by the speaker, it went 'whoop!'[6]

Reich's low-key re-enactment of Roger Daltrey's infamous microphone cowboy-ism led him to conceive of a piece of music for microphones and speakers only. As Reich gave the standard Rock and Roll intro of 'one, two, three, four', the five performers let their microphones swing freely in front of their speaker cabinets, giving off a 'whoop' with each pass. As gravity ran its course, the microphones eventually came to rest at a pre-determined point, where they produced a low drone—the piece ended when the microphones had come to a complete stop, and Reich unplugged the speakers with a dramatic flourish.

Just like the sand in the hourglass, the action of the microphones in *Pendulum Music*, having been set in motion by the composer, is determined by the laws of physics. But just because you know, broadly speaking, what's going to happen to the sand when you turn the hourglass upside-down doesn't mean that you can predict in advance the movement of every little grain of sand on the way down, and the same holds true for *Pendulum Music*; what seems simple on the surface is, in fact, infinitely complex. The sound of any given performance of *Pendulum Music* is subject to be influenced by a number of variables including air pressure, the acoustics of the room, the force with which the microphone is swung, the angle at which it's released, and any slight discrepancy in the moment at which the five players start the piece. This is what Reich meant when he wrote in 1969 that music realised by gradual processes had 'enough mysteries to satisfy all'.[7]

'Gradual' was a key word for Reich—if the rate of change is slow, then the listener tends to listen more carefully. This realisation had dawned on him after *Come Out* and was reinforced by his next experiment. Reich had begun to wonder whether it would be possible to write music for live players that utilised the gradual 'phase-shifting' technique of *Come Out*. In 1966, he recorded a short phrase played on the piano, looped it, and left it to play while he reproduced the same pattern in real time at the keyboard, doing his best to put his playing ever so slightly behind the loop with each pass. It was difficult, and of course the result was nowhere near as precise as the unthinking turning of the tapes in *Come Out* had been, but it was, in its own way, just as interesting. Reich found that the effort of trying to gradually speed up his playing against the loop had slowed down his hearing, making him, as he put it 'completely focused on the music while I played'.[8] Soon Reich was writing music for small groups of musicians where the players effectively became human loops, playing short, interlocking musical phrases over and over, and gradually incorporating small changes—an extra note here, the addition of another player there—and these became the hallmarks of a new musical style: Minimalism. Like most isms, the tag has become a blessing and a curse for its practitioners; dwelling on their few similarities while obscuring the important differences that mark them out as composers. However, the term has stuck, mostly because it does such a good job of describing the traits that their work has in common. Whereas most modern

Western music (including much of Cage's) changes so often that after a while, you don't notice the events at all, Reich's music, and the music of contemporaries like Philip Glass, La Monte Young and Terry Riley, by containing fewer changes, and having them occur more slowly, achieves more with drastically reduced means.

80. SON OF RILEY

The Time Lag Accumulator and the Pinball Wizard

Minimalism was, at first, a low-key affair. The composers shared a small network of players, rehearsal spaces and equipment, and often played in each other's groups. But in the late sixties, things started to change, beginning with the release of the movement's first big hit in 1968, Terry Riley's *In C*. By this point, Riley had arrived at a similar style to Reich's; small, repeated musical cells, transparent structure, gradual change and steady pulse. He'd met La Monte Young in the late fifties, and was impressed by Young's *Trio for Strings*, with its sustained notes and long silences.[1] He took this new idea of slowness and stillness with him to Paris in 1962, where, in the same studio where Pierre Schaeffer had created many of his works for Musique Concrete, Riley perfected a new system for improvising with tape loops similar to the one later discovered by Steve Reich. The difference was that Riley's 'time-lag accumulator', as he called out, allowed for greater improvisational freedom than Reich's loops, which, while they changed in relation to each other, remained the same themselves. Instead of just playing along with a loop, Riley was recording loops as he went—the sounds made by the player were recorded onto tape and then played back into the room as the loop fed through another machine. Riley would play a 'C' and then hear the note coming back to him a few seconds later, like a vastly delayed echo. Then he'd play a 'G' along with the 'C'—soon he'd hear the combined 'G' and 'C' on the next turn of the loop, by which time he'd be improvising something else over the top of that. Over time, the built-up echoes of Riley's notes would combine in beautiful and endlessly complex clouds of harmonies that, nevertheless, were anchored in a simple, repetitive time structure; the length of the loop itself. As with Reich's method, Riley's time-lag accumulator seemed to encourage closer listening—sound events that normally passed by too quickly to notice (because the musician is already thinking about what note to play next even as he's playing a note) were now hanging frozen in the air a second later, where they could be subjected to greater scrutiny.[2] It was this process of 'tape jamming' that led Riley to develop a form of ensemble music made of repeated musical phrases in a static environment. One of the first results of this new method was *In C*, which had its first public performance in San Fransisco in 1964, with Steve Reich at the piano, hammering out the repeated 'C' that anchors the piece.

> While performing and listening to gradual music processes one can participate in a particular liberating and impersonal kind of ritual. Focusing on the musical process makes possible that shift of attention away from he and she and you and me outward toward IT.
>
> **Steve Reich, *Music as a Gradual Process*, 1969**[3]

With its unashamedly beautiful harmony and flickering, strobe-like pulse, *In C* was tailor-made for the psychedelic era.[4] In fact, mind-expanding drugs were key to Riley's music—his experiments with mescalin had led him to try to re-create the experience musically with his time-lag accumulator, a system that provided an equivalent of the altered perception of time experienced by the psychedelic drug user. Perhaps because of this, Riley's music was also great for taking drugs to—perhaps the first time this could honestly be said of a piece of music from the Western classical tradition—and the studio recording of *In C* arrived in 1968, just in time for the global Hippie moment that had swept the world in the wake of Monterey. Columbia records launched the album with a party and a live performance—the air was thick with marijuana smoke as Riley played the electric organ dressed in a long white robe.[5]

The commercial success of *In C* as the must-have psychedelic accessory of 1968 inspired an outbreak of Minimalism in Rock and Roll in the early seventies. In 1971 The Who released *Who's Next*, featuring the hard Rock classic, 'Baba O'Reilly'—'Baba' for Pete Townshend's guru, 'O'Reilly' as in 'son of Riley'. 'Baba O'Reilly' is built around a startling bit of Minimalist music, performed by Townshend on an Arp synthesiser, that actually more closely resembles Steve Reich's loop from *Piano Phase* than anything by Riley himself.[6] Two years later, nineteen-year-old prodigy Mike Oldfield recorded his Minimalist symphony *Tubular Bells*, the runaway success of which virtually bankrolled Richard Branson's Virgin Records.[7] But being Rock musicians, neither Oldfield nor The Who were entirely content with Minimalism for its own sake. Where Riley and Reich were quite pleased to have their music develop slowly and steadily, and to leave it more or less unresolved, the Rock Minimalists could not resist the big pay-off. *Tubular Bells* begins in an elegantly minimal fashion, with a pulsating piano figure closely related to *In C*, and slowly introduces additional instruments. But by the end of side one, Oldfield is indulging in guitar histrionics and dramatic flourishes that would be quite out of place on a Terry Riley album, where the instruments are deployed in a far more democratic fashion, and no one gets to solo. The Who, meanwhile, can only sit still for one minute of 'music as a gradual process' before busting out the guitars and rocking out. In fact, the use of Minimalist patterns as tension-builders in Rock and Dance music—Fatboy Slim's 'Right Here, Right Now' being a classic example—is now such a commonplace that it's hard to hear *Piano Phase* or Reich's ensemble pieces from the seventies without expecting a huge lead guitar break to ring out or a beat to kick in. But if these were more superficial manifestations of Minimalism in Rock, by the time of the release of *In C* in 1968, Riley could already claim to have been part of a group of musicians that influenced Rock and Roll in a far more significant way.

81. GERMS FROM NEW YORK

La Monte Young, Lou Reed and 'Louie Louie'

Riley, as we've seen, had already made an important connection with La Monte Young before going to Paris, and after the first performance of *In C* in 1964, he moved back to New York to add his soprano saxophone playing to the endless drone that was going on in Young's loft. At this point, the group consisted of Young, Marian Zazeela and Tony Conrad. John Cale, the other founding member of the group, had left to form a Rock band with Lou Reed, originally known as The Primitives, later The Falling Spikes, and finally (at the suggestion of Al Hansen), The Velvet Underground. Along with guitarist Sterling Morrison and newly recruited drummer Moe Tucker, Cale and Reed played their first gigs as The Velvets in 1965, where their combination of Cale's brain-altering Minimalist drones and Reed's tales of urban sleaze terrified the patrons of the high schools and tourist cafés where they'd been booked to play.[1] By 1967, their debut album, wrapped in a Warhol-designed sleeve and featuring Factory superstar Nico on half the vocals, was released by Verve records to a not-exactly-waiting world.

> The first time I heard the Velvet Underground and Nico record was at a party on the University of Michigan Campus. I just hated the sound. You know, HOW COULD ANYBODY MAKE A RECORD THAT SOUNDS LIKE SUCH A PIECE OF SHIT? THIS IS DISGUSTING! ALL THESE PEOPLE MAKE ME FUCKING SICK!
>
> **Iggy Pop quoted in Legs McNeil and Gillian McCain's *Please Kill Me*, 1996**[2]

Despite their shared roots in La Monte Young's music, The Velvet Underground and Nico were a long way from *In C*. Where Riley's music was harmonious and ecstatic, The Velvets' was harsh and pounding. While some of the gentler songs on the album—*Sunday Morning*, *Femme Fatale*—might have been passable as music to smoke to, these merely lulled the unsuspecting listener into a false sense of security. John Cale's sickly viola drone in 'Venus in Furs' or his one-note piano loop in 'All Tomorrow's Parties' could set even the most relaxed individual's teeth on edge, and if your trip came on in the middle of 'Heroin' or 'Black Angel's Death Song' you were in big trouble. This is why The Velvet Underground went down like such a lead balloon in San Francisco in 1966. To the flower-children of California's bohemian mecca, The Velvets and their Factory entourage were, in the words of The Fillmore Auditorium's Bill Graham, 'disgusting germs from New York', morbidly obsessed with sleaze, depravity and noise. Whereas to The Velvets, the Hippies were simply unrealistic, having naively simplified the Marquis de Sade's imprecation to keep the imagination free and turn their desires into reality, without understanding that 'going back to nature' meant more than just growing your hair long and taking off your clothes—sleaze and depravity were just as much a part of nature as flowers and free love. Factory regular Mary Woronov later summed up the divide between the two camps succinctly: 'They thought we were evil, and we thought they were stupid.'[3]

By 1969, Cale had been forced out of the band by Reed's megalomania, and had taken up a career as a singer-songwriter and producer for hire. Having been impressed by his work on Nico's solo record *The Marble Index*, Elektra records president Jac Holzman hired Cale to produce the debut album by a bunch of Punks from Detroit called The Stooges. The Stooges had made their debut the previous year supporting Blood Sweat and Tears at Detroit's Grande Ballroom, where fans of the headlining band's polite Jazz-Rock fusion were treated to the undignified spectacle of The Stooges' singer Iggy Pop playing shrieking feedback using a microphone dropped in and out of a metre high metal cone while wearing a maternity dress, golf shoes and an afro wig made of aluminium foil. Behind him, drummer Scott Asheton hammered out primitive rhythms on a pair of oil drums, emblazoned with the words 'TITS' and 'PUSSY'.[4] The Stooges were, if nothing else, products of their environment. In an interview for the televised history of Rock and Roll, *Dancing in the Street*, Iggy recalls growing up within earshot of the Ford auto plant and hearing the factory machinery going 'boom, boom boom' all day long—'y' know, each one is another fender'. Early Stooges music was a nightmare inversion of Russian composer Alexander Mosolov's *Steel Foundry* of 1927, where the happy union of proud factory workers and great machines conjured by Mosolov's orchestral evocation of steam-hammers and falling girders was replaced by something closer to Gustav Metzger's 'monuments for industrial societies'—the sound of a giant machine hell-bent on its own destruction. It was not 'good' music in the sense that the conservatorium-trained members of Blood Sweat and Tears would understand it, but it mined the seam where the furthest-flung reaches of experimental music meets the stoned grunting of complete amateurs, the same territory that Beefheart and the Magic Band were exploring that same year at the house on Ensenada Drive. In other words, it was both avant-garde and deeply stupid—Cale was hooked.

The Stooges had instinctively picked up on the link between Minimalism and the most basic forms of garage-band Rock and Roll. As Steve Reich had observed in *Music as a Gradual Process*:

> Drug-oriented Rock and Roll may make us aware of minute sound details because in being modal (constant key center, hypnotically droning and repetitious) [it] naturally focuses on these details.[5]

It was this unlikely link between the high-art world of the Minimalists and the raucous Rock and Roll '45s that Tony Conrad used to blast out of his record player that had drawn Cale to Rock music in the first place. Cale and Conrad shook their heads in amazement at the way The Everly Brothers effortlessly achieved the precise harmonic intervals they had been experimenting with in the Theatre of Eternal Music, and when Cale met Reed and explained the technique he'd been perfecting of tuning all the strings on his viola to the same note in order to get a richer, purer drone, he was astonished to find that Reed had been doing the same thing with his guitar—so that it would be easier to play.[6]

Rock and Roll was unashamedly repetitive music, a fact that reflected its roots in African music, where polyphony and rhythm are generally prioritised over melody and musical progression. To Cale, having absorbed the influence of John Cage, the value of repetition made perfect sense. Defending his staging of Erik Satie's *Vexations* in 1963, Cage had protested that logically, there should be no problem for an audience hearing the same short piece of music eight hundred and forty times, since, 'there are more than 840 repetitions in life'. But nobody needed to explain that to sixties garage Rockers The Seeds, who never seemed to get bored of repeating the keyboard riff from their hit *Pushin' too Hard* in every other song they wrote, and who, in 1968, recorded the ten-minute epic 'Up in her Room', which was, as David Keenan put it, 'a bacchanalian lesson in primitive psychedelic repetition that'd make Terry Riley dizzy'.[7] Nor did the kids in the audience at Seattle nightclub The Chase in April 1963 need John Cage to tell them that there's joy in repetition, as local band The Kingsmen played the numbskull riff of their soon-to-be recorded version of 'Louie Louie' non-stop for *one and a half hours.*[8] The learn-to-play-me simplicity of 'Louie Louie' made it a staple of the American garage-band repertoire in the sixties, and most of those bands would have been quite happy to play that riff at least eight hundred and forty times on any given weekend if it kept the girls dancing.

The Stooges were a great garage band, and as such they immediately made sense to Cale, who jumped at the opportunity to produce them, while Iggy couldn't have been happier, having one of his musical heroes produce his first album. The result was a marriage of New York Minimalism and primitive Rock and Roll so perfect that it was hard to tell where the one ended and the other began. 'I Wanna Be Your Dog' is virtually the bastard son of The Velvets' 'I'm Waiting For the Man'—both are built around a monolithic eight-beat pattern where the entire band seems to be playing the drums. On 'I Wanna be Your Dog' a single note on the piano is hammered out on every beat, as though Little Richard were playing keyboards in the Theatre of Eternal Music.[9] This radical reduction of Rock to its crudest, most basic form would make The Stooges debut an important reference point for Rock bands in the late seventies, but before that, it would provide the impetus for a far more unlikely musical development across the Atlantic: the rise of Kraftwerk. The Futuristic sheen of the man-machine might seem a long way from The Stooges' grimy garage Punk, but the members of Kraftwerk often listed the Detroit proto-Punks as one of their favourite bands.[10] The Germans had simply taken the repetitive throb of The Stooges and automated it, so that instead of having to actually stand there and hammer out those industrial beats and hypnotic riffs, the Kraftwerkers could simply program their studio with the necessary patterns and walk away—no sweat. Kraftwerk could see how The Stooges, and before them, The Velvet Underground, were carrying on a tradition of European avant-garde music that had begun with the Futurists' 'Art of Noises': the desire to wrench music away from what Russolo called the 'boredom' of orchestras playing notes, towards a concept of music that could include *all* sound as music. What got up the Futurists' noses in particular about most classical music was that it seemed tragically stuck in the pastoral tradition, evoking landscapes and sunsets while ignoring the fierce beauty of the newly mechanised world—the world of electrified city streets and roaring car engines. So when Kraftwerk recorded 'Metal On Metal' for its 1975 album *Trans-Europe Express*, it was completing a circular journey that had begun with Russolo's *Intonarumori* in 1913, taking in Schaeffer's Musique Concrete, John Cage, La Monte Young and John Cale, before sweeping past Ann Arbour, Detroit, where Iggy could be found dragging abandoned factory equipment back to Stooge headquarters so that Scott Asheton could whack it with a mallet—boom, boom, boom, boom.[11]

Having been perfected by Kraftwerk in the seventies, machine music returned to Detroit in the early eighties, where the comfortably well-off children of Ford factory employees were spending their disposable income at local nightclubs dancing to, among other things, *Trans-Europe Express*. The popularity of repetitive, European, electronic music with middle-class black teenagers in Detroit would eventually create the demand for a homemade version of Kraftwerk's Minimalist pulse, and by 1986, this music was ready for export, and would come to be known all over the world as Techno.[12] This first wave of Detroit Techno, as typified by the work of Juan Atkins, Derrick May and Kevin Saunderson, was some of the most startlingly Minimal music to achieve a mass audience in the twentieth century. Derrick May's 1986 classic, 'The Dance', amounts to little more than a modulating bass line over an overlapping series of electronic rhythms. UK DJ and producer Mixmaster Morris has pointed out the strong similarities between the gradual processes of Steve Reich and Terry Riley and the early Detroit sound: both styles are characterised by very short, repetitive phrases, and as with the Minimalists' early tape-loop works like *Come Out*, Detroit Techno was often the result of a program simply running its course[13], the sound of machines talking to each other.

82. EINE KLEINE LIFTMUSIK

A short history of background burble, from Erik Satie to Air

> Minimalism is the passionless, sexless and emotionally blank soundtrack of the machine age, its utopian selflessness no more than an expression of human passivity in the face of the bomb.
>
> **Ian MacDonald, *The People's Music*, 2003**[1]

In his essay 'Minimalism and the Corporate Age', Ian MacDonald is not so much exposing the emperor as having no clothes, but pointing out that the emperor has been wearing the *same* clothes for quite some time, and that perhaps it was no longer possible to say that this was, in itself, interesting. MacDonald criticises Riley, Reich and Glass, and the people who buy and listen to their music (quite a lot of people by the 1980s), for swallowing, as though it were self-evident, the line in Reich's manifesto about Minimal music 'facilitating closely detailed listening'. Does it really? Or does the repetitive nature of Minimalism just make it easier to ignore, and therefore a perfect choice of background music for people who aren't really interested in music?

MacDonald argues that repetitive music, in fact, does the opposite to what it says on the tin—it dulls the mind—and if, after prolonged exposure to Minimalism, you find the ticking of a watch or the bumping of a stylus against the end of a record musically interesting, then what does that really say about Minimalism? Far from sharpening the senses, Minimalism dulls them by giving them nothing of significance to focus on. Meanwhile, its appeal, he argues, rests on its being easy to consume. Everything chugs along at a nice, steady pace, and new elements are added gradually. There are no jarring changes of tempo or unexpected lurches into noise or dissonance in Minimalism, no alarms and no surprises. After a while, you stop noticing that it's even there.

But what's wrong with that? In daily life, there is a need for music that you can put on in the background and ignore while you type, cook, entertain your parents or sell people pants, and Minimalism fits the bill. Not that you're likely to hear Steve Reich's *Music for 18 Musicians* or *In C* down at the mall or around the office, but you will hear Moby, Faithless, Air, David Gray or the latest Ministry of Sound *Chill Out* compilation. All of these, in their various ways, owe an important debt to Minimalism, and all fulfil the need for music that sounds good, but makes no demands of you and lets you go about your business, a need first identified in 1920 by composer Erik Satie, in a letter to the Cubist painter Fernand Leger:

> You know, there's a need to create furniture music, that is to say, music that would be a part of the surrounding noises and take them into account. I see it as melodious, as masking the clatter of knives and forks without drowning it completely, without imposing itself. It would fill up the awkward silences that occasionally descend on guests. It would spare them the usual banalities ...[2]

People continue to squirm their way through awkward silences in restaurants, and in elevators ask people they don't know very well how their weekend was, and no amount of Satie, Celine Dion or Air is likely to change the situation for good. But whether or not it actually works, Satie's idea has proved to be a popular one—it just took a little while to get it off the ground. In 1920 Satie arranged a performance of background music to be played during the intermission of a play by his friend Max Jacob. The music was pretty, melodic and repetitive, and many of its motifs were 'borrowed' from works by other composers—composers, incidentally, that Satie didn't like—catchy little riffs that the patrons of the theatre would find familiar and pleasant, even if they couldn't place exactly where they'd heard them before. Boring, derivative and unchallenging, furniture music probably wasn't that good if you paid attention to it, but that was the whole point: you weren't supposed to. Unfortunately, the crowd at the Galerie Barbazanges that night knew of no other way to listen to music than to pay close attention. Satie, in a bizarre reversal of the usual fate of the musician, trying desperately to get his masterpieces heard over the din of the world, frantically ran around the theatre trying to convince everybody to stop listening to his music and get on with whatever they were doing.[3]

Here, as with *Vexations*, what might at first have seemed like another Satie wind-up turned out to be an important thought experiment with enormous consequences for the future of music. Satie's jokes had a way of turning serious—after the First World War, his throwaway idea was transformed into a thriving business by Major General George Owen Squier's Wired Music company, renamed shortly before his death in 1934 as Muzak. Purveyors of piped instrumental music to hotels, offices and restaurants, the folks at Muzak were not about to sit around waiting for people to start hearing the whirring of elevator motors or the massed flushing of hotel toilets with what Russolo would have called 'Futurist ears'. Nor were they optimistic, as John Cage was, that American office workers were about to experience some sort of Zen-like moment of enlightenment and learn to enjoy their own typing and telephony as a form of music. Despite what the twentieth-century avant-garde might have hoped for, Muzak programmers knew that what people *wanted* was to mask the jarring racket of modern life with some kind of audio perfume—pleasant enough to drown out the bad sounds, but not so distracting as to be a drag on productivity. And they had proof, too: in his Surrealist appreciation of Muzak and other easy-listening forms *Elevator Music*, Joseph Lanza amasses an extraordinary collection of data gathered by Muzak and other independent researchers over the previous six decades. The studies showed, among other things, that in 1937, UK factory workers were more cheerful and 'less resentful' of their employers when subjected to canned music, that 88.7 per cent of employees at the US Army Map Service surveyed in 1947 agreed with the statement 'Muzak helps me in my work', and, amazingly, that farmers in McKeesport, Pennsylvania, a few years earlier reported that their cows gave more milk to Muzak.[4]

Of course, not all music is Muzak. Like Satie, the company's programmers realised that their song choices and arrangements had to be catchy and pleasing, but entirely innocuous. The session musos hired to cover 'I Got You Under My Skin' and 'There's a Small Hotel' for the Muzak library were duly briefed on the company's formula:

> Factors that distract attention—change of tempo, loud brasses, vocals—are eliminated. Orchestras of strings and woodwinds predominate, the tones blending with the surroundings as do proper colours in a room. The worker should be no more aware of the music than of good lighting.[5]

Lanza's book makes for fascinating, but uncomfortable reading. Fascinating, because it reveals a sort of shadow world of musical history, of behavioural scientists and paid-by-the-hour vibraphonists quietly working away to produce music that no one will ever notice, but which, in some mysterious way, helps our society to run better—aural caffeine. Uncomfortable because the idea of people making background music on purpose seems deeply wrong, for the same reason that the mental image of Satie rushing around the Galerie Barbazanges shouting 'nothing to hear here' is faintly hilarious. How can Lanza muster so much enthusiasm for something so bland? And how can music which is specifically designed to offend nobody possibly be enjoyed by anybody?

Muzak is not just a registered trademark—it's an insult. It's almost a one-word record review—if you were discussing a new Rock album for, say, *Rolling Stone*, and you wanted to say that the band had produced a bland, formulaic album, calculated to appeal to a wide audience, but ultimately so smoothed over that it entirely fails to gain the listeners' attention you could sum up the idea in a single word—Muzak. Conversely, you'd never tell your friend that his Indie band makes good background music, unless you specifically wanted to annoy him. You'd certainly never say it to Thom Yorke, Bruce Springsteen or Björk (or, at least, you probably shouldn't). Even those artists mentioned previously, whose work, while by no means Muzak, tends to be used as ambience, would be displeased at the suggestion. Air, I'd imagine, would be slightly bemused, Moby and David Gray would be horrified.

What puts the sting in MacDonald's accusation that Minimalism was 'the Muzak of the eighties' is the assumption that music matters, that it exists to communicate powerful ideas, whether they be personal or political, and to surprise and even shock us with startling new formal innovations. 'Challenging', 'confronting', 'original' are words people use when giving positive reviews (or writing press releases)—they're all good things, which is why Radiohead will tend to get better reviews than Coldplay. Radiohead are judged to be a great band, partly because, when poised on the brink of enormous popular success after the release of *OK Computer* (voted by readers of *Q Magazine* as the Best Album of All Time), they decided to release *Kid A* and *Amnesiac*, which are difficult, challenging albums that require concentration and effort to appreciate. By this standard, if all you've done is produce a pleasant noise that is popular because it sounds like other things that are popular, without in any way upsetting the apple cart, then it's assumed that you've failed, or at least underachieved. More worryingly, there's even the hint of a suggestion that this 'easy' music might be in some way bad for you. 'It's like people have been eating wonderbread for so long', said Yoko Ono in 2002, singing the praises of Radiohead's 'Living in a Glass House', 'and suddenly realised that it's better to go to mom and pop's shop and get a really good loaf of bread.' What do you mean, 'there's brown bits in it'? Don't be such a cry-baby, it's *good* for you![6]

This is the thinking that prevails in Indie-Rock world, that nebulous zone that extends from the scruffier end of *Rolling Stone* through *Mess+Noise*, *Pitchfork*, *Vice* magazine and *Magnet*, to the more brightly lit corners of *The Wire*. But outside this is a much bigger world, where these standards do not apply. In these lawless wastelands, the rules of engagement are so different as to be unrecognisable. Here, no one gives a crap if it's 'challenging', 'confronting' or 'original'—the more pertinent questions are: 'Can I dance to it?', 'Can I sing along to it?', 'Is it hot right now?'. Turn up your nose if you like, but this is the world of the Top 40, the commercial radio station, and 'the song that was in that ad'—it's Pop music, and it is, by definition, popular.

83. FEAR OF POP

Why 50,000 Elvis fans can't be right.

Why do so many people like Pop music? You might say to yourself—'It's all good, people can listen to whatever they like'—but it's a different story when you're arguing with your flatmate about the music he's blasting out of his room at four in the morning, or having a tug of war over the car stereo with your sister. Sooner or later, you're going to need a reason why their music sucks and yours doesn't.

The most common reason given is that *their* music is disposable Pop (Yoko's 'wonderbread'), while *yours* is real art made by real artists. So far so good, but we still haven't got round the problem of why their albums are more popular than yours. Why do more people shell out for Anthony Callea than Antony and the Johnsons? Is it really reasonable to assume that you and your mates know something about music that thousands of people around the world don't?

It's an untenable position, and one guaranteed to turn you overnight into a Rock snob. But the Rock snob attitude, the firm belief that fifty thousand Elvis fans can't be right, just because there're so damn many of them, underlies a great deal of Indie music journalism, and the man who did most to shape the belief that Pop=crap was a philosopher from Frankfurt named Theodor Adorno.

> No matter how their products look and sound, they are successes, listeners are forced to sing them to themselves, not only because the most finely tooled machinery hammers it into them, but because the monopoly of the sound film prevents all other musical commodities, from which they might choose something else, from reaching them.[1]

No, it's not a posting on *Mess+Noise* about 'Australian Idol', that's Adorno from his 1932 essay 'On the Social Situation of Music'. Here, he accuses the music industry of offering the public substandard fare, which they, not knowing any better, eagerly stand in line for. Why is it substandard? *Because* it's mass-produced. According to Adorno, the conditions of Capitalism are built into the products of the music industry. Mass-production demands standardisation, so Pop music uses repetition to appeal to the largest number of people possible. This takes place both in the structure of the music—he heard it in the riffs and runs of Jazz, but would recognise it just as well in the recurring bassline of a Hip-hop track, for instance, or the endless bubbadubba of the commercial dance music that's evolved from Detroit Techno—but also from one hit song to the next. Pop music, he argues, requires no real engagement on the part of the listener, since everything it presents has been heard before. In other words, if you like the new song by The Strokes or Madonna, it's only because you've heard that beat or that chord progression—or that bit where they put the last line of the song before the chorus through the 'intercom' effect—in countless other songs; everything else is just window-dressing. The Pop fan has mistaken recognition for meaning: she is merely, to use Adorno's phrase, 'moving in the worn grooves of the familiar'.[2] It was this anxiety over repetition and mass-production in Pop that Kraftwerk exploited in the seventies with its 'factory worker' pose, and that Pink Floyd (and prog-Rock bands in general) took up a position against. 'Gawd', said Dave Gilmour, goggling at the flare-trousered masses grooving in the worn grooves of the familiar four-to-the-floor beat at his local disco. 'Ghastly!'[3]

Adorno's criticism of popular music is so rigorous that after a while you start to wonder whether a form of music exists, or has ever existed, that would satisfy all his demands for a non-repetitive, un-popular, serious, integral artform. Adorno argued that such music has existed at various times through history, but that, for the twentieth century, there was only one contender—the music of the second Viennese school, led by the composer Arnold

Schoenberg. This went through two distinct phases: first, the abandonment of the usual system of keys and harmony with the advent of atonality around 1909, and then, in the 1920s, the replacement of that system with a new one—Serialism.

84. ATONALLY YOURS

Schoenberg breaks the harmony barrier—but only because someone had to do it

Franz Liszt, one of the last great nineteenth-century composers, once said that every new composition should contain at least one new chord.[1] That's all very well, but what happens when you run out of chords? There's only so many notes in the scale, and of those, even less that sound nice when you play them together. In the work of late romantic composers like Mahler and Strauss, the strain is starting to show, as the search for new chords led to larger, stranger and more complex combinations of notes, always stopping short of what, to many, seemed like the logical next step—a step no one was prepared to take for fear of ruining it for everybody. After all, the rules of tonal harmony had been there for centuries, they were the guiding principle of Western art music—if they were broken, the result could be anarchy.

Still, Western classical music had come this far—didn't the composer have a duty to continue the tradition, even if it meant the abandonment of everything he held dear? This, at least, was the way Arnold Schoenberg saw it. Schoenberg's early reputation was built on the success of his chamber piece, *Verklarte Nacht (Transfigured Night)*, written at the end of the nineteenth century under the influence of Wagner. Personally, Schoenberg liked tonal harmony as it was, and would have preferred to leave it that way. But like Frodo Baggins on his quest to destroy the one true ring in the fires of Mordor, Schoenberg also knew that it was too late to turn back, and in 1908 he glumly shouldered his burden and set off into the scary, uncharted musical world that lay ahead of him—atonality.

Schoenberg's first atonal work was a setting of poems by Stefan George for his second string quartet, closely followed by another George adaptation, *Das Buch der Hangenden Garten.* It was weird, disturbing stuff—the unfamiliarity of music with no tonal center, written in no fixed key, naturally produced a mood of tension and unease. Schoenberg often referred to these early atonal works as Expressionist, and in some ways he can be seen as the musical equivalent of Van Gogh, cautiously but steadily dismantling the rules of tonality, as Van Gogh had with colour, and, in the strange new world this opened up, discovering new means of self-expression (Schoenberg was, himself, a fairly accomplished painter). Atonality expanded the language available to composers, creating, as Schoenberg said in 1937, 'a new approach to the expression of moods and characters'.[2] That those moods and characters were mostly unpleasant could be put down to the strife in Schoenberg's personal life (his very first atonal movement was composed during a month when his wife had left him)[3], as much as the turmoil of living in a world at war with itself.

The problem for Schoenberg, and, by extension, for European classical music as a whole, was that unease and psychic turmoil seemed to be the *only* kind of feelings Atonality was capable of generating. It was, in a nutshell, bad mood music, and as a result, Schoenberg and his followers Berg and Webern found that they had a lot of trouble getting their works performed and produced. Schoenberg later agreed that this was fair enough: 'It might have been a desire to get rid of this nightmare, of this unharmonious torture, of these unintelligible ideas, of this methodical madness—and I must admit: these were not bad men who felt this way.'[4] Atonality was no fun for the audience ('play *Verklarte Nacht*', they yelled), but that was to be expected. The bigger problem for Schoenberg was that it was no fun for the composer—having pushed beyond the barriers of traditional harmony, the composer was left floating in a tonal vacuum, with no system by which to organise his notes. After an attempt to wed atonal composition to a lighter, more satirical style in *Pierrot Lunaire*, Schoenberg fell quiet for the next eight years.

85. THE HISTORY OF THE FUTURE OF MUSIC

From Serialism to Minimalism

When Schoenberg piped up again in 1921, he claimed to have 'discovered something which will assure the supremacy of German music for the next hundred years'.[1] Again, Schoenberg, for all that his ideas seemed weird and unfamiliar, is mostly concerned with the preservation of tradition—it's just that he knew that if the tradition were to survive in the weird new world of the twentieth century, it had to find a language suitable to the tenor of the times—and that language, he believed, was his new 'method of composing with twelve tones'.

Twelve-tone music, or Serialism as it's sometimes called, is actually based on a very simple system. You lay out all twelve notes of the scale and place them in whatever order you choose—this is the 'series'. Now, to make a serial composition, you take this series and use it any way you like—run it forwards or backwards, play it high or low on any instrument you choose, race through it at a millions miles an hour on a woodwind or have it unfold gently and slowly on a double bass. You can even play it backwards or invert it—but you have to keep using those notes in that order. This might seem like a boring way to make music, always using the same row of notes, but Schoenberg was convinced that it represented the way forwards. In a sense, it was no more restrictive than the old system of keys—there were rules, sure, but a good composer could work within those rules to create works of great, expressive beauty, and it was certainly a big improvement on the anarchy of Atonality. Well, for the composers it was, anyway. For most music audiences, Serialism was every bit as baffling and irritating as Atonality. Nevertheless, Schoenberg and his followers Webern and Berg devoted themselves to Serialism, as did many younger composers in the coming decades, including Pierre Boulez and Karlheinz Stockhausen. Schoenberg, however, wouldn't explain Serialism to just anyone. After he moved to the United States in the 1930s, he became a music teacher, and here the man who was once regarded as 'the Satan of Modernistic music' (his own words) taught his young pupils nothing but the laws of harmony as Beethoven would have learned them. Having recently given up his initial hope of becoming an architect, John Cage showed up at Schoenberg's house around 1934, and promised the composer that he would devote his life to music; Schoenberg, having received this guarantee, agreed to teach Cage free of charge. According to David Revill, Cage dutifully learned scales and counterpoint before one day plucking up courage to ask the irascible composer about twelve-tone composition. 'That's none of your business', said Schoenberg.[2]

Schoenberg was not the only European composer to relocate to America around this time. The same mass exodus of European artists and intellectuals that brought the Bauhaus luminaries to the New World brought with it innovators from the field of music as well. As a result, Serialism would strike deep roots in the United States. This, combined with Boulez's almost messianic devotion to Serialism in Paris, made twelve-tone the dominant musical style of the post-war years[3]—for those within the academies, if not for the great unwashed without.

The Minimalists' revolt into pretty, repetitive tonal music was in many ways a reaction to the strictures of Serialism. In the early sixties, Philip Glass and Steve Reich both came up hard against the dominance of twelve-tone music in universities, and eventually decided that it was not for them. It might be the way forwards for the European classical tradition, but what was so great about that? Glass and Reich had, respectively, discovered the music of Ravi Shankar and John Coltrane. Both improvised melodically within a static harmonic framework, which was a relief after all the restless heaving about of Serialism, and neither could care less about ensuring 'the supremacy of German music'. When Boulez said that it was 'historically necessary' to compose according to the twelve-tone system, Reich thought to himself: 'Well, just count me out of history, then.'[4]

In this, as with their interest in Rock and Roll and Soul music, the Minimalists were on the right track. In the end, the music that spoke most truthfully and uncompromisingly about the lives of human beings in the modern world came from nowhere near the conservatories of Vienna, or from the 'Society for Private Musical Performances', where Schoenberg and his disciples could audition each others', difficult, demanding atonal works without having tomatoes thrown at them. It came from the Mississipi Delta—which is probably why it's called 'the blues', and not 'the alienations'. Here, an oppressed, transplanted people created, from the materials available to them, music that was both complex and repetitive, tonal and atonal, and deeply, intuitively Expressionistic.

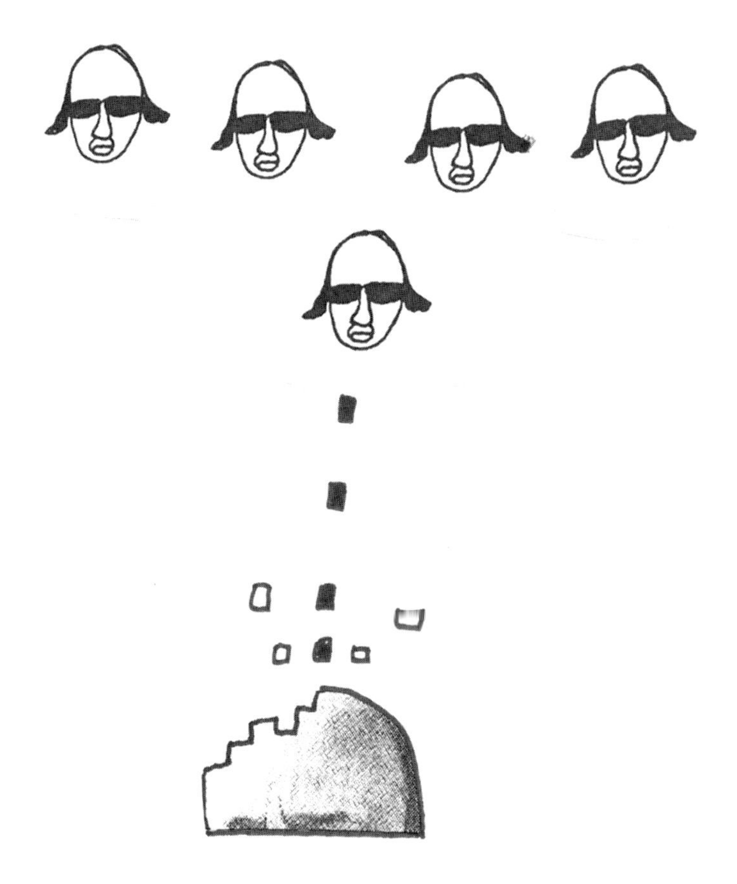

86. VERY ANGRY

Theodor Adorno and the truth about Pop music

By 1925, Schoenberg's earlier, atonal works had a new admirer. It was this curiously un-hummable music that Theodor Adorno believed was the only form of composition with any claim to be serious, worthwhile art in the twentieth century. Indeed, Adorno saw the universal dislike heaped upon Schoenberg's atonal music as proof of its serious-ness. Schoenberg, he wrote in 'On The Social Situation of Music', 'offers such a perfected and rational total organization that it cannot possibly be compatible with the present social constitution.' Because Schoenberg's music has too much reality in it for the fans of Tchaikovsky and Louis Armstrong to handle, because it reflects too starkly the true tenor of the times, they have no choice but to 'take up an offensive position and call upon nature for assistance against the attack on consciousness encountered in Schoenberg'.[1]

Adorno maintains that the vast majority of the radio-listening, record-buying public are not really engaging seriously with music at all—they're just consuming. Unlike his colleague Walter Benjamin, with whom he maintained a long-running correspondence, Adorno was convinced that popular media like film, photography and sound recording, were having a negative effect on art and its appreciation. Radio, he believed, reduced music, even 'good' music like Beethoven, to a series of effects and motifs, so that people just listen out for the bits that they like, without engaging with the work of art as a whole. He called this 'commodity listening', and compared it to ready-mix pancakes—easy to prepare, undoubtedly tasty, but ultimately bad for you.[2]

Again, Adorno's position here finds many parallels in the division between 'serious' (underground, Indie, cutting edge) music and Pop music today. In 2003, a letter was sent to triple j from a fan of the US Punk band NOFX, after a song of the band's was added to the station's playlist. The fan (who signed off as 'Very Angry') complained that the band was 'too good' for the station, and demanded that the song be taken *off* the playlist. In this, Very Angry was taking a basically Adornite position towards the effect of radio upon 'serious' music. For Adorno, as for Very Angry, serious art is (to use Robert Witkin's phrase) an 'island of resistance'. Playing it on the radio merely reduces it to the level of kitsch, so that the NOFX song suffers the same fate as Beethoven's *Fifth*, which, Adorno felt, was being listened to by the radio audience as though it were nothing more than its melody—the catchy bits that people like. So, in the case of NOFX, what was once a serious work of art, which included, at every level, a demand that the world be changed, has become another song in the hit parade. 'It would be absurd', as Adorno says of Beethoven on the radio, 'to maintain that it could be received by the listener as anything but entertainment.'[3]

More recently, a musician was talking to me about the runaway popularity of a local group, whose new single had recently been featured in an episode of 'The OC'. Until that point, they'd been an Indie band with a small but solid fan base, a group of people who'd invested a certain amount of time and effort on a 'serious' appreciation of the band's music. Now that they'd been on TV, all sorts of people who'd never heard of them until last week were coming to their shows—because they liked that song, just like they liked Nickelback last week and Keane the week before. 'The people who are going to those shows', said my friend, 'don't really like music—they just like ... *stuff*.' This is what Adorno meant when he talked about 'commodity listening'.

People who like Pop music might say that it's none of Adorno's business *how* they listen to it. Beethoven's *Fifth*, NOFX, and that new song from 'The OC' just make them feel good—what's wrong with that? But according to Adorno, this is the biggest problem of all. Adorno says that this mode of listening is lulling you into believing that the world is OK when in reality we are living in a nightmare of alienation created by Capitalism. The pop music they play on the radio, he claims in 1945's 'A Social Critique of Radio Music', 'serves to keep listeners from criticising social realities ... In this respect radio music offers a new function not inherent in music as an art—the function of creating smugness and self-satisfaction.'[4] And just in case you think listening to Bob Dylan or The International Noise Conspiracy or Michael Franti lets you off the hook because they're trying, through the messages in their lyrics, to make the world a better place, you'd better think again. 'All objectivist music [that's you too, Franti] has the intention of diverting attention away from social conditions', he wrote in 1932. 'It attempts to make the individual believe he's not lonely, but rather close to all others in a relationship portrayed to him by music ...' Even NOFX, for all its DIY integrity, would be fatally compromised in Adorno's eyes by those catchy riffs and shout-along choruses.

In other words, as long as you're sitting at home and singing along to protest music, or watching the band at a festival and punching your fist in the air, you're actually feeling *good* about the world, because the song makes you feel that you're part of a community in which the revolution has already taken place. Meanwhile, you do nothing but buy more CDs and T-shirts, and the world stays as it is. This might seem a little far-fetched, but imagine if he's right! What if Rock music, which we are usually led to believe is a creative force for good, or at the very least a harmless way to pass the time, has been lulling us into a passive, coma-like state while the world continues to get worse and we do nothing? It's like *The Matrix*, only with alienation instead of actual aliens—now *that's* worth fighting over the radio for.

ENDNOTES

1. THE END OF AN EAR-A

1. Fat Mike, posted on NOFX official website, May 2000. nofxofficialwebsite.com.
2. Marshall McLuhan and Gerald E. Stearn, a dialogue published in *McLuhan Hot and Cool*, Penguin, London, 1967.
3. Howard Luck Gossage, 'You Can See Why the Mighty Would be Curious', reprinted in *McLuhan Hot and Cool*, Penguin, London, 1967.
4. Marshall McLuhan and Quentin Fiore, *The Medium is the Massage*, London, Penguin, 1967.

2. THE MEDIUM IS ... THE MASSAGE

1. John Cage, 'Writing for the second time through Finnegans Wake', sound recording, 1978, found on UBUWEB audio archive: ubuweb.com
2. Marshall McLuhan and Quentin Fiore, *War and Peace in the Global Village*, Bantam, New York, 1968.
3. James Joyce, *Finnegans Wake*, Penguin Classics, London, 2000.
4. John Cage, op. cit.

3. THE FINNEGANS WAKE

1. Sigmund Freud, 'Seven White Wolves', reprinted in Guido Almansi and Claude Beguin, *Theatre of Sleep*, Picador, London, 1987.
2. Sigmund Freud, *The Interpretation of Dreams*, Penguin, Middlesex, 1976.
3. Anthony Burgess, *A Shorter Finnegans Wake*, Faber and Faber, London, 1965.
4. James Joyce, *Finnegans Wake*, Penguin Classics, London, 2000.
5. Lewis Carroll, *The Annotated Alice*, ed. Martin Gardner, Penguin, London, 2000.
6. Chris Rodley, *Lynch on Lynch*, Faber and Faber, London, 2000.

4. BREAK THE CODE, SOLVE THE CRIME

1. *Twin Peaks*, First Season Special Edition, Paramount DVD, 2004.
2. Sigmund Freud, *The Interpretation of Dreams*, Penguin, Middlesex, 1976.
3. Chris Rodley, *Lynch on Lynch*, Faber and Faber, London, 2000.

5. LIE DOWN ON THE COUCH ...

1. Herbert Read, *Surrealism*, Faber and Faber, London, 1936.
2. Andre Breton, *Selections*, ed. Mark Polizotti, University of California Press, Berkley, 2003.
3. Ruth Brandon, *Surreal Lives*, Pan Macmillan, London, 2000.
4. Andre Breton, op. cit.
5. Ruth Brandon, op. cit.
6. Andre Breton, *Nadja*, Penguin Classics, London, 1999.
7. *Surrealism, Revolution By Night*, exhibition catalogue, National Gallery of Australia, Canberra, 1993.
8. Meryle Secrest, *Salvador Dali, The Surrealist Jester*, Paladin, London, 1986.

6. SURREALISM IN SPACE

1. Kathi Christen and Adrienne Thiemer, *H. R. Giger's Retrospective*, ABC Verlag, Beverly Hills, CA, 1997.

7. THIS IS NOT AN APPLE

1. A. M. Hammacher, *Magritte*, Thames and Hudson, London, 1986.
2. A. M. Hammacher, op. cit.

8. DAYDREAM BELIEVERS

1. Chris Rodley, *Lynch on Lynch*, Faber and Faber, London, 2000.
2. *The Shining*, Warner Brothers DVD, 2001.
3. *Twin Peaks*, First Season Special Edition, Paramount DVD, 2004.
4. Jacque Meuris, *Magritte*, Taschen, Koln, 2004.
5. Jacque Meuris, op. cit.

9. WALK AWAY RENEE

1. Hipgnosis and George Hardie, Hipgnosis: Walk Away Renee, Paper Tiger / Dragons World, Surrey, UK, 1978.
2. Ian MacDonald, *The People's Music*, Pimlico, London, 2003.
3. Hipgnosis and George Hardie, op. cit.
4. The Mars Volta, *Frances the Mute*, Universal CD, 2005.
5. Chris Rodley, *Lynch on Lynch*, Faber and Faber, London, 2000.

10. HAPPENING THINGS

1. Clement Greenberg, 'Modernist Painting', reprinted in Gregory Battcock, *The New Art*, Dutton, New York, 1966.
2. Adrian Henri, *Total Art: Environments, Happenings and Performance*, Praeger, New York, 1974.

11. SPACE INVADERS

1. Adrian Henri, *Total Art: Environments, Happenings and Performance*, Praeger, New York, 1974.

2. Alexandra Monroe, *Scream Against the Sky: Japanese Art After 1945*, Abrams, New York, 1994.
3. Gilbert Perlein and Bruno Cora, *Yves Klein: Long Live the Immaterial*, Delano Greenidge Edition, New York, 2001.
4. Sidra Stich, *Yves Klein*, Hayward Gallery, London, 1995.

12. ROCK AND ROLL

1. Albert Camus, *The Myth of Sisyphus*, Penguin Classics, Middlesex, 1986.
2. Albert Camus, *The Outsider*, Penguin, London, 1982.
3. Albert Camus, *The Outsider*, op. cit.
4. The Cure, *Standing On The Beach*, Elektra LP, 1986.
5. Albert Camus, *The Outsider*, op. cit.
6. The Beatles, *Revolver*, Parlophone / EMI LP, 1966.
7. Frederick Karl and Leo Hamalian, *The Existential Imagination*, Picador, London, 1973.
8. The Dust Brothers, 'This is Your Life', *Fight Club*, Restless CD, 1999.
9. Ian Macdonald, *Revolution in the Head: The Beatles' Records and the Sixties*, Pimlico, London, 1995.
10. Jean-Paul Sartre, *Being and Nothingness*, Routledge Classics, London, 2003.
11. The Dust Brothers, *Fight Club (OST)*, Restless CD, 1999.
12. Jean-Paul Sartre, *Nausea*, Penguin Classics, London, 2000.
13. Jean-Paul Sartre, *Nausea*, op. cit.
14. Jean-Paul Sartre, *Being and Nothingness*, op. cit.
15. Nik Cohn, 'Another Saturday Night', reprinted in *Ball the Wall: Nik Cohn in the Age of Rock*, Picador, London, 1989.
16. *Saturday Night Fever*, Paramount DVD, 2002.

13. STAYIN' ALIVE

1. Peter Shapiro, *Turn the Beat Around: The Secret History of Disco*, Faber and Faber, London, 2005.
2. Nik Cohn, *Awopbopaloobopalopbamboom*, Paladin, London, 1972.
3. Nik Cohn, 'Feverish', *Rolling Stone* magazine, December 1997.
4. Nik Cohn, *I am still the greatest says Johnny Angelo*, Penguin, London, 1970.
5. Nik Cohn, *Ball on the Wall*,
6. Don DeLillo, *Underworld*, Picador, London, 1997.

14. VIOLENT PORNOGRAPHY

1. Gregory Corso, 'Bomb', reprinted in Barry Miles, *Beat Collection*, Virgin Books, London, 2005.
2. Barry Miles, *The Beat Hotel: Ginsberg, Burroughs and Corso in Paris, 1958–1963*, Grove Press, New York, 2000.

3. James Campbell, *Paris Interzone: Richard Wright, Lolita, Boris Vian and others on the Left Bank, 1946–1960*, Minerva, London, 1995.
4. Simone De Beauvoir, 'Must We Burn Sade?', reprinted in *The Marquis De Sade—The 120 Days of Sodom*, Arrow, London, 1989.
5. Jeff Nuttall, *Bomb Culture*, Paladin, London, 1970.
6. Francine du Plessix Gray, *At Home with the Marquis de Sade*, Pimlico, London, 2000.
7. Marquis de Sade, *Justine*, 1791
8. *Surrealism, Revolution By Night*, exhibition catalogue, National Gallery of Australia, Canberra, 1993.
9. Herbert Read, *Surrealism*, Faber and Faber, London, 1936.

15. YOU LITTLE LIBERTINE

1. *Surrealism, Revolution By Night*, exhibition catalogue, National Gallery of Australia, Canberra, 1993.
2. The Pixies, 'Debaser', *Doolittle*, 4AD, LP, 1989.
3. Ruth Brandon, *Surreal Lives*, Pan Macmillan, London, 2000.
4. The Pixies, *Doolittle*, 4AD LP, 1989.
5. The Breeders, *Last Splash*, 4AD LP, 1993.
6. Kim Deal, interview with Richard Kingsmill, triple j, 1993.

16. DE LA SADE

1. Francine du Plessix Gray, *At Home with the Marquis de Sade*, Pimlico, London, 2000.
2. De La Soul, 'I Can Do Anything (Delacratic)', *3 Feet High and Rising*, Tommy Boy LP, 1989.
3. De La Soul, op. cit.

17. DESTROY PASSERS-BY

1. Ruth Brandon, *Surreal Lives*, Pan Macmillan, London, 2000.
2. Andre Breton, *Selections*, ed. Mark Polizotti, University of California Press, Berkley, 2003.
3. Jon Savage, *England's Dreaming*, Faber and Faber, London, 1991.
4. Jon Savage, op.cit.
5. Juliet Ash, 'The Philosophy of the Catwalk' in Juliet Ash and Elizabeth Wilson, *Chic Thrills: A Fashion Reader*, University of California Press, Berkley, 1992.
6. Jon Savage, op. cit.
7. John Lydon, 'Anarchy in the UK', *Never Mind the Bollocks,* LP
8. Simon Ford, *The Situationist International: A User's Guide*, Black Dog Publishing, London, 2005.

18. THE DIVINE MARQUIS

1. John Weightman, *The Concept of the Avant-Garde: Explorations in Modernism*, Alcove Press, London, 1973.

2. Simone De Beauviour, 'Must We Burn Sade?', reprinted in *The Marquis De Sade—The 120 Days of Sodom*, Arrow, London, 1989.
3. Francine du Plessix Gray, *At Home with the Marquis de Sade*, Pimlico, London, 2000.
4. James Campbell, *Paris Interzone: Richard Wright, Lolita, Boris Vian and others on the Left Bank, 1946–1960*, Minerva, London, 1995.

19. DIRTY BOOKS

1. Maurice Girodias, *The Olympia Reader: Selections from the Traveller's Companion Series*, North Star Line, New York, 1991.
2. Maurice Girodias, op. cit.
3. Ted Morgan, *Literary Outlaw: The Life and Times of William S. Burroughs*, Pimlico, London, 1991.

20. THE MAN WHO TAUGHT HIS ASSHOLE TO TALK

1. Ted Morgan, *Literary Outlaw: The Life and Times of William S. Burroughs*, Pimlico, London, 1991.
2. Ted Morgan, op. cit.
3. William Burroughs, *The Naked Lunch*, Corgi, London, 1972.
4. Andre Breton, *Selections*, ed. Mark Polizotti, University of California Press, Berkley, 2003.
5. Oliver Harris, *The Letters of William S. Burroughs: 1945 to 1959*, Picador, London, 1993.
6. William Burroughs, *Queer*, Picador, London, 1986.
7. Oliver Harris, op. cit.

21. LESBIAN SARDINES

1. Dawn Ades, 'Dada and Surrealism' in *Concepts of Modern Art*, Thames and Hudson, London, 1990.
2. Barry Miles, *The Beat Hotel: Ginsberg, Burroughs and Corso in Paris, 1958–1963*, Grove Press, New York, 2000.
3. Barry Miles, op. cit.
4. Oliver Harris, *The Letters of William S. Burroughs: 1945 to 1959*, Picador, London, 1993.
5. Oliver Harris, op. cit.
6. William Burroughs, *The Soft Machine*, Paladin, London, 1986.

22. RETURN ME BACK TO THE CIGARETTE

1. Clinton Heylin, *Bob Dylan: Behind The Shades*, Penguin, London, 2000.
2. *No Direction Home: Bob Dylan*, Apple DVD, 2005.
3. *Re: Search—Industrial Culture Handbook*, Re: Search, San Francisco, 1991.
4. Jonathan Miller, *McLuhan*, Fontana, London, 1971

5. William S. Burroughs with Daniel Odier, *The Job*, Penguin, London, 1974.
6. William S. Burroughs, *Break Through in Grey Room*, Sub Rosa CD, 2001.

23. THE SOUND OF SILENCE

1. David Revill, *The Roaring Silence, John Cage: A Life*, Arcade Publishing, New York, 1992.
2. Douglas Kahn, *Noise, Water, Meat: A History of Sound in the Arts*, The MIT Press, Massachusetts, 2001.
3. Calvin Tomkins, *The Bride and the Bachelors*, Penguin, New York, 1976.
4. David Revill, op. cit.
5. Geoff Smith and Nicola Walker-Smith, *American Originals*, Faber and Faber, New York, 1994.

24. THE SOUND MEASURER

1. David Revill, *The Roaring Silence, John Cage: A Life*, Arcade Publishing, new York, 1992.
2. Douglas Kahn, *Noise, Water, Meat: A History of Sound in the Arts*, The MIT Press, Masssachusetts, 2001.
3. Christopher Cox, *Audio Culture: Readings in Modern Music*, Continuum, New York, 2004.

25. HARDER, BETTER, SLOWER, STRONGER

1. John Cale and Victor Bockris, *What's Welsh for Zen?*, Bloomsbury, London, 1999.
2. Tony Conrad, 'Lyssophobia: On Four Violins', reprinted in *Audio Culture: Readings in Modern Music*, Continuum, New York, 2004.
3. Geoff Smith and Nicola Walker-Smith, *American Originals*, Faber and Faber, London, 1994.
4. Mark Weber, 'Dream Encounters' in *The Wire*, December 1998.

26. THE WELL-FED PIANO

1. Hannah Higgins, *Fluxus Experience*, University of California Press, Berkley, 2002.
2. Emmett Williams, 'Rich food is bad for your heart' in *The Readymade Boomerang: Certain Relations in 20th Century Art*, Biennale of Sydney catalogue, Sydney, 1990.
3. Hannah Higgins, op. cit.
4. Hannah Higgins, op. cit.
5. Emmett Williams, 'Rich food is bad for your heart' in *The Readymade Boomerang: Certain Relations in 20th Century Art*, Biennale of Sydney catalogue, Sydney, 1990.

27. THE YEAR OF THE SCAVENGER

1. Al Hansen, *Intermedia Poetry / Venus Rap*, sound recording, 1992, found on UBUWEB audio archive: ubuweb.com
2. Hannah Higgins, *Fluxus Experience*, University of California Press, Berkley, 2002.
3. Barney Hoskyns, 'Yep, it's the folk-punk poke-fun(k) hip-hop knee-drop kid' in *World Art*, 1998.
4. Beck, *Midnite Vultures*, Geffen CD, 1999.
5. Beck, *Mellow Gold*, Geffen CD, 1994.
6. Barney Hoskyns, *Waiting for the Sun*, Bloomsbury, London, 2003.
7. Apollinaire, *Selected Poems*, Penguin, Middlesex, 1970.
8. Andre Breton, *Black Forest*, ed. Mark Poizotti, University of California Press, Berkley, 2003.
9. Andre Breton, *Selections*, ed. Mark Polizotti, University of California Press, Berkley, 2003.
10. Bob Dylan, *Tarantula*, Granada Publishing, London, 1971.
11. William S. Burroughs with Daniel Odier, *The Job*, Penguin, London, 1974.
12. Christopher Sandford, *Bowie: Loving the Alien*, Warner Books, New York, 1997.
13. *Futurama*, 'Bendin in the Wind', 20th Century Fox DVD, 2002.
14. Beck, *Odelay*, Geffen CD, 1996.
15. Andre Breton, op. cit.

28. SATORI

1. Alexandra Monroe, *Scream Against the Sky: Japanese Art After 1945*, Abrams, 1994.
2. Hannah Higgins, *Fluxus Experience*, University of California Press, Berkley, 2002.
3. B.H. Friedman, *Jackson Pollock: Energy Made Visible*, Weidenfeld and Nicholson, London, 1973.
4. Emmett Williams, 'Rich Food is Bad for Your Heart' in *The Readymade Boomerang*, Biennale of Sydney catalogue, Sydney, 1990.

29. THE ART PILL

1. Joseph Beuys, Energy Plan for the Western Man, Four Walls Eight Windows, New York, 1993.
2. Joseph Beuys, Energy Plan for the Western Man, Four Walls Eight Windows, New York, 1993.
3. Emmett Williams, 'Rich Food is Bad for Your Heart' in *The Readymade Boomerang*, Biennale of Sydney catalogue, Sydney, 1990.
4. Joseph Beuys: Drawings, Objects and Prints, Institute for Foreign Cultural Relations, Dusseldorf, 1989.

5. William Furlong, *Audio Arts: Discourse and Practice in Contemporary Art*, Academy Editions, New York, 1994.

30. ART AND THE PEOPLE [NEED TO CHECK THESE]

1. Calvin Tomkins, *Duchamp: A Biography*, Pimlico, London, 1996.
2. Calvin Tomkins, op. cit.
3. William Furlong, *Audio Arts: Discourse and Practice in Contemporary Art*, Academy Editions, New York, 1994.
4. Calvin Tomkins, op. cit.
5. Ruth Brandon, *Surreal Lives*, Pan Macmillan, London, 2000.
6. Calvin Tomkins, op. cit.

31. A RIDDLE TO FREE THE MIND

1. Beck, *Odelay*, Geffen CD, 1996.
2. Joseph G. Schloss, *Making Beats: The Art of Sample-Based Hip-Hop*, Wesleyan University Press, Connecticut, 2004.
3. Marcel Duchamp, *The Writings of Marcel Duchamp*, Da Capo, New York, 1989.
4. Angus Batey, 'Rhymin' and Stealin" in *Mojo*, 2003.
5. Calvin Tomkins, *Duchamp: A Biography*, Pimlico, London, 1996.
6. Ted Morgan, *Literary Outlaw: The Life and Times of William S. Burroughs*, Pimlico, London, 1991.

32. RE-COMMODE-IFICATION

1. Marcel Duchamp, *The Writings of Marcel Duchamp*, Da Capo, New York, 1989.
2. Brian Eno and Peter Schmidt, *Oblique Strategies*, fifth edition, Opal/Obliquecards, London, 1996.
3. Eric Tamm, *Brian Eno: His Music and the Vertical Colour of Sound*, Da Capo, New York, 1995.
4. Brian Eno, 'Duchamp's Fountain' in Brian Eno, *A Year With Swollen Appendices*, Faber and Faber, London, 1996.

33. INDETERMINACY—THAT'S WHAT I WANT!

1. Clive Bell, 'Radio-active' in *The Wire*, September 1996.
2. David Revill, *The Roaring Silence, John Cage: A Life*, Arcade Publishing, New York, 1992.
3. Sonic Youth, *SYR 1*, Sonic Youth Recordings, 1997.
4. Sonic Youth, *Goodbye 20th Century*, Sonic Youth Recordings, 1998.
5. An anthology of noise and electronic music / first a-chronology volume #1, Sub Rosa, 2001.
6. Sonic Youth, Radio Interview with Richard Kingsmill, triple j, 2002.

34. AGAINST AESTHETICS

1. Calvin Tomkins, *The Bride and the Bachelors*, Penguin, New York,1976.
2. Dawn Ades, 'Dada and Surrealism' in *Concepts of Modern Art*, Thames and Hudson, London, 1990.
3. Arturo Schwartz, *The Complete Works of Marcel Duchamp*, Delano Greenidge Editions, New York, 2000.
4. Marcel Duchamp, *The Writings of Marcel Duchamp*, Da Capo, New York, 1989.

35. BUSINESS ART AND THE ART BUSINESS

1. Benjamin Buchloh, 'Andy Warhol's One-Dimensional Art' in *Andy Warhol: A Retrospective*, Museum of Modern Art, New York, 1989.
2. Arturo Schwartz, *The Complete Works of Marcel Duchamp*, Delano Greenidge Editions, New York, 2000.
3. Andy Warhol, TV interview, 1964. Posted by Appleshe on YouTube.
4. Andy Warhol, op. cit.
5. Steven Watson, *Factory Made: Warhol and the Sixties*, Pantheon Books, New York, 2003.
6. Andy Warhol and Pat Hackett, *Popism: The Warhol 60s*, Pimlico, London, 1996.
7. Benjamin Buchloh, op. cit.
8. Steven Watson, op. cit.
9. Victor Bockris and Gerard Malanga, *Up-Tight: The Story of the Velvet Underground*, Omnibus Press, New York, 1996.
10. Andy Warhol, *From A to B and Back Again: The Philosophy of Andy Warhol*, First Harvest / HBJ, Florida, 1977.

36. THE APPEAL OF REAL

1. Jack Smith, *Wait for me at the Bottom of the Pool*, High Risk Books, London, 1997.
2. Susan Sontag, *Against Interpretation*, Vintage, London, 2001
3. Jack Smith, op. cit.
4. Jack Smith, op. cit.
5. Andy Warhol, *From A to B and Back Again: The Philosophy of Andy Warhol*, First Harvest / HBJ, Florida, 1977
6. Jonathan Ross, *The Incredibly Strange Film Book*, Simon and Schuster, London, 1993.
7. Scott Alexander and Larry Karaszewski, *Ed Wood* (original screenplay), Faber and Faber, London, 1995.

37. THE FLANEUR

1. *Surrealism, Revolution By Night*, exhibition catalogue, National Gallery of Australia, Canberra, 1993.

2. Jack Smith, *Wait for me at the Bottom of the Pool*, High Risk Books, London, 1997.
3. Andre Breton, *Selections*, ed. Mark Polizotti, University of California Press, Berkley, 2003.
4. Andre Breton, *Nadja*, Penguin Classics, London, 1999.
5. Walter Benjamin, *Illuminations*, Pimlico, London, 1999.
6. Walter Benjamin, op. cit.
7. Terry Gilliam, *Animations of Mortality*, Eyre Methuen, London, 1978.
8. Dawn Ades, *Photomontage*, Thames and Hudson, London, 1976.

38. NAVEL-GAZING VERSUS BELLY-DANCING, PART1

1. Dawn Ades, 'Dada and Surrealism' in *Concepts of Modern Art*, Thames and Hudson, London, 1990.
2. Peter Conrad, *Modern Times Modern Places*, Thames and Hudson, London, 1999.
3. Jon Savage, *England's Dreaming*, Faber and Faber, London, 1991.
4. Walter Benjamin, *Selected Writings: Volume 2, Part 1, 1927–1930*, The Belknap Press of Harvard University Press, Cambridge, Mas., 1999.

39. BEAUTY IS IN THE STREET

1. Jamie Reid and Jon Savage, *Up They Rise: The Incomplete Works of Jamie Reid*, Faber and Faber, London, 1987.
2. Guy Debord, *The Society of the Spectacle*, Zone Books, New York, 1995.
3. Simon Ford, *The Situationist International: A User's Guide*, Black Dog Publishing, London, 2005.
4. Jon Savage, *England's Dreaming*, Faber and Faber, London, 1991.
5. Ruth Brandon, *Surreal Lives*, Pan Macmillan, London, 2000.
6. John Harris, *The Last Party: Britpop, Blair and the Demise of English Rock*, Fourth Estate, London, 2003.
7. Simon Ford, *The Situationist International: A User's Guide*, Black Dog Publishing, London, 2005.
8. Simon Ford, op. cit.
9. Jamie Reid and Jon Savage, op. cit.
10. Fast Product, *The First Year Plan* (compilation), EMI LP, 1979.

40. CROSSING OVER

1. Simon Ford, *The Situationist International: A User's Guide*, Black Dog Publishing, London, 2005.
2. The Human League, *Dare*, Virgin LP, 1981.
3. Public Image Limited, 'This is not a love song', Virgin 12", 1983.
4. ABC, *The Lexicon of Love*, Phonogram LP, 1982.

41. NAVEL-GAZING VERSUS BELLY-DANCING, PART 2

1. Peter Watson, *A Terrible Beauty: The People and Ideas that Shaped the Modern World*, Phoenix Press, London, 2004.
2. Robert Motherwell and the New York school, *Storming The Citadel*, RM Arts Video, 1991.
3. Andy Warhol and Pat Hackett, *Popism: The Warhol 60s*, Pimlico, London, 1996.
4. Leo Steinberg, 'Contemporary Art and the Plight of its Public' in Gregory Battcock, *The New Art*, Dutton, New York, 1966.
5. Walter Benjamin, *Illuminations*, Pimlico, London, 1999.
6. Benjamin Buchloh, 'Andy Warhol's One-Dimensional Art' in *Andy Warhol: A Retrospective*, Museum of Modern Art, New York, 1989.
7. Hugh Kenner, 'Understanding McLuhan' in *McLuhan Pro & Con*, Penguin, Baltimore, 1969.
8. Walter Benjamin, op. cit.

42. MACHINE ART

1. Ruth Brandon, *Surreal Lives*, Pan Macmillan, London, 2000.
2. Mel Gooding, *Surrealist Games*, Redstone Press, London, 1992.
3. Camilla Gray, *The Russian Experiment in Art*, Abrams, New York, 1962.
4. Maynard Solomon (ed.), *Marxism and Art*, Alfred A. Knopf, New York, 1973.
5. Maynard Solomon, op. cit.
6. Dawn Ades, *Photomontage*, Thames and Hudson, London, 1976.
7. Charles Jencks, *Modern Movements in Architecture*, Doubleday Anchor, London, 1971.

43. THE SHARP EDGE OF THE WEDGE VS THE FRAYED END OF THE PAINTBRUSH, PART 1

1. Dawn Ades, *Photomontage*, Thames and Hudson, London, 1976.
2. Camilla Gray, *The Russian Experiment in Art*, Abrams, New York, 1962.
3. Franz Ferdinand, *You Could Have it So Much Better*, Domino CD, 2005.
4. Steve Edwards and Paul Wood, *Art of the Avant-Gardes*, Yale University Press, London, 2004.

44. CRAZY BALDHEADS

1. Frank Whitford, *The Bauhaus*, Thames and Hudson, London, 1984.
2. Frank Whitford, op. cit.
3. Frank Whitford, op. cit.

45. HOLY MAHOGANY

1. Frank Whitford, *The Bauhaus*, Thames and Hudson, London, 1984.
2. Alan Bullock, *Hitler: A Study In Tyranny*, Penguin, Middlesex, 1965.
3. *Bauhaus: The face of the 20th Century*, RM Arts Video, 1994.
4. *Bauhaus*, op. cit.
5. Charles Jencks, *Modern Movements In Architecture*, Doubleday Anchor, New York, 1971.
6. David Revill, *The Roaring Silence, John Cage: A Life*, Arcade Publishing, New York, 1992.
7. Jonathan Glancey, *20th Century Architecture*, Carlton, London, 1998.

46. WORKER HOUSING

1. Richard Weston, *Modernism*, Phaidon, London, 1996.
2. Frank Whitford, *The Bauhaus*, Thames and Hudson, London, 1984.
3. Charles Jencks, *Modern Movements in Architecture*, Doubleday Anchor, New York, 1971.
4. Charles Jencks and Karl Kropf, *Theories and Manifestos of Contemporary Architecture*, Wiley-Academy, Sussex, 2006.
5. *St Louis Post-Dispatch.*

47. THE END OF MODERN ARCHITECTURE

1. Rob Krier, 'Urban Space', reprinted in Charles Jencks and Karl Kropf, *Theories and Manifestoes of Contemporary Architecture*, Wiley-Academy, Sussex, 2006.
2. Philip Johnson, 'The Seven Crutches of Modern Architecture, reprinted in Charles Jencks and Karl Kropf, op. cit.
3. Charles Jencks, *Modern Movements in Architecture*, Doubleday Anchor, New York, 1971.
4. Jencks and Knopf, op. cit.
5. Jencks and Knopf, op. cit.

48. THE END OF MODERN ART

1. Clement Greenberg, 'Modernist Painting', reprinted in Gregory Battcock, *The New Art*, Dutton, New York, 1966.
2. Ellen G. Landau, *Reading Abstract Expressionism*, Yale University Press, New Haven, 2005.
3. Andy Warhol, *From A to B and Back Again: The Philosophy of Andy Warhol*, First Harvest / HBJ, Florida, 1977.
4. Leo Steinberg, 'Contemporary Art and the Plight of its Public', reprinted in Gregory Battcock, op. cit.
5. Charles Jencks, *Modern Movements In Architecture*, Doubleday Anchor, New York, 1971.

49. UP FOR SALE

1. Simon Malpas, *The Postmodern*, Routledge, London, 2005.
2. International Noise Conspiracy,radio interview with Robbie Buck, triple j, 2006.
3. International Noise Conspiracy, *Up For Sale*, Burning Heart Records CD, 2002.
4. Blondie, *Parallel Lines*, Chrysalis LP, 1978.
5. Bryan Ferry, *These Foolish Things*, Polydor LP, 1973.
6. Simon Frith and Howard Horne, *Art Into Pop*, Methuen, London, 1987.
7. Michael Compton, *Pop Art*, Hamlyn, London, 1970.
8. Barry Lazell and Dafydd Rees, *Bryan Ferry & Roxy Music*, Proteus Books, New York, 1982.
9. Roxy Music, *Greatest Hits*, EG Records LP, 1977.
10. Walter Benjamin, *Illuminations*, Pimlico, London, 1999.
11. Roxy Music, *Roxy Music*, Island LP 1972,
12. Scissor Sisters, *Scissor Sisters*, Polydor CD, 2004.
13. Pink Floyd, *Mojo Special Edition*, Pink Floyd, 2004.
14. Andrew Holleran, 'Dancer from the Dance', reprinted in *The Faber Book of Pop*, Faber and Faber, London, 1995.
15. Simon Malpas, *The Postmodern*, Routledge, London, 2005.
16. International Noise Conspiracy, *Bigger Cages*, Longer Chains, Burning Heart Records CD, 2002.

50. MODERN LOVERS

1. *Lipstick Traces* (compilation), Rough Trade, 1993.
2. Umbro Apollonio, *The Documents of 20th-Century Art: Futurist Manifestos*, Viking, London, 1970.
3. Umbro Apollonio, op. cit.
4. Umbro Apollonio, op. cit.

51. THE ART OF NOISES

1. Umbro Apollonio, *The Documents of 20th-Century Art: Futurist Manifestos*, Viking, London, 1970.
2. Karin Bijsterveld, 'A Servile Imitation: Disputes About Machines in Music, 1910–30' in *Music and Technology in the Twentieth Century*, John Hopkins University Press, Baltimore, 2002.

52. LISTEN LIKE THIEVES

1. Laszlo Moholy Nagy, 'Production-Reproduction: Potentialities of the Phonograph', reprinted in *Audio Culture: Readings in Modern Music*, Continuum, New York, 2004.
2. David Revill, *The Roaring Silence, John Cage: A Life*, Arcade Publishing, New York, 1992.
3. Rob Young, 'My Concrete Life' in *The Wire*, 2005.

4. Joseph G. Schloss, *Making Beats: The Art of Sample-Based Hip-Hop*, Wesleyan University Press, Connecticut, 2004.
5. Method Man, *Tical*, Def Jam, 1994.
6. Missy Eliot, *Under Construction*, Warners, 2003.

53. TURNING THE TURNTABLES

1. Dave Haslam, *Adventure on the Wheels of Steel*, Fourth Estate, London, 2001.
2. David Toop, *Rap Attack*, Serpents Tail, London, 2000.
3. Greg Tate, 'The Color of Money' in *The Nation*, 2006.
4. Emily Youssef, 'Late Bloomer' in *Resonance*, 2006.
5. Frank Broughton and Bill Brewster, 'The True Life Adventures of Flash', sleevenotes included with Grandmaster Flash, *The Official Adventures of Grandmaster Flash*, Strut CD, 2001
6. Frank Broughton and Bill Brewster, op. cit.
7. Grandmaster Flash quoted in *Dancing in the Streets*, BBC TV documentary, 1998.

54. DOING THE ROBOT

1. Andy Gill, 'We Can Be Heroes' in *Mojo*, 1997.
2. Karin Bijsterveld, 'A Servile Imitation: Disputes About Machines in Music, 1910–30' in *Music and Technology in the Twentieth Century*, John Hopkins University Press, Baltimore, 2002.
3. Kraftwerk, *The Man-Machine*, Capitol LP, 1978.
4. Lester Bangs, 'Kraftwerkfeature' in *Psychotic Reactions and Carburetor Dung*, William Heinemann, London, 1987.
5. Camilla Gray, *The Russian Experiment in Art*, Abrams, 1962.
6. *Sounds of New Music* (compilation), Folkways LP, 1958.
7. Lester Bangs, op. cit..
8. Wolfgang Flur, *Kraftwerk: I Was a Robot*, Sanctuary Encore, 2005.
9. Frank Whitford, *The Bauhaus*, Thames and Hudson, London, 1984.
10. Andy Gill, op. cit.
11. Rob Young, 'My Concrete Life' in *The Wire*, 2005.

55. ZANG TUMB TUUM

1. Mark Cunningham, *Good Vibrations: A History of Record Production*, Castle, Surrey, 1996.
2. Art of Noise, *Close to the Edit*, Island 7", 1984.
3. Edward Lucie-Smith, *Experimental Poetry 1: 1870–1922*, Rapp & Whiting, 1971.
4. Umbro Apollonio, *The Documents of 20th-Century Art: Futurist Manifestos*, Viking, London, 1970.
5. Martin O'Gorman, 'The Designer' in *Mojo*, 2005.
6. Alan Bullock, *Hitler: A Study In Tyranny*, Penguin, Middlesex, 1965.

7. Martin Gayford and Karen Wright, *The Penguin Book of Art Writing*, Penguin, London, 1999.

56. DEGENERATE ART AND THE OBSTINATE COLOURIST

1. Vincent Van Gogh, *The Letters of Vincent Van Gogh*, Penguin, London, 1997.
2. Colin Wilson, *The Outsider*, Pan Books, London, 1970.
3. Judy Sund, *Vincent Van Gogh*, Phaidon, London, 2002.
4. Vincent Van Gogh, *The Letters of Vincent Van Gogh*, Penguin, London, 1997.
5. Andy Warhol, *From A to B and Back Again: The Philosophy of Andy Warhol*, First Harvest / HBJ, Florida, 1977.
6. Judy Sund, op. cit.

57. SUICIDED BY SOCIETY

1. *Close Encounters of the Third Kind*, Columbia Pictures DVD, 2004.
2. Joseph McBride, *Steven Spielberg: A Biography*, Faber and Faber, London, 1998.
3. Antonin Artaud, 'Van Gogh: A Man Suicided by Society' in Martin Gayford and Karen Wright, *The Penguin Book of Art Writing*, Penguin London, 1999.
4. Antonin Artaud, op. cit.
5. Jeff Nuttall, *Bomb Culture*, Paladin, London, 1970.

58. LET'S GO CRAZY!

1. Prince, *Purple Rain*, Paisley Park / Warner Bros, 1984.
2. Andre Breton, *Nadja*, Penguin Classics, London, 1999.
3. Mel Gooding, *Surrealist Games*, Redstone Press, London, 1992.
4. Antonin Artaud, *The Theatre and its Double*, Grove Press, New York, 1958.
5. Antonin Artaud, op. cit.
6. John Weightman, *The Concept of the Avant-Garde: Explorations in Modernism*, Alcove Press, London, 1973.

59. THE PING-PONG OF THE ABYSS

1. Barry Miles, *The Beat Hotel: Ginsberg, Burroughs and Corso in Paris, 1958–1963*, Grove Press, New York, 2000.
2. Antonin Artaud, *To Have Done with the Judgement of God*, sound recording, 1947, found on UBUWEB sound archive, ubuweb.com
3. Antonin Artaud, *The Theatre and its Double*, Grove Press, New York, 1958.
4. Ian Hamilton, *Against Oblivion: Some lives of the twentieth-century poets*, Penguin, London, 2003.
5. Barry Miles, *Beat Collection* (anthology), Virgin Books, London, 2005.

6. Douglas Kahn, *Noise, Water, Meat: A History of Sound in the Arts*, The MIT Press, Cambrdige MA, 2001.
7. Barry Miles, op. cit.

60. INVASION OF THE BODY SNATCHERS

1. *Penguin Modern Poets 5* (anthology), Penguin, Middlesex, 1963.
2. *Penguin Modern Poets 5*, op. cit.
3. Ted Morgan, *Literary Outlaw: The Life and Times of William S. Burroughs*, Pimlico, London, 1991.
4. Jonathan Miller, *McLuhan*, Fontana, London, 1971.
5. Frederik Pohl & Frederik Pohl IV, *Science Fiction Studies in Film*, Ace Books, New York, 1981.

61. BOMB CULTURE, PART 2

1. Carl Gustav Jung, *Flying Saucers*, Routledge, London, 2005.
2. John Gruen, *The New Bohemia*, Shorecrest, New York, 1966.
3. Tom Wolfe, *The Right Stuff*, Bantam, New York, 1985.
4. Barry Miles, *Beat Collection* (anthology), Virgin Books, London, 2005.
5. Ted Morgan, *Literary Outlaw: The Life and Times of William S. Burroughs*, Pimlico, London, 1991.
6. *The Beat Generation* (compilation), Rhino / Word Beat CD, 1992.
7. Barry Miles, op. cit.

62. GO MAN, GO!

1. *The Beat Generation* (compilation), Rhino / Word Beat CD, 1992
2. Sleevenotes included with Allen Ginsberg, *Howl and other poems*, Sub Rosa CD, 1998.
3. Patti Smith, *Land*, Arista CD, 2002
4. James Campbell, *Paris Interzone: Richard Wright, Lolita, Boris Vian and others on the Left Bank, 1946–1960*, Minerva, London, 1995.
5. Barry Miles, *Beat Collection* (anthology), Virgin Books, London, London, 2005.
6. Allen Ginsberg, *Howl*, Sub Rosa CD.

63. THE ID BEAST

1. Frederik Pohl & Frederik Pohl IV, *Science Fiction Studies in Film*, Ace Books, New York, 1981.
2. *OHM+: The Early Gurus of Electronic Music*, Ellipsis CD/DVD, 2005.
3. Antonin Artaud, *The Theatre and its Double*, Grove Press, New York, 1958.
4. David Revill, *The Roaring Silence, John Cage: A Life*, Arcade Publishing, New York, 1992.

5. Geoff Smith and Nicola Walker-Smith, *American Originals*, Faber and Faber, London, 1994.

64. HAPPENING THINGS, PART 2

1. Adrian Henri, *Total Art: Environments, Happenings and Performance*, Praeger, 1974.
2. Susan Sontag, *Against Interpretation*, Vintage, London, 2001.
3. Douglas Kahn, *Noise, Water, Meat: A History of Sound in the Arts*, The MIT Press, Cambridge MA, 2001.
4. Barry Miles, *The Beat Hotel: Ginsberg, Burroughs and Corso in Paris, 1958–1963*, Grove Press, New York, 2000.

65. ARTAUD ROCK

1. Antonin Artaud, *The Theatre and its Double*, Grove Press, New York, 1958.
2. Nik Cohn, *Awopbopaloobopalopbamboom*, Paladin, London, 1972.
3. 'Is Johnny Ray a Mass Hypnotist?' in *The Faber Book of Pop*, Faber and Faber, London, 1995.
4. Lester Bangs, *Main Lines, Blood Feasts and Bad Taste*, Serpents Tail, London, 2002.
5. Barney Hoskyns, *Waiting for the Sun*, Bloomsbury, London, 2003.
6. Barry Miles, *Beat Collection* (anthology), Virgin Books, London, 2005.
7. Barry Miles, op. cit.
8. The Doors, *The Doors*, Elektra CD.
9. Peter Buckley, *The Rough Guide to Rock*, Rough Guides/Penguin, London, 2003.

66. MAYBE I'M CRAZY

1. Gnarls Barkley, *St Elsewhere*, CD, 2006.
2. Cee-Lo, interview with Zan Rowe, *J-mag*, 2006.
3. Jean-Michael Rabate, *Jacques Lacan*, Palgrave, New York, 2001.
4. *Surrealism, Revolution By Night*, exhibition catalogue, National Gallery of Australia, Canberra,1993.
5. Gnarls Barkley, op. cit.

67. SHE'S LOST CONTROL

1. Simon Reynolds, *Rip It Up and Start Again: Post Punk 1978–1984*, Faber and Faber, London, 2005.
2. Mick Middles, *From Joy Division to New Order: The Factory Story*, Virgin Books, 1996.
3. Colin Wilson, *The Outsider*, Pan Books, London, 1970.

68. ENTERTAINMENT THROUGH PAIN

1. Mick Middles, *From Joy Division to New Order: The Factory Story*, Virgin Books, London, 1996.

2. Throbbing Gristle, *Greatest Hits: Entertainment Through Pain*, Industrial Records LP, 1980.
3. Simon Ford, *Wreckers of Civilisation*, Black Dog Publishing, London, 1999.
4. *The Tyranny of the Beat* (compilation), Mute CD, 1991.
5. Simon Ford, op. cit.
6. Simon Ford, op. cit..
7. Marcus Errico, 'Yoko Ono Fan Defaces Painting', E! Online, 1997.
8. Re Search, *Industrial Culture Handbook*, Re Search, 1991.
9. *Industrial Culture Handbook*, op. cit.
10. Beck and Al Hansen, 'Playing with Matches', travelling exhibition, 1998.

69. THE HUMAN HONK

1. Lester Bangs, *Main Lines, Blood Feasts and Bad Taste*, Serpents Tail, London, 2002.
2. Mike Barnes, *Captain Beefheart*, Quartet Books, London, 2000.
3. Marcel Duchamp, *The Writings of Marcel Duchamp*, Da Capo, New York, 1989.
4. *OHM+: The Early Gurus of Electronic Music*, Ellipsis CD/DVD, 2005.
5 Eric Tamm, *Brian Eno: His Music and the Vertical Colour of Sound*, Da Capo, New York, 1995.
6. Mike Barnes, op. cit.
7. Mike Barnes, op. cit.
8. Barney Hoskyns, *Waiting for the Sun*, Bloomsbury, London, 2003.

70. AUTO-DESTRUCTIVE ART

1. David Mellor, *The Sixties Art Scene in London*, Phaidon, London, 1993.
2. Michael Nyman, *Experimental Music: Cage and Beyond*, University Press, Cambridge, 1999.
3. Robert Hewison, *Too Much*, Methuen, London, 1986.
4. Nik Cohn, *Awopbopaloobopalopbamboom*, Paladin, London, 1972.
5. Simon Frith and Howard Horne, *Art Into Pop*, Methuen, London, 1987.
6. David Mellor, op. cit.

71. MUD, BLOOD AND IDIOCY

1. Roger Lewis, *The Life and Death of Peter Sellers*, Arrow, London, 1994.
2. Spike Milligan, *More Goon Show Scripts*, Sphere, London, 1976.
3. Spike Milligan, op. cit.
4. Spike Milligan, *Goon Show Scripts*, Sphere, London, 1973.
5. Roger Lewis, *The Life and Death of Peter Sellers*, Arrow, London, 1994.

6. Jeff Nuttall, *Bomb Culture*, Paladin, London, 1970.
7. Spike Milligan, op. cit.
8. Mel Gordon, *Dada Performance*, PAJ, New York, 1987.
9. Mark Cunningham, *Good Vibrations: A History of Record Production*, Castle, 1996.

72. ROCK CONCRETE

1. Ian Macdonald, *Revolution in the Head: The Beatles' Records and the Sixties*, Pimlico, London, 1995.
2. Ian Peel, *The Unknown Paul McCartney*, Reynolds and Hearn, Surrey UK, 2002.
3. Ian Macdonald, op. cit.
4. The Beatles, *The Beatles (The White Album)*, EMI LP, 1968.

73. FLUXUS BEACH PARTY

1. The B-52's, 'Rock Lobster', Island 7", 1979.
2. Kate Pierson, interview with Richard Kingsmill, triple j, 2002.
3. Cyndi Lauper quoted in the sleevenotes from Yoko Ono, *Walking on Thin Ice*, Rykodisc CD, 1992.
4. Simon Reynolds, *Rip It Up and Start Again: Post-Punk 1978–1984*, Faber and Faber, London, 2005.
5. Martin O'Gorman, 'In The Beginning' in *Mojo*, 2002.
6. Martin O'Gorman, op. cit.

74. SONG OF THE YOUTHS

1. Ian Macdonald, *The People's Music*, Pimlico, London, 2003.
2. Julian Cope, *Krautrocksampler*, Head Heritage, 1996.
3. Mark Pendergast, *The Ambient Century*, Bloomsbury, London, 2003.
4. Paul Griffiths, *Modern Music*, Thames and Hudson, London, 1984.
5. Hannah Higgins, *Fluxus Experience*, University of California Press, Berkley, 2002.
6. Can DVD, Spoon Records DVD, 2003. [check this against text]
7. Julian Cope, op. cit.
8. Ian Macdonald, *Revolution in the Head: The Beatles' Records and the Sixties*, Pimlico, London, 1995.
9. The Wire, *Invisible Jukebox*, Quartet Books, London, 1998.
10. *The Tyranny of the Beat* (compilation), Mute CD, 1991.
11. Can, *Future Days*, Spoon LP, 1973.
12. The Wire, *Invisible Jukebox*, op. cit.

75. WAR AND PEACE IN THE GLOBAL VILLAGE

1. Eric Tamm, *Brian Eno: His Music and the Vertical Colour of Sound*, Da Capo, New York, 1995.
2. Dave Bowman, *fa fa fa fa fa fa: The adventures of Talking Heads in the 20th Century*, Bloomsbury, London, 2001.

3. Holger Czukay, *Movies*, EMI LP, 1979.
4. Paul Griffiths, *Modern Music*, Thames and Hudson, London, 1984.
5. Eric Tamm, op. cit.
6. Brian Eno and David Byrne, *My Life In the Bush of Ghosts*, Sire LP, 1981.
7. David Toop, *Rap Attack*, Serpents Tail, London, 2000.
8. Public Enemy, *Fear of a Black Planet*, Def Jam, 1990.
9. An anthology of noise and electronic music / first a-chronology volume #1, Sub Rosa, 2001.
10. Ian Peel, *The Unknown Paul McCartney*, Reynolds and Hearn, Surrey UK, 2002.
11. Ian Macdonald, *Revolution in the Head: The Beatles' Records and the Sixties*, Pimlico, London, 1995.
12. Simon Frith, *Sound Effects*, Pantheon, New York, 1981.

76. DANGER MUSIC

1. Adrian Henri, *Total Art: Environment, Happenings and Performance*, Praeger, New York, 1974.
2. Michael Nyman, *Experimental Music: Cage and Beyond*, University Press, Cambridge, 1999.
3. *The Flaming Lips: The Fearless Freaks*, Stomp Visual DVD, 2004.
4. The Flaming Lips, *Yoshimi Battles the Pink Robots*, Warner Bros CD, 2002.
5. *The Flaming Lips: The Fearless Freaks*, Stomp Visual DVD, 2004.
6. Andre Malraux, 'The Royal Way' reprinted in Frederick Karl and Leo Hamalian, *The Existential Imagination*, Picador, London, 1973.
7. Video Overview in Deceleration (VOID), *The Flaming Lips: 1992–2005*, Warner Bros DVD, 2005.
8. Wayne Coyne, quoted in *Mojo*, 2006.

77. ACID

1. Charles Shaar Murray, *Crosstown Traffic*, St Martins Press, New York, 1989.
2. Adrian Henri, *Total Art: Environments, Happenings and Performance*, Praeger, New York, 1974.
3. The Soft Machine, *The Soft Machine*, Probe LP, 1968.
4. Edwin Pouncey, 'Light Laboratories' in *Frieze*, 1999.
5. Ian Macdonald, *Revolution in the Head: The Beatles' Records and the Sixties*, Pimlico, London, 1995.
6. Calvin Tomkins, *The Bride and the Bachelors*, Penguin, New York, 1976.
7. Harry Shapiro, 'Time Out of Mind: A Brief History of LSD' in *Mojo*, 2004
8. Hunter S. Thompson—'The "Hashbury" is the Capitol of the Hippies' in *The Faber Book of Pop*, Faber and Faber, London, 1995.

9. Hunter S. Thompson, op. cit.
10. Geoff Smith and Nicola Walker-Smith, *American Originals*, Faber and Faber, London, 1994.
11. Ian Macdonald, *Revolution in the Head: The Beatles' Records and the Sixties*, Pimlico, London, 1995.

78. PERCEPTUAL INSTABILITY

1. Jerome Agel, *The Making of Kubrick's 2001*, Signet, New York, 1970.
2. Jerome Agel, op. cit.
3. Text from William Townsend Memorial Lecture by Bridget Riley, 1997, quoted in Michael Bracewell, *The Nineties: When Surface Was Depth*, Flamingo, London, 2003.
4. Cyril Barrett, *Optical Art*, Studio Vista / Dutton, London, 1971.
5. Cyril Barrett, op. cit.
6. Marcel Duchamp, *The Writings of Marcel Duchamp*, Da Capo, New York, 1989.
7. Michael Bracewell, op. cit.
8. Michael Desmond and Christine Dixon, *1968*, Thames and Hudson, London, 1995.
9. Michael Bracewell, op. cit.

79. BEING BORING

1. Pamela Des Barres, *I'm With the Band: Confessions of a Groupie*, Helter Skelter Publishing, London, 1987.
2. Steve Reich, *Early Works*, Elektra / Nonesuch LP, 1987.
3. Archives GRM (compilation), institute national de l'audiovisuel CD 2004.
4. Angus Batey, 'Rhymin' and Stealin'' in *Mojo*, 2003.
5. Steve Reich, 'Music as a Gradual Process' in Christopher Cox, *Audio Culture: Readings in Modern Music*, Continuum, New York, 2004.
6. *OHM+: The Early Gurus of Electronic Music*, Ellipsis CD/DVD, 2005.
7. Steve Reich, op. cit.
8. Steve Reich, *Early Works*, Elektra / Nonesuch LP, 1987.

80. SON OF RILEY

1. Mark Pendergast, *The Ambient Century*, Bloomsbury, London, 2003.
2. *OHM+: The Early Gurus of Electronic Music*, Ellipsis CD/DVD, 2005.
3. Steve Reich, 'Music as a Gradual Process' in Christopher Cox, *Audio Culture: Readings in Modern Music*, Continuum, New York, 2004.

4. Steve Reich, op. cit.
5. Trevor Pinch and Frank Troccho, *Analog Days*, Harvard University Press, Massachusetts, 2002.
6. The Who, *Who's Next*, Decca LP, 1971.
7. Mike Oldfield, *Tubular Bells*, Virgin LP, 1973.

81. GERMS FROM NEW YORK

1. Victor Bockris and Gerard Malanga, *Up-Tight: The Story of the Velvet Underground*, Omnibus Press, London, 1996.
2. Legs McNeil and Gillian McCain, *Please Kill Me*, Abacus, London, 1996.
3. Victor Bockris and Gerard Malanga, op. cit.
4. Edwin Pouncey, 'Coming Through Slaughter' in *The Wire*, 1999.
5. Steve Reich, 'Music as a Gradual Process' in Christopher Cox, *Audio Culture: Readings in Modern Music*, Continuum, New York, 2004.
6. John Cale and Victor Bockris, *What's Welsh for Zen?*, Bloomsbury, London, 1999.
7. David Keenan, *Mojo*, 2002.
8. Dave Marsh, *Louie Louie*, Hyperion, 1993.
9. The Stooges, *The Stooges*, Elektra LP, 1969.
10. Lester Bangs, 'Kraftwerkfeature' in *Psychotic Reactions and Carburetor Dung*, William Heinemann, London, 1987.
11. Edwin Pouncey, 'Coming Through Slaughter' in *The Wire*, 1999.
12. Simon Reynolds, *Energy Flash*, Picador, London, 2001.
13. The Wire, *Invisible Jukebox*, Quartet Books, London, 1998.

82. EINE KLEINE LIFTMUSIK

1. Ian MacDonald, *The People's Music*, Pimlico, London, 2003.
2. Joseph Lanza, *Elevator Music*, Quartet, London, 1995.
3. Joseph Lanza, op. cit.
4. Joseph Lanza, op. cit.
5. Joseph Lanza, op. cit.
6. Martin O'Gorman, 'In The Beginning' in Mojo, 2002.

83. FEAR OF POP

1. Theodor Adorno, *On The Social Situation of Music*, Telos 35, 1978.
2. Robert Witkin, *Adorno on Popular Culture*, Routledge, London, 2003.
3. Pink Floyd, *Mojo Special Edition*, 2004.

84. ATONALLY YOURS

1. Paul Griffiths, *Modern Music*, Thames and Hudson, London, 1984.
2. Arnold Schoenberg, *Style and Idea*, University of California Press, Berkley, 1984.

3. Norman Lebrecht, *The Complete Companion to 20th Century Music*, Simon and Schuster, London, 2000.
4. Arnold Schoenberg, *Style and Idea*, University of California Press, Berkley, 1984.

85. THE HISTORY OF THE FUTURE OF MUSIC

1. Norman Lebrecht, *The Complete Companion to 20th Century Music*, Simon and Schuster, London, 2000.
2. David Revill, *The Roaring Silence, John Cage: A Life*, Arcade Publishing, New York, 1992.
3. Paul Griffiths, *Modern Music*, Thames and Hudson, London, 1984.
4. Geoff Smith and Nicola Walker-Smith, *American Originals*, Faber and Faber, London, 1994.

86. VERY ANGRY

1. Robert Witkin, *Adorno on Popular Culture*, Routledge, London, 2003.
2. Theodor Adorno, 'A Social Critique of Radio Music' in *Radiotext(e), Semiotext(e) #16*, 1993.
3. Theodor Adorno, op. cit.
4. Theodor Adorno, op. cit.

ACKNOWLEDGEMENTS

First of all, I owe a great debt to Steve Cannane and Francis Leach for coming up with the initial idea for the Culture Club in 2001. Since then, I've been fortunate to work with some great presenters and producers at triple j, including Steve, Francis, Cath Dwyer, Vicki Kerrigan, Dan Buhagiar and Zan Rowe—all of whom have contributed to the segment in important ways. I'd like to make special mention of the extraordinary contribution Mel Bampton has made to the Culture Club since she started hosting triple j's morning program in 2004. Mel's imagination, enthusiasm and curiosity consistently brings the segment to life, week in and week out.

I'm very grateful to Linda Bracken for her support, and to everyone at triple j for their ideas and assistance over the years, but would like to give a special mention to the following people: Alicia Brown (for art theory in everyday life), Fenella Kernebone (for inspirational texts), Jason 'Jay' Whalley and Dr Lindsay McDougall (for puns, alliterations, ass-onances and goat-announces) and Richard Kingsmill (for sage advice, and for letting me play 'Unskinny Bop' by Poison on his radio station—or for at least not being fast enough to run into the studio and stop me).

I'd also like to send an enormous round of applause in the direction of Brad Cook, the Marcel Duchamp of the suburban parking garage, a resounding high-five to Mr Keith Hurst, and a super-sized 'cheers' to everyone at ABC books: to Jill Brown for getting it started, and especially to Susan Morris-Yates for seeing it through—and for not stabbing me with a coffee stirrer when I kept trying to change things at the last minute.

And finally, a big, warm, fuzzy 'thank you' to Michael 'Timmy' Rosenthal for the vinyl frenzies and guitar solo rhapsodies, Marissa and Shane for the spirited debates and international cuisine, Mum and Dad for not making me stay in school, and Janine Blackstock—for much, much more than I can say here.

INDEX